For Terri

Contents

Preface

Did you know that an $80,000 mortgage with an interest rate of ten per-cent for a term of 30 years costs over $172,000 in interest? That's right; it will cost you $172,000 to borrow $80,000! This book will show you how you can beat the banks at their own game, and save thousands of dollars. It will provide you with the facts on financing your home, and will explain the many options available in the "beat the system" approach to saving money.

Few consumers realize the importance of financing a home or refinancing an existing home mortgage. Financial institutions in this country have encouraged borrowers to concentrate on the affordability of the monthly payment rather than on the total cost of the loan over the term of the mortgage.

Historically, in order to reduce monthly installments for the principal and interest on a mortgage, lending institutions have offered long-term financing of 30 years or more. In recent years, a 15-year term has been available accompanied by a higher monthly payment.

Most of us do not realize that in the first few years of a mortgage loan, the majority of the payment is comprised of interest. Over the first five to ten years of a 15-year mortgage, or the first five to 20 years of a 30-year mortgage, there is very little reduction in the principal balance.

Years ago, financing a home was simple because there were fewer options. There was one type of mortgage for either the veteran or the non-veteran. Today, hundreds of mortgage programs are available. How do you choose the best mortgage program? How can you save thousands of dollars in closing costs and interest on your present mortgage? Should you refinance for a lower interest rate or for a shorter term? Does it make economic sense to refinance in order to take cash back from the equity you have, thereby increasing your present first mortgage? These are some of the main questions to consider when financing or refinancing your home.

Read on and learn why, in most cases, refinancing your present first mortgage is *not* a good idea and how you can save money on interest charges without costly refinancing. Keep reading for the critical, money-saving answers and learn how to "beat the system!"

Arthur Kramer
February 1992

Chapter 1

Saving Money on Your Mortgage

Traditionally, mortgage loans or deed of trusts[1] have been repaid to the financial institutions[2] by the borrower on a monthly basis. A monthly payment is less costly and more convenient for the banks, and consequently, more expensive for the borrower. Interest charged by the banks on mortgage loans is calculated daily on the outstanding amount borrowed over the term of the loan. The interest cost to the borrower amounts to thousands of dollars in excess of the original loan.

This book will demonstrate how to save 30 percent or more of the thousands of dollars in interest the borrower is obligated to pay over the term of the loan, *without costly refinancing*. In addition, this book will show how those thousands of dollars in interest savings can be applied to the increased equity in your home.

Regardless of the type of home mortgage program you have, you can save thousands of dollars if you begin using the approaches in this book now. The "beat the system" approach can be implemented with a first mortgage, a second or third mortgage, an equity loan, or a line of credit. In addition, you can beat the system if your mortgage is calculated on a fixed interest rate, an adjustable interest rate, or a Graduated Payment Mortgage (GPM).

Irrespective of the interest rate on your mortgage, the higher your loan, the more you will save. However, if you are fortunate to have an interest rate on your loan as low as seven percent, you can still save thousands of dollars!

Most of us share a desire to live comfortably and enjoy a sense of financial security and independence. We appreciate purchasing things that have value and show that we are successful. The obvious difference is that some of us appear more financially secure than others.

Let's take a look at the diagram depicting two identical family residences. We'll call them Home "A" and Home "B." Each family

---

1   Another term used instead of mortgage in some states, and henceforth in this book referred to as "mortgage."
2   Hereafter referred to as "lender" or "bank."

Home "A"

Home "B"

purchased its home at the same time and paid the same price. In addition, each owner had the same mortgage financing term of 30 years and the same fixed rate of interest. The difference is that the owner of Home "B" will end up paying over $90,000 less for his home! Also, homeowner "B" will own his home free and clear of any mortgage almost 11 years sooner!

How? In the subsequent chapters we will be explaining our savings methods so you can be a homeowner "B" and save thousands of dollars. Refer to Table 1–1 for a detailed, financial comparison.

Table 1–1   Comparison of Costs and Savings of Home "A" and Home "B"
             Under Conventional Monthly and "Biweekly" System Approach

Original Loan Amount: $110,000   Annual Interest Rate: 12%
Original Loan Term: 30 Years   Monthly Payment: $1,131.47
No. of Previous Payments: 41   Biweekly Payment: $565.74

Loan Balance at Start of Comparison: $108,367

End of Year	Home "A" Monthly		Home "B" Biweekly		Comparison	
	Remaining Balance	Interest Paid	Remaining Balance	Interest Paid	Equity Growth	Interest Saved
1	107,761	12,971	106,630	12,861	1,131	–0–
2	107,078	25,866	104,672	25,723	2,406	143
3	106,308	38,674	102,465	38,225	3,843	449
4	105,441	51,384	99,979	40,448	5,462	936
5	104,464	63,985	97,178	62,356	7,286	1,629
6	103,363	76,461	94,021	73,908	9,342	2,553
7	102,122	88,798	90,464	85,060	11,658	3,738
8	100,723	100,077	86,456	95,761	14,267	5,216
9	99,148	112,070	81,939	105,954	147,209	7,025
10	97,372	124,781	76,850	115,573	20,522	9,208
11	95,372	136,358	71,115	124,548	24,257	11,810
12	93,117	147,682	64,652	132,794	28,465	14,888
13	90,577	158,719	57,371	140,222	33,206	18,497
14	87,715	169,434	49,165	146,726	38,550	22,708
15	84,489	179,786	39,919	152,189	44,570	27,597
16	80,855	189,730	29,501	156,479	51,354	33,251
17	76,759	199,212	17,761	159,448	58,998	39,764
18	72,144	208,175	4,532	160,929	67,612	47,246
19	66,944	216,552	Debt	161,046	–0–	55,506
20	61,085	224,270	Free	161,046	–0–	63,224

Table continues

Table 1–1   Continued

End of Year	Home "A" Monthly		Home "B" Biweekly		Comparison	
	Remaining Balance	Interest Paid	Remaining Balance	Interest Paid	Equity Growth	Interest Saved
21	54,482	231,245	–0–	161,046	–0–	70,199
22	47,042	237,382	–0–	161,046	–0–	76,336
23	38,658	242,576	–0–	161,046	–0–	81,530
24	29,210	246,707	–0–	161,046	–0–	35,661
25	18,565	249,639	–0–	161,046	–0–	88,593
26	6,570	251,221	–0–	161,046	–0–	90,175
27	–0–	251,454	–0–	161,046	–0–	90,408
28	–0–	–0–	–0–	–0–	–0–	–0–
29	–0–	–0–	–0–	–0–	–0–	–0–
30	–0–	–0–	–0–	–0–	–0–	–0–

Chapter 2

The Structure of Mortgages, Interest and Principal

The repayment of a mortgage note is always set up by the banks to insure that in the early years, the greater proportion of the monthly payment is interest. This "up-front" interest will occur in years one through 23 of a 30-year mortgage or the first ten years of a 15-year mortgage. As the following Tables 2–1 and 2–2 illustrate, in the early years, a smaller amount of the monthly payment is credited to the reduction of the original amount borrowed, also known as the principal.

Table 2–1   30-Year Mortgage

Basis: Loan Amount	Term	Interest Rate	Monthly Payment	Total Payments
$80,000	30 Yrs.	10%	$702.06	360

Analysis

At End of	Total Payments	To Interest	To Principal Reduction	Remaining Principal Balance
1st year	$8,424.72	$7,944.22	$480.00	$79,520.00
5th year	$42,123.60	$39,403.60	$2,720.00	$77,280.00
10th year	$84,247.20	$76,967.60	$7,280.00	$72,720.00
15th year	$126,370.80	$111,730.80	$14,640.00	$65,360.00
20th year	$168,494.40	$141,614.40	$26,880.00	$53,120.00
25th year	$210,618.00	$163,658.00	$46,960.00	$33,040.00
30th year	$252,741.60	$172,741.60	$80,000.00	–0–

Table 2–2   15-Year Mortgage

Basis: Loan Amount	Term	Interest Rate	Monthly Payment	Total Payments
$80,000	15 Yrs.	10%	$859.69	160

Analysis

At End of	Total Payments	To Interest	To Principal Reduction	Remaining Principal Balance
1st year	$10,316.28	$7,916.28	$2,400.00	$77,600.00
5th year	$51,581.40	$36,621.40	$14,960.00	$65,040.00
10th year	$103,162.80	$63,642.80	$39,520.00	$40,480.00
15th year	$154,744.20	$74,744.20	$80,000.00	–0–

The larger proportion of the monthly payment comprised of interest is known as the bank's "leverage." The following pages will show how to drastically reduce the leverage, resulting in considerable savings.

In Table 2–1, a total of over $172,000 (an average of over $5,700 per year) in interest was paid to borrow $80,000. By beating the system, the borrower could save a minimum of $58,000 in interest *and* pay off the entire 30-year loan in 21 years!

In Table 2–2, a total of almost $75,000 in interest was paid to borrow $80,000.00 (an average of almost $5,000 per year). The borrower could save a minimum of $12,563 in interest and pay off the 15-year loan in 12 years!

Chapter 3

How to Save Money without Refinancing

In most cases, refinancing for a lower interest rate to achieve a lower monthly payment can be risky. Although the lower interest rate is enticing in considering the reduction of your monthly payment, the following example indicates the reasons why it may not be a desirable option.

Example:

Mr. Jones has a 30-year mortgage which he obtained at an interest rate of 12% on an original loan amount of $80,000. He has had the mortgage for the past four years, and after making 48 monthly payments, has a present balance of $78,560. Mr. Jones has been offered a nine percent 30-year mortgage with closing costs totaling $4,384 on a new loan of approximately $83,000. This new mortgage loan amount is achieved by adding the closing costs which Mr. Jones wants to include in his loan, and the mortgage balance of $78,560. The new monthly payment is $667.84, compared to Mr. Jones' current mortgage payment of $822.90. This results in a monthly savings of $155.06. Let's examine this so-called "savings."

To begin with, it would take over 28 months of payments before Mr. Jones could recapture the $4,384 in closing expenditures. Mr. Jones has already increased his loan to $83,000 from $78,560, which is the balance after four years of payments on the original $80,000 mortgage, and he decreased his equity by increasing the loan amount to $83,000. In addition, for the next four years, Mr. Jones will repeat the front-loading interest payments totaling $38,059.20 that he already paid on his original mortgage. With the new mortgage, Mr. Jones will assume additional interest charges of $29,483.32 for the next four years. Add to that amount the interest from the four years of the original loan ($38,059.20), and Mr. Jones will have paid $67,542.52 in interest in eight years if he refinances! It will take Mr. Jones a very long time to recover that expenditure! Don't forget, Mr. Jones will have 26 years remaining on his current mortgage even though he would have made payments for eight years.

Mr. Jones' savings on his monthly payment added up to $35.81 per week. Is it worth it to Mr. Jones? From an economic standpoint, it hardly seems to be make sense.

If Mr. Jones chooses to refinance, he will lose $3,680 in equity and will increase his mortgage balance from $78,560 to $83,000. Additionally, he will increase his mortgage term by four years and reincur front-loading interest costs.

If Mr. Jones is like the average person who owns a home, he will be looking to sell his home within a seven-year period from the date that he made the purchase. Does this tremendous refinancing expenditure make sense? It does if Mr. Jones doesn't have $35.81 a week to keep up with his current mortgage payments. Refer to Chapter 9 for *The Ultimate "Beat the System" Approach* to saving money without refinancing.

Let's explore another common pitfall in the world of refinance. If you have a 30-year mortgage and you are interested in refinancing for a 15-year mortgage with higher payments, you may want to reconsider. If your objective is to build your equity and savings, you do not need to spend thousands of dollars in closing costs when you can achieve the same goal by implementing the biweekly approach to savings. This approach does not incur closing costs or front-loading interest charges. Review Chapter 9 for more information on this method.

Another reason to refinance may be to utilize the equity in your home to acquire ready cash. Follow the example to understand why refinancing may not be the most economic way to obtain cash out of your home.

Example:

Let's say you need $10,000 and your home has a current value of $110,000. You have a mortgage balance of $75,000, an interest rate of ten percent, and a current monthly payment of $702.06. There are two options available to you to acquire the immediate $10,000 in cash using the equity in your home. The first option is to refinance your entire present mortgage of $75,000. In addition to the original loan amount, add the $10,000 that you need, and the closing costs of $5,000. This new loan amount totals $90,000. Considering the same interest rate of ten percent is available to you, you will have new monthly payments of $833.90.

Let's analyze this example. You have increased your monthly payments by $131.84. You also have paid $5,000 in closing costs to borrow

$10,000, and you have lost your original equity by increasing your loan amount from $75,000 to $90,000. In addition, you are going to have to pay the same front-loading interest charges again as demonstrated in Paragraph 1 of this Chapter.

Alternatively, let's see what happens if you decide to borrow $10,000 on a bank credit, equity line or second mortgage. In borrowing $10,000 plus $1,000 in closing costs (we have allowed ten percent closing costs on this example, which is high), the total loan is $11,000. Employing a term of 15 years at an available rate of 12 percent, the monthly payment would be $132.03. At $132.03, the monthly payment is only 19 cents per month higher than refinancing your entire mortgage (see previous example) with a term of 15 years instead of 30 years. That's right, the loan would be 15 years shorter in term and would have a *savings* of $4,000 in closing costs. In other words, the interest rate is higher, the closing costs are lower, the loan is for a shorter term, with virtually the same monthly payments. Does this sound like a better deal?

Another type of loan situation that may warrant refinancing is negative amortization. Negative amortization occurs when the borrower is not paying enough to meet his interest obligation. For the first few years, the monthly payments are purposely set lower; however, the interest the borrower doesn't pay is added to the loan balance. In a negative amortization situation, the borrower can end up paying *more* than the original amount borrowed.

Prior to refinancing in negative amortization, it is important to analyze your particular loan situation. Determine the term in which your principal balance continues to increase in negative amortization. If you are still within the term of increase you should be seriously looking to refinance into a *positive* amortization loan. For a less costly method to minimize your negative amortization, refer to Chapter 11.

Evaluate whether your loan has already peaked at the highest loan amount to which it can increase in negative amortization. If your loan has reached the highest increase allowed by the terms of your mortgage, be careful in considering refinancing. The damage has already been done, and refinancing may compound the mistakes already made by entering into a negative amortization loan. By reviewing Chapter 11 however, you can learn how to recover a major portion of your past expenditures by implementing the biweekly method, which will save money without refinancing.

Chapter 4

Where to Go to Find Your Mortgage

Choosing the right lender for your mortgage needs can be difficult and confusing. There are so many options to choose from that making a decision on the best one for you can be mindboggling. Let's evaluate the sources from which you can obtain a mortgage.

Savings and Loan Associations are a logical first choice to examine. They are either Federally or State chartered, and can make mortgage loans of up to 95 percent (more for some FHA and VA guaranteed mortgages) of the appraised value of a home. In some states there are Mutual Savings Banks which are much the same as Savings and Loan Associations, but are quite restricted in the mortgage plans they offer.

Our next options are *Commercial Lenders* and *Mortgage Companies*. In recent years, Commercial Lenders have organized separate subsidiary companies and referred to them as mortgage companies. These mortgage companies offer a wide range of residential home mortgage loan programs.

In addition to the previous options, there are also *Mortgage Brokers* or *Mortgage Bankers*. These are individuals or companies who charge a fee, known as an origination or broker's fee, for their services. Their purpose is to find the lowest interest rate and the most suitable mortgage program. We do not recommend the use of these types of organizations because the added cost for the loan may vary between 0.5 to 2.5 percent of the loan amount over and above other closing costs.

Credit Unions also often write residential mortgages. If you are a member of a Credit Union, you may have to do some of your own legwork, as they are often not equipped to do research; however, they can be a good source for a reasonably priced loan. If you end up not acquiring a mortgage from a Credit Union, you can use it as a primary savings comparison to other lenders.

In recent years, many state and local governments have introduced bond issue mortgages at low interest rates in order to serve the public. A bond issue mortgage offered in your area will usually not allow for any negotiations in the method of repayment or in the costs associated with this financing.

When selecting a mortgage program, your main concern should be in acquiring the best interest rate and mortgage term at the lowest cost. One of a buyer's most valuable, and often, overlooked resource for obtaining mortgage money, is through the seller. Sellers are often interested in providing mortgage deals if it means they will sell their home. Seller financing can include providing a full mortgage, assumption of the previous mortgage or secondary financing. For more detailed information on seller financing, refer to Chapter 6.

In choosing the right lender for your loan requirements, remember that you represent a profit potential to each of the lenders. They all want your business, so choose the program that is best for *you*. Evaluate the following questions prior to a final decision. Does the lender offer you mortgage loans without the payment of discount points? Discount points, or points, is a charge passed on to the borrower by the bank to reduce the interest rate the borrower pays. The discount points may be included in the loan amount or paid out-of-pocket by the borrower. Refer to Chapter 6 for more information on discount points.

Another question to consider is whether the lender charges an origination or broker fee? As discussed previously, the mortgage broker may charge anywhere from 0.5 to 2.5 percent for his services in addition to the discount points and closing costs that are normally assessed by this type of lender. Because of these added fees, it is usually in the borrower's best interest to avoid mortgage brokers.

Inquire as to whether the lender incorporates a prepayment penalty within its mortgage. A prepayment penalty is an additional charge by the bank for paying off the loan earlier than the designated loan period. Refer to Chapter 6, for further information on prepayment penalties.

Determine whether the bank will allow you to pay a higher interest rate to eliminate closing costs. The interest rate as well as the points are often negotiable, therefore, it is worth pursuing both angles to find the best situation for you. Refer to Chapter 6 for further information on higher interest rates versus closing costs.

Does the bank allow you to conduct normal banking transactions, such as with checking accounts, savings accounts, or money market accounts? Sometimes, the best deal you can make for yourself is at the bank with whom you maintain a banking relationship, because it means additional profit to the bank derived from your use of other banking services.

Chapter 5

Choosing a Mortgage
Loan Program

In addition to the many places to go for a mortgage, there are also several mortgage programs available to you today. Which is the one for you? How do you choose a mortgage loan program? The mortgage program you choose should suit your specific requirements of credit, income, loan amount, closing costs, term, interest rate, and affordable monthly payments.

Of the numerous mortgage programs available, the *Fixed Rate* or *Conventional Mortgage* is the most common. A fixed rate mortgage usually has a term of 15 or 30 years, with the interest rate and the monthly payments constant throughout the term of the loan. This type of mortgage usually has the highest interest rate compared to other mortgage programs explained hereafter because it puts the greatest long-term constraints on the bank. In today's climate of fluctuating interest rates, the banks are less likely to offer low interest (below eight percent) fixed rate mortgages for long terms. Fixed rate mortgages are the most desirable of all mortgages and should be your first consideration when the rate has not exceeded 11 percent in the prevailing market place.

An *Adjustable Rate Mortgage* (ARM) or *Variable Rate Mortgage*, as the name implies, carries an interest rate that is adjusted periodically (semiannually, annually, or biannually). During the term of the loan, the fluctuating rate reflects the general interest rate levels. There are several types of adjustable rate mortgage programs available on the market. They are as follows:

(1) One-year adjustable with adjustments occurring every six months.

(2) One-year adjustable with adjustments occurring once a year.

(3) Three-year adjustable with adjustments occurring every three years.

(4) Five-year adjustable with adjustments occurring every five years.

Adjustable rate mortgages are comprised of several ingredients. As a borrower, it is important to be familiar with these because each one represents a potential risk. Due to the escalation of the interest rate, each element of the adjustable rate mortgage could result in an additional cost to you.

Within adjustable rate mortgages, there exists an initial interest rate known as the starting interest rate. It is usually set below the market rate as an incentive for you to enter the program. The one year adjustable starting interest rate is lower than a three-year adjustable starting interest rate. Consequently, the one- and three-year adjustable starting interest rates are both lower than the five-year adjustable interest rate programs. When exploring an adjustable rate mortgage, keep in mind that the first year's adjustment will usually be an increase due to several factors.

Let's identify those factors and what they represent to the borrower. They include *index, margins* and *caps*. In an adjustable rate mortgage, the interest rate varies according to a national index. The most common indexes used by lenders are the six-month Treasury Bill, the one-year Treasury Bill, or the Federal Home Loan Bank Board national average of mortgage rates for existing homes. As the index number changes, your interest rate, and therefore, your payment changes.

Margin is just another word for profit used by the banks. The margin is a percentage of any where from two percent to 3 1/4 percent which the bank adds to the index to insure them of a profit.

Example:

A bank offers a 7 1/4 percent 30-year adjustable rate mortgage tied to the one-year Treasury Bill (the Index) which we will hypothetically say is at 5 1/4%. Add to that an average margin that we'll call 2 3/4 percent, and you have an actual interest rate of eight percent. Your starting rate incentive is at 7 1/4 percent, therefore, in order for you to maintain a continuing 7 1/4 percent in the second year of your mortgage, the Treasury Bill Index would have to drop to 4 1/2 percent. This occurs because the bank adds the margin of 2 3/4 percent to that 4 1/2 percent (Index) to get the original starting rate of 7 1/4 percent. This can be risky for the homeowner who thinks his interest rate will remain stable or even decline each year.

Whether you choose a one-year, three-year, or five-year adjustable rate mortgage, it is important to know that caps are there for the borrower's protection. The two types of adjustment caps include initial adjustment term and life term. One-year adjustable rate mortgages are available with either one percent (1%) or two percent (2%) annual caps.

An initial adjustment cap means that regardless of the fluctuation of the index and the margin, your interest rate cannot exceed the cap which is added to your starting interest rate. In other words, if the interest rate jumps four (4) points in one year, your adjustable rate can only increase by the preset cap. This cap is usually only one (1%) or two percent (2%) in a one-year period.

Life term caps are set by the bank and are generally three (3%) to six percent (6%) above your starting interest rate. Over the life of your loan, the starting interest rate will not increase more than three (3%), four (4%), five (5%) or six percent (6%).

Example:

Seven and one-quarter percent (7 1/4%) starting interest rate with a five percent (5%) lifetime cap means that your interest rate could not be higher than 12 1/4% anytime during the term of the loan. In the worst scenario, with a two percent (2%) annual cap, the full five percent (5%) increase would not occur until your loan reached the fourth year.

An interest rate increase results in an increase in the monthly payment, and therefore, could be detrimental for the unprepared homeowner.

Another popular type of mortgage program is the *Convertible Adjustable Rate Mortgage.* As it's name implies, it is similar to the adjustable rate mortgage, but with one additional feature. Within a specified period of time during the loan term, the borrower may convert the adjustable rate to a fixed rate *without* reincurring closing costs. Some banks offer the conversion feature after the first year anniversary through the fifth year, which represents five conversion periods. This type of convertability is the most beneficial because it allows the borrower a greater period of time to find the lowest fixed rate. Less desirable conversion periods may be available and would occur in the second, third or fourth year of the mortgage. To achieve the greatest savings with a convertible loan, the borrower needs to be aware of the fluctuating interest rates in order to choose the lowest fixed rate. Instead of charging standard closing costs at the time of the conversion, a fee will be assessed by the bank. The amount of this conversion fee will be disclosed to you at the time of your original loan application and will be either a percentage of the loan amount or a preset dollar amount.

The *Graduated Payment Mortgage* (GPM) is a type of adjustable loan which allows for lower monthly payments in the first three, four or five years of the mortgage. Later on, the payments rise at fixed amounts over a set number of years throughout the loan term. A graduated payment mortgage is ideal for the home buyer who expects his income to rise, and is interested in entering into a 15-year term mortgage. This type of loan offers fixed payment rates which are generally competitive with the current fixed rate 15-year term mortgage.

Another adjustable rate mortgage is known as the *Graduated Equity Mortgage* (GEM). This mortgage is often confused with the *Graduate Payment Mortgage* (GPM) in that the monthly payments are lower in the early years, and rise throughout the term of the mortgage. The difference is that in a GEM, the equity in your home increases at a faster rate because you pay more each year to reduce your principal more rapidly. The increased amount you pay is based on a predetermined percentage that is set up by the bank.

Another type of mortgage that is based on an adjustable rate is the *Balloon Mortgage*. This kind of mortgage, unlike a fully amortized loan, calls for either a lump sum payment or a refinance at the end of a specific period of time. When the loan balloons, should a refinance be necessary, it is negotiated at the current interest rate. This could benefit you if the rates are favorable, or harm you if the rates have risen. As a borrower, obtaining a balloon mortgage may not be your first choice; however, it may be your only option due to market conditions, lender acceptance and your income at the time of application. The following example illustrates the specific detriments of a balloon mortgage.

Example:

A. $80,000 - 30-year amortized mortgage at ten percent. The monthly payment is $702.06 for the entire term of the mortgage.

B. $80,000 balloon mortgage - 30-year amortization with a ten-year balloon at ten percent. Monthly payment is $702.06 (yes, that's right; the same monthly payment), but at the end of the ten-year term you have to make a lump sum payment of $72,720!

The mortgage program you select should be the one that best suits your situation as a borrower. To achieve maximum savings, evaluate the program you have chosen with the information contained in Chapter 11.

Chapter 6

Important Things to Know About Financing Your Mortgage

We have determined in previous chapters that there are several different types of mortgages and as many places to go for mortgage money. In this chapter, we will explore some of the important aspects of financing your home.

One important feature involved in financing your home is the *lock-in*. Most lenders offer lock-ins of some type. The lock-in is designed to secure the interest rate requested on the borrower's original application until the time of the closing. Hence the term "lock-in," as you are locking-in the interest rate.

A 30-day lock-in is available, however, is not often utilized due to the difficulty in processing a loan to closing in such a short time frame. The 45-day lock-in is better than the 30-day lock-in; however, the time constraints are still somewhat prohibitive. This is especially true when the interest rate market is down and demands on the lenders for loans are greater than normal. The 60-day lock-in, is the most common because it allows for the necessary time for both you and the bank to complete the processing of your loan application. There are occasions when lenders will give you an extended lock-in of up to 90 days. This may be possible for a certain fee of 1/4 point or 1/2 point of the loan amount, which is usually refundable or credited against your closing costs at the time of closing. As we have discussed, the lock-in protects the borrower against rising interest rates before final loan processing is accomplished. On the other side however, what if you are "locked-in" and the interest rate goes down? Inquire as to whether your lender will also give you the lowest rate prevailing at the time of closing. As all lenders differ on this matter, it is best to explore it with your lender. It will provide you with another consideration in making the choice of which lender is offering you the best possible mortgage loan program.

Discount Points, or simply, points, are the prepaid interest charges that a lender will assess for originating the mortgage. Essentially, they represent the additional fees charged to the borrower upon obtaining a loan. One point represents one percentage point of the amount borrowed. For example, on a $100,000 loan, with three points, the fee would be $3,000. In most situations, points can be included in your conventional mortgage instead of paid in a lump sum at closing. Points are generally prevalent on fixed rate loans and are one of the means by which lenders gain a profit on your loan.

The points charged by a lender can serve as the additional profit for the lender or as a "buy down" of the interest rate. In other words, a bank may give you a lower interest rate if you pay points up front. The import-ant issue here is that points are often negotiable, and all aspects of the the loan situation should be evaluated prior to signing the loan agreement. The following example illustrates the practical application of points to interest.

Example :

Interest Rate	Points	Loan Amounts	Points Costs	Monthly Payment 15-Year—30 Year
9%	2	$100,000	$2,000*	$1,034.56—$820.83
9 1/2%	–0–	$100,000	–0–	$1,044.23—$840.86

(If no points)

The previous example indicates that the monthly payment differen-tial on a 30-year term in $20 a month, and $10 on a 15-year term. The borrower of the 9 1/2 percent loan with zero points will pay the addi-tional monthly amount without the upfront $2,000. Alternatively, the bor-rower paying the points will assume a lower interest rate, slightly lower monthly payments, but will incur a $2,000 charge at closing.

For further implication of points versus interest rates, examine the following examples.

Example 1: Bank A offers **10%** with **1.5** discount points on a **30-year** fixed rate loan.

Example 2: Bank B offers **10.25%** with **0** points, on a **30-year** fixed rate loan.

Let's say you need an $80,000 mortgage and you choose Bank A which offers a ten percent, 30-year term, with 1.5 percent discount points. If you decide to include the points in your mortgage of $80,000, simply multiply $80,000 times one and one-half points (1.5%), which equals an additional $1,200. Your mortgage total is $81,200 with a monthly payment of $712.60 for principal and interest. For the $1,200 increase due to the inclusion of the discount points in your mortgage, you are paying an additional $10.54 each month for the entire term of the mortgage.

Let's say you decide to keep your home only five years with the figures in Example 1. If you sell your home in five years, you will have paid $10.54 times 60 months which equals $632.40. Additionally, you will have paid approximately $41 off the principal balance of the additional $1,200 you borrowed on top of the $80,000 mortgage you have.

If you sell your home in ten years, you will have paid $10.54 per month times 120 months, or $1,264.80. Also, you will have paid approximately $110 off the $1,200 you originally borrowed and added to your $80,000 mortgage, to pay for the points. Compare these figures with the choice of Bank B which offered $80,000 with 0 discount points at 10.25 percent for a 30-year term. In this situation your monthly payments will be $716.89. That's right. The monthly payment is approximately $4.29 higher.

By choosing Example 2 with the $4.29 higher payment per month, after five years, you have reduced your principal balance from $80,000 to $77,360. Whereas, in Example 1, you have reduced your principal balance from $81,200 to $78,439. Your equity savings is $979. By making a monthly payment just $4.29 more, in just five years, the interest savings is over $500! In addition, you now have a much lower mortgage balance. In ten years, the difference is even more dramatic as to the savings in equity and future interest charges.

Prepayment penalties, or the Rule of 78 amortization schedule is another important facet of mortgage financing. The Rule of 78 amortization is a way in which a bank may receive additional dollars from you for an early payoff. It is a prepayment *penalty.* Under this rule, prepayment penalties will incur in two ways. Either you pay off your mortgage in its entirety earlier than the original term, or if during the term of the mortgage, you will make additional payments directly towards principal to reduce the principal balance. Many prepayment penalties will add up to five percent or more of the outstanding balance of your mortgage. This could mean thousands of dollars in additional costs when you pay off your mortgage. A prepayment penalty must be disclosed to you in the

Truth in Lending and Disclosure Statement. The Truth in Lending Disclosure Statement is discussed in detail at the end of this chapter.

Closing costs, as the name implies, are expenses incurred at the time
of closing. These charges can be substantial depending on the type of loan
and property. They can be as high as as six percent of your mortgage loan
amount on loans under $100,000 and as high as four percent of the loan
amount on loans exceeding $125,000. Represented below are your major
closing items. For a further explanation of the terminology, refer to the
Glossary.

Closing Cost Items:

Appraisal Fee; Credit Report; Discount Points; Abstracting; Title Insurance; Recording Fees; Documentary or Tax Stamps; Intangible
Tax; Survey; Attorney Fee; Origination Fee; Roof & Termite Inspection; Lender's Fees; Courier Fees; Tax Service; Document Preparation; Private Mortgage Insurance (PMI); Escrows.

Although these costs are steep, do not automatically assume that
they have to be your total responsibility. A motivated seller may assist
you in paying closing costs in order to have his property sold.

In some loan situations, it may be to your advantage to pay a higher
interest rate than the prevailing rate. Closing costs usually total about four
to six percent of the amount borrowed (see previous paragraph on closing
costs). Assume that if you could reduce the closing costs and negotiate a
higher rate, the bank agrees to eliminate the points, origination fee,
lender's fee, and document preparation fee. On an $80,000 mortgage loan,
the closing costs would total $5,000. If you negotiate a 1/2 percent higher
interest over the prevailing rate in order to reduce the closing costs by
$3,000, you may see that you come out ahead financially. Take a look at
the following examples to see how this idea works.

FIXED RATE

Term: 15 Years

Loan Amount	Interest Rate	Monthly Payment	Total Payment*	Principal Reduction	Paid Interest
(1) $85,000	9.75	900.46	10,805.52	2,295.00	8,510.52
(2) 82,000	10.25	893.77	10,725.24	2,460.00	8,265.24

Term: 30 Years

Loan Amount	Interest Rate	Monthly Payment	Total Payment*	Principal Reduction	Paid Interest
(1) $85,000	10.00	754.94	8,951.28	510.00	8,441.28
(2) 82,000	10.50	750.10	9,001.20	410.00	8,591.20

(1) Closing costs included in loan amount.
(2) Closing costs not included in loan amount.
*Calculations for one year.

The example illustrates that Item (1), which is the $85,000 loan includes the $5,000 in closing costs usually required on a loan of this amount. Item (2) illustrates that with the $82,000 figure, you have made an agreement with your lending institution to have them pay the major closing costs, as previously stated, due to your willingness to increase your interest rate by 1/2% above the currently prevailing rate.

As you can see in the example, for a 15-year term loan the actual monthly payment for your $82,000 loan is $6.69 less than your $85,000 loan payment, which includes closing costs.

The reduction of your principal balance for the first year as it would be in subsequent years is only $165 less. This is due to the fact that you borrowed $3,000 less (the closing costs). The net interest you are paying for the first year, as it would be in subsequent years, gives you $245 less tax deduction. However, your benefit is that you have saved $3,000 in closing costs.

In the example for a 30-year term mortgage, you are actually paying $4.84 less each month and your principal reduction is the same in either case. You have saved yourself $3,000 because your loan amount is $3,000 less, due to the fact that there are fewer closing costs included. Your total interest payments for the year are approximately $150 greater.

When you are considering the option of *higher interest rate versus closing costs,* there are several points to evaluate including the term of your mortgage, the amount of time you expect to be in your home, the interest rate, the amount of closing costs and how they will be paid, and your income structure. Determine the best mortgage program for your needs as a consumer, and analyze it with the approaches in this book to achieve maximum savings throughout the life of your loan.

Several years ago, when due to high interest rates, lenders were not attracting borrowers, they created a lower interest rate program founded on *negative amortization*. As we discussed in previous chapters, negative amortization simply means that the principal balance of your mortgage loan does not decrease with each payment you make, but, rather *increases*. In some of the programs that attracted many borrowers, the loan amount increased by 25 percent of the original amount borrowed. However, negative amortization is not always considered a negative. Knowing the extent of the negative amortization schedule and reviewing the disclosure in advance will provide you with all the necessary information in making this financial decision. You may find some mortgage loan programs with only a two or three percent negative amortization. That type of loan may be as competitive or even more competitive when a higher interest rate trend occurs in the mortgage industry.

Loan to Value (LTV) is a phrase that is constantly used in mortgage financing. It merely means that the loan amount you require is compared to the purchase price or the value of the home set by the appraisal, whichever is lower. The difference between the loan and the value is your equity. When you make a purchase, the difference between loan and value will be your down payment. Most banks will loan up to 80 percent of the value of the home, and the additional 20 percent is the borrower's down payment. Some lenders however, have programs where they lend up to 90 or 95 percent of the appraised value of the home.

When loan to value exceeds 80 percent of the value of the property, most lenders require that in addition to its own approval, a mortgage loan must also be approved by a *Private Mortgage Insurance Company*. A private mortgage insurance company will insure your loan to the lender against a default by the borrower. In the event a default occurs, the lender has insurance on the mortgage loan up to 30 percent of the value. This simply means that if there is a default and a foreclosure of the property is in question, the insurance company would be responsible for the top 30 percent of the loss suffered by the lender. In the event the lender could not achieve its full value from the sale of the property to pay off the mortgage loans, attorney fees and other costs which may have occurred in the foreclosure action, the lender would be protected.

Mortgage lenders require loans with loan to value (LTV) of between 80 and 95 percent to have insurance coverage of at least 25 to 30 percent of the amount borrowed. In the event of default by the borrower, this limits the bank's risk to 81 to 95 percent, less the 25 to 30 percent coverage by the insurance company.

In cases where a 20 percent down payment is not possible, obtaining private mortgage insurance may be the borrower's only chance of owning their own home. The cost of private mortgage insurance is expensive, however, and the following example illustrates just how much it will cost you.

Example:

Let's use the costs required by one of the major private mortgage insurance plans. If you borrow a loan amount that is 90 percnt of value, and the amount borrowed is $80,000, the payment to meet your cash escrow requirement is $1,440 for the first year's premium, paid in advance. This is an additional up front closing cost. In addition, you now will have added to your monthly payment of principal, interest, insurance and taxes payment, a PMI charge of an additional $30 per month for the life of the mortgage.

Most recently, some major savings and loan institutions have incorporated 90 percent financing on certain mortgage programs without private mortgage insurance being required. These new programs are limited to adjustable rates, but the savings to you for private mortgage insurance coverage such as described herein are substantial. In addition to the expense, the PMI company is going to be far more discriminating as to your financial situation in regards to credit, debt and income.

This close scrutiny is due to the fact that the major risk is to the PMI company in insuring the top portion of the loan. In many cases, borrowers receive an approval from the bank subject to private mortgage insurance approval. If the insurance company denies the insurance coverage, the bank is forced to deny your mortgage loan request, even though it was originally approved.

Escrows are usually collected by banks as part of your monthly payment for property taxes, hazard insurance, and if applicable, private mortgage insurance (PMI). By paying monthly, the bank will hold your escrows and assume the responsibility of the payments to the appropriate designees.

Some would argue against escrows held by the banks because they want to earn the interest on the money rather than their bank. Let's assume for the purpose of disputing this theory that the escrows you will have to pay each year total $1,200 per annum, or $100 per month. How much interest can be earned?

If you were able to earn $100 per year in interest, would it be worth it to you to receive $8.33 per month to assume the responsibility of making these escrow payments on a timely basis? It is very unlikely that it is worth it to any of us. Most banks mandate that escrows be paid by the borrower to them on a monthly basis.

If you are taking out a new mortgage, you may also be required to make direct lump sum payments to the escrow account for the previously listed items. These are separate from your regular monthly escrow payments, and are done in order to bring all escrows up to the required level as of the date of your closing.

As discussed in Chapter 5, obtaining a mortgage loan doesn't necessarily involve generating a new loan. Some loans can be "assumed" by the buyer from the seller. Assumption means that the loan can be transferred from the buyer to the seller for the remaining term of the loan. The purpose of assuming a loan is to obtain a low-interest rate loan. Since the balance of the assumed mortgage has been reduced by payments over the time it has been held, it may be relatively low in relation to the current selling price.

Prior to the 1980s, assuming a conventional fixed rate mortgage was commonplace. In today's financial market however, assumption may be only available on certain limited mortgage programs that include a "qualifier." A qualifier limits assumability to a qualified buyer or a current interest rate adjustment. A qualified buyer must qualify for the loan as if he were applying for a new mortgage in terms of credit, debt, and income. In addition, the lender reserves the right to increase the seller's mortgage interest rate to the prevailing higher one for the buyer. In addition to conventional loans, today, assumption is often available with qualifiers on certain adjustable rate mortgage programs and can be used by banks to entice the borrower into these types of programs.

From a seller's standpoint, there are advantages and disadvantages to assumption. It can be less secure, and reduce your market of potential buyers. On the other hand, it also may put some additional cash in your pocket at closing, and be the only way to sell your home. Let's see what occurs after you have owned your home for five years of your 30-year term and are contemplating selling.

With Assumption

Original Purchase Price	5-Year Appreciation Purchase Price		Principal Balance Remaining (5 Years)		Cash to Close From Buyer
$80,000	$102,000	minus	$784,000	=	$28,000 plus closing costs

Buyer Provides Own Bank Financing

Purchase Price	Bank (95%) Financing	Cash Down Payment	Closing Costs		Cash to Close
$102,100	$96,995	$5,105	$4,000	=	$9,105

The above examples demonstrate that with assumption, the buyer often must produce more cash on closing than if they obtained a new mortgage. In this example, approximately $19,000 more in cash is needed for assumability. A new mortgage would require less cash down; however, the monthly payments would be higher due to the larger loan and higher interest rates. In assuming an existing loan, the monthly payments are lower and the balance is paid off sooner. As you can see, there are trade offs to both methods.

Whether you are a buyer or a seller, consider all the financial positions before making a decision. From a buyer's standpoint, the assumption of the seller's mortgage may be a distinct advantage to you if the seller interest rate is comparable or lower than the prevailing rates offered by banks. Because the seller's mortgage has been reduced by the number of years the mortgage has been held, you will also save the front-loading interest because it has already been paid by the seller in the early years of the mortgage. In addition, the assumption of a seller's mortgage will save you points, origination fees and substantial closing costs which a bank would charge, but a seller would not. In the event the seller's mortgage rate is slightly higher, it may be to your advantage to take the higher rate than the prevailing one through a bank due to the savings discussed previously. Lastly, if you had previous credit problems, you would find in most cases that it is easier to assume a mortgage from the seller than originating a new mortgage and running the chance of having your application denied.

The down payment could be lower with "seller financing" by negotiating a *purchase money second mortgage* with the seller for the difference between your down payment, the principal balance remaining on the seller's mortgage, and the price that you agree to pay for the seller's home. The following example illustrates this:

Example :

1. Negotiated sales price between buyer and seller - $80,000

2. Down payment you propose and seller has accepted - $4,000

3. Remaining balance due seller - $76,000

4. Seller's remaining balance on mortgage you are assuming is eight years old, and has a remaining term of 22 years - $60,775

5. Balance needed to close - $15,225

The figure of $15,225 is the mortgage loan you will need to negotiate with the seller. It is commonly referred to as a purchase money second. Let's see how this works out as a monthly payment. The monthly payment on the original mortgage obtained by the seller for $65,000 at ten percent for 30 years is $570.43. Purchase money second mortgage negotiated by you, for ten years at a fixed rate of ten percent, has a monthly payment of $201.20. The total of these two payments is $771.63.

It is the buyer's responsibility to negotiate the purchase money second mortgage for the best terms available as illustrated in other segments throughout this book. You may choose a weekly, a biweekly, or a monthly payment method.

When selecting a mortgage program, your main concern should be in acquiring the best interest rate and mortgage term at the lowest cost. If the seller has no mortgage on his home, it may be in your best interest to negotiate a purchase money first mortgage on the best term you can, based upon the information in this book. In many cases, your credit and income worthiness will not be challenged in this type of situation.

Usually within three days of receiving your application, the lender is required to provide you with a *Truth in Lending and Disclosure Statement*. The Truth in Lending statement discloses the "Annual Percentage Rate" (APR) which reflects the cost of your mortgage loan as a yearly rate. This rate may be higher than the rate stated in your mortgage because the APR includes the interest, the loan discount (points), fees, and other credit costs. The Truth in Lending Statement also discloses the finance charges, schedule of payments, late payment charges, and if they exist, any prepayment penalties. Often, the disclosures in the Truth in Lending Statement will be estimates because the information may not be finalized. Should the actual APR differ greatly from the original bank estimate, the lender must give you a corrected Truth in Lending Statement no later than at settlement. However, if the estimated APR proves to be correct, the lender need not give you a new Truth in Lending Statement, even if other disclosures have changed. For this reason, you may want to ask the bank shortly before settlement if all the Truth in Lending disclosures remain accurate.

Following Chapter 12, you will find samples of Truth in Lending Statements and disclosure statements. The disclosure statements enclosed are formal explanations of the terms of some of the most common loan programs. In addition, they contain information regarding the complete structure of the loan program which is not always included in the Truth in Lending Statement. It is important to receive a disclosure statement and review it thoroughly to insure proper representation by your lender.

Chapter 7

Beating the System Using the Federal Tax Laws

According to the Tax Reform Act of 1986, your payments of interest and real estate taxes are deductible from federal income taxes on your first and second mortgages only. Contrary to the laws prior to 1986, homeowners are not allowed to borrow unlimited amounts against their homes. These deductions are now restricted to the original purchase price and the cost of home improvements, in addition to any funds needed for medical or educational expenses. Other tax deductions are available when you sell a home, therefore, it is always wise to consult with your accountant to find out the best tax advantages for you.

The Tax Reform Act of 1986 places some limitations on the refinancing of an existing mortgage in regard to the tax deductions that were normally allowed prior to the act. If you are contemplating refinancing your mortgage, and you are financing a larger loan amount than your original purchase price, refer to your accountant for any new tax deduction limitations. Also, if it applies to you, verify with your accountant on the new aspects of the Tax Reform Act concerning vacation homes and non-owner occupied residential property.

The only closing cost tax deductions allowed on residential mortgage financing are discount points, which is the prepaid interest. However, if discount points are financed within the mortgage over the term of the mortgage, tax deductions will be limited to the expense of discount points incurred each year over the term of the mortgage.

It may be of interest to note how interest deductions affect your taxable income. Contrary to popular thought, interest on mortgages is *not* a deduction from net income. The following example illustrates the effect of interest deduction.

Example:

With Interest Deduction	Without Interest Deduction
Tax Bracket—25%	Tax Bracket—25%
Gross Income—$30,000	Gross Income—$30,000
Interest Deduction—$3,000	Interest Deduction –0–
*Net Taxable Income—$27,000	*Net Taxable Income—$30,000
*Tax Deduction—$6,750	*Tax Deduction—$7,500

*If no other deduction

The Tax Reform Act of 1986 disallows any deduction for consumer interest, which includes interest on automobile and boat loans, credit card, general consumer financing, and tax deficiencies. The disallowance of personal interest is phased over five (5) years commencing in 1987. A full 35% of previously deductible interest became non-deductible as of 1987. Disallowance of personal interest decreased to 60 percent in 1988; 80 percent in 1989; 90 percent in 1990; and 100 percent thereafter. Interest on mortgage debt incurred prior to August 17, 1986 is not subject to the limitation identifiable and relating to the purchase price plus improvements.

In summation, those personal interest deductions which we were accustomed to deducting prior to the Tax Reform Act are no longer personal tax deductions. Borrowing against the equity in your home, to the limits described herein, is the primary method to achieve personal tax deduction.

Chapter 8

How to Save Money and Build Equity in Your Home

Equity is the value of the property in excess of the mortgage(s). There are two ways of building equity, and these include the appreciation method and the biweekly approach. Appreciation occurs when the value of your home increases above the amount paid. This appreciation occurrence is not easily predictable due to several socio-economic conditions. While in some areas, home values may rise, in other areas, home values may remain constant or even decrease in value. The decreasing value of a home is known as depreciation. This is an ever changing situation depending upon the location of the home. None of us have control over the appreciation or depreciation factor.

The second way to achieve equity is by paying less interest on your mortgage, and converting some of that interest savings to the accelerated reduction of the principal balance of the mortgage. Once the biweekly system is implemented, every year the principal balance of the mortgage is reduced. By doing this, you increase the difference between what the mortgage balance is and the cost of the home, or in other words, the equity. This equity build-up further reduces the dependency on appreciation as the primary means to achieve equity. If, however, the value of the property appreciates in value, you will have achieved both methods of increasing equity. If the property is not appreciating in value, you may still emerge ahead of the financial game by utilizing the biweekly approach. The biweekly approach results in a quicker reduction of principal, thereby increasing your equity.

Chapter 9

The Future Value of Your Dollars Derived from the "Beat the System" Approach

Throughout this book, you are constantly provided with information and specific instructions that will save you thousands of dollars in closing costs and interest payments over the term of a mortgage. To re-emphasize the importance of these interest savings, let's examine the future value of each dollar actually saved. and the money realized if those dollars were deposited in a savings account earning compounded interest.

Example:

A. Each dollar at 6 1/2 percent, compounded interest for *five* years, has an increased value of $1.37.

B. Each dollar at 6 1/2 percent, compounded interest for *ten* years has an increased value of $1.88.

To further emphasize the point, examine the following table, which demonstrates the enormous savings possible over the life of a mortgage with a loan amount of $110,000, an interest rate of ten percent, and a term of both 15 years and 30 years, respectively.

Analyzing this exhibit demonstrates that the future value of the interest dollars saved in the 30-year term mortgage is $272,729.12,[1] and $36,277.39[1] in the 15-year term. These future values are possible due to the use of the biweekly payment system which is discussed in detail in Chapter 11.

---

1   Compounded interest plus inflationary value of one percent per annum.

Table 9–1   **Future Value of Dollar on Interest Saved**
Biweekly Payment Program
6 1/2% per Annum, Compounded Yearly
Mr. and Mrs. William Smith—Homeowners
Loan Amount: $110,000.00

A. Term: 15 Years

End of Year	Interest Saved Prior Yr.	Interest Saved to Date	6 1/2% Earned	Earnings to Date	Total Saved/ Earned to Date	Value (1% CPI) to Date
2	0.00	0.00	0.00	0.00	0.00	0.00
3	167.45	167.45	10.88	10.88	178.33	178.33
4	356.08	523.53	34.74	45.62	569.15	570.93
5	568.67	1,092.20	73.96	119.58	1,211.78	1,217.49
6	808.25	1,900.45	131.30	250.88	2,151.33	2,163.50
7	1,078.18	2,978.63	209.92	460.80	3,439.43	3,461.07
8	1,382.34	4,360.97	313.42	774.22	5,135.19	5,169.80
9	1,725.12	6,086.09	445.92	1,220.14	7,306.23	7,357.93
10	2,111.32	8,197.41	612.14	1,832.28	10,029.69	10,103.27
11	2,546.54	10,743.95	817.45	2,649.73	13,393.68	13,494.71
12	3,036.91	13,780.86	1,067.99	3,717.72	17,498.58	17,633.53
13	3,589.53	17,370.39	1,370.73	5,088.45	22,458.84	22,635.18
14	3,938.70	21,309.09	1,715.84	6,804.29	28,113.38	28,339.73
15	2,656.01	23,965.10	2,000.01	8,804.30	32,769.40	33,052.80
16	983.71	24,948.81	2,193.95	10,998.25	35,947.06	36,277.59

B. Term: 30 Years

2	0.00	0.00	0.00	0.00	0.00	0.00
3	143.53	143.53	9.33	9.33	152.86	152.86
4	305.26	448.79	29.78	39.11	487.90	489.43
5	487.48	936.27	63.40	102.51	1,038.78	1,043.67
6	692.81	1,629.08	112.55	215.06	1,844.14	1,854.58
7	924.20	2,553.28	179.94	395.00	2,948.28	2,966.83
8	1,184.90	3,738.18	268.66	663.66	4,401.84	4,431.51
9	1,478.71	5,216.89	382.24	1,045.90	6,262.79	6,307.11
10	1,809.76	7,026.65	524.72	1,570.62	8,597.27	8,660.34
11	2,182.79	9,209.44	700.70	2,271.32	11,480.76	11,567.36
12	2,603.16	11,812.60	915.45	3,186.77	14,999.37	15,115.04
13	3,076.79	14,889.39	1,174.95	4,361.72	19,251.11	19,402.26
14	3,610.53	18,499.92	1,486.01	5,847.73	24,347.65	24,541.67
15	4,211.97	22,711.89	1,856.38	7,704.11	30,416.00	30,661.42
16	4,889.63	27,601.52	2,294.87	9,998.98	37,600.50	37,907.11
17	5,653.29	33,254.81	2,811.50	12,810.48	46,065.29	46,444.36
18	6,513.79	39,768.60	3,417.64	16,228.12	55,996.72	56,461.16
19	7,483.43	47,252.03	4,126.21	20,354.33	67,606.36	68,170.97
20	8,576.03	55,828.06	4,951.86	25,306.19	81,134.25	81,815.96
21	9,719.53	65,547.59	5,905.50	31,211.69	96,759.28	97,577.44
22	9,230.21	74,777.80	6,889.32	38,101.01	112,878.81	113,854.58
23	8,678.84	83,456.64	7,901.25	46,002.26	129,458.90	130,597.45
24	8,057.57	91,514.21	8,938.57	54,940.83	146,455.04	147,761.01
25	7,357.49	98,871.70	9,997.81	64,938.64	163,810.34	165,287.95
26	6,568.63	105,440.33	11,074.63	76,013.27	181,453.60	183,106.48
27	5,679.69	111,120.02	12,163.66	88,176.93	199,296.95	201,128.01
28	4,678.03	115,798.05	13,258.37	101,435.30	217,233.35	219,244.63
29	3,549.33	119,347.38	14,350.87	115,786.17	235,133.55	237,326.00
30	2,277.51	121,624.89	15,431.72	131,217.89	252,842.78	255,216.04
31	844.51	122,469.40	16,489.67	147,707.56	270,176.96	272,729.12

Chapter 10

Using the "Beat the System" Approach to Increase Your Borrowing Power

The implementation of the biweekly system of payments will save thousands of dollars in interest, which in turn accelerates the reduction of the principal balance. As the following illustration demonstrates, reducing the principal balance causes accelerated equity build-up.

Basis - $80,000 mortgage, interest rate of ten percent and a term of 30 years.

Without Biweekly System		With Biweekly System			
End of Year	Remaining Principal Balance	End of Year	Remaining Principal Balance		Equity Difference
5	$77,259.23	5	$72,932.69	+	$4,326.54
10	$72,749.76	10	$61,304.82	+	$11,444.94
15	$65,330.37	15	$42,173.29	+	$23,157.08
20	$53,123.15	20	$10,696.10	+	$42,427.05
22*	$46,263.68	22*	$ 226.28	+	$46,037.40

*Eight years still remain until payoff

*Entire loan payoff

The equity build-up, which is caused by decreasing the principal balance of the mortgage, increases the buyer's borrowing power. The increased borrowing power can be converted to cash through a second mortgage or equity line of credit financing for major purchasing, cash investments, or any emergency which may occur. Each of these methods of equity financing can be achieved with full IRS personal tax deductability of the interest charged.

Second mortgage or equity lines of credit due to increased borrowing power are less costly for several reasons. As we have already established, the interest charges are deductible on second mortgages or equity lines of credit. Refer to Chapter 7 for more detailed information on deductible interest. Second mortgage or equity line of credit interest and finance charges are generally much lower than consumer finance and interest charges, such as those on credit cards, automobiles, and boats. Second mortgage or equity lines of credit avoid the more costly refinance of the entire first mortgage method to obtain equity out in the form of cash. Refer to Chapter 3 for further information on refinancing.

How to increase your borrowing power? The next chapter demonstrates in detail how you can achieve increased borrowing power in addition to saving thousands of dollars in interest payments.

Chapter 11

The Ultimate "Beat the System" Approach

In previous chapters, we discussed that the method of mortgage loan repayment occurs once a month, and the interest charged on these loans is calculated daily on the outstanding balance. We have established that this interest cost amounts to thousands of dollars for the term of a mortgage. The approaches we will be exploring will provide property owners with a safe, secure and disciplined method to reduce their mortgage interest costs, and rapidly increase the equity accumulation in their property. One way you can accomplish this is by making biweekly (twice a week) mortgage payments instead of the standard once monthly mortgage payment.

Assume, for the sake of example, that you have a 30-year mortgage at a nine percent interest rate with an original balance of $80,000. In the first five years of your mortgage, you will have spent $35,000 in interest and reduced your original principal balance by only $3,280. In the first ten years of your mortgage, you will have spent over $70,000 in interest, with a net principal reduction of only $8,480. Therefore, your balance after ten years is still over $71,500 on an $80,000 mortgage.

By instituting the biweekly payment schedule, you would be able to reduce the interest expenditures and build up the equity in your home.

Example:

Your current monthly mortgage payment is $800, and you remit that amount once each month. Let's explore the implications of paying half of your monthly payment every two weeks. In other words, you will be sending $400 every two weeks instead of $800 once a month. By generating a payment every two weeks, you will actually be remitting 26 payments of $400 instead of 12 payments of $800. This results in making one full extra payment per year of $800. It calculates out that 26 times $400 equals $10,400, while 12 times $800 totals $9,600. The result is an additional $800 per year paid into your mortgage to reduce the principal balance. In remitting this extra payment, you will need to specify that it is for principal only. By following this method, you will save thousands of dollars in interest costs and reduce the original 30-year mortgage by nine years, and the 15-year mortgage by three years!

If your interest rate is higher than is shown on the previous example, your savings will be thousands of dollars greater. If your interest rate is fortunately lower than the example, the savings will be a few thousand dollars less, but, still amount to a substantial savings. Even if you don't intend to live in your home for the full term remaining on your mortgage, the principal reduction you make through biweekly payments is to your benefit when you sell your home. You will have less to pay off on your mortgage balance when you sell; therefore, the remaining cash after your mortgage payoff goes to you. In almost every situation, it will be to your advantage to make biweekly payments. If you have an assumable mortgage, and the future buyer of your home is going to assume the mortgage, he will assume your principal balance. The difference between the lowered figure and the sales price you have agreed upon, goes into your pocket. In addition, in order for you to benefit from this system, it makes no difference what type of interest rate loan program mortgage or term you have. Fixed rates, adjustable rates, and graduated payment mortgages with terms from ten to 30 years are still mortgages on which you can save thousands of dollars in interest costs.

If you have a negative amortization loan, or one with prepayment penalties, you can still utilize this approach to save money. As long as the prepayments to principal reduction that you make do not exceed the allowable prepayment of your mortgage prepayment penalty, you will save thousands of dollars in interest costs.

The savings on most balloon mortgages are even greater than those mortgages without a balloon payment. Balloon mortgages generally have much less principal reduction structured within each monthly payment than conventional mortgages, therefore, the biweekly system has a more dramatic effect on savings.

This whole concept is based upon your continuing with your present mortgage company without incurring the tremendous costs of refinancing. You do not need to refinance or change your mortgage loan company. To implement this program, you will need to visit your bank's customer service department. Inform them that you would like the bank to open a special account for you to make payments directly from your checking or savings account to your mortgage company. This is usually accomplished through an automatic withdrawal by the bank, whereby the 26 biweekly payments will accumulate, and the bank will remit your monthly mortgage payments directly from their bank to your mortgage company on your behalf. At the end of each year, when the bank has accumulated that extra payment, you will direct them to make that payment directly to your mortgage company to reduce the *principal balance* of your mortgage.

This extra annual payment to principal reduction has a dramatic compounding effect. More and more of each future payment goes toward the reduction of principal rather than the costly payment of interest charges. Over the term of the typical mortgage, this process results in a substantial savings in interest costs, and an earlier payoff of the property owner's mortgage.

To set up the account and accomplish this task, the bank may charge you a small monthly service charge. However, the fee will be a slight cost compared to the enormous savings you will have in interest costs. In the event your present bank will not cooperate with you in the manner described, you may find another bank that will. The other option is to arrange with your present mortgage lender an "automatic withdrawal" from your bank account, which will accomplish the same result. It is safe, simple, and automatic. You never have to write a mortgage check again because everything is arranged between your bank and your checking or savings account. The withdrawals will be made in a timely fashion. You will always receive a receipt notifying you that those payments have been taken from your checking or savings account and paid directly to your mortgage company.

By utilizing the biweekly method, you will have in effect, a forced savings account which is building equity. You will save thousands of dollars in interest, increase your net worth, reduce your mortgage balance, save the time and bother of issuing mortgage payments to your mortgage company, increase your personal cash credit and equity borrowing power and have the security of your bank making automatic mortgage payments for you, which protects your good credit standing.

The following tables demonstrate the comprehensive savings available by using the biweekly system.

Table 11–1   Comparison of Costs and Savings for Mr. & Mrs. John Abbot—Homeowners Conventional vs. Biweekly Programs Summary

```
==================================================================================================
| ORIGINAL LOAN AMOUNT:           80,000.00          ANNUAL INTEREST RATE:          10.000 % |
| ORIGINAL LOAN TERM:             15 (YEARS)         CURRENT MONTHLY PAYMENT:        859.68   |
| NUMBER OF PREVIOUS PAYMENTS:     0                 'NEW' BIWEEKLY PAYMENT:         429.84   |
| CURRENT LOAN BALANCE:           80,000.00                                                   |
==================================================================================================
```

	CURRENT MONTHLY			'NEW' BIWEEKLY			DIFFERENCE	
END OF YEAR	REMAINING BALANCE	INTEREST PAID TO-DATE	(EQUITY) PRINCIPAL PAID TO-DATE	REMAINING BALANCE	INTEREST PAID TO-DATE	(EQUITY) PRINCIPAL PAID TO-DATE	EQUTIY GROWTH TO-DATE	INTEREST SAVED TO-DATE
1	77,574.69	7,890.85	2,425.31	76,715.01	7,890.85	3,284.99	859.68	0.00
2	74,895.42	15,527.74	5,104.58	73,086.02	15,437.70	6,913.98	1,809.40	90.04
3	71,935.59	22,884.07	8,064.41	69,077.02	22,604.54	10,922.98	2,858.57	279.53
4	68,665.81	29,930.45	11,334.19	64,648.21	29,351.57	15,351.79	4,017.60	578.88
5	65,053.65	36,634.45	14,946.35	59,755.67	35,634.87	20,244.33	5,297.98	999.58
6	61,063.26	42,960.22	18,936.74	54,350.83	41,405.87	25,649.17	6,712.43	1,554.35
7	56,655.02	48,868.14	23,344.98	48,380.01	46,610.89	31,619.99	8,275.01	2,257.25
8	51,785.18	54,314.46	28,214.82	41,783.99	51,190.71	38,216.01	10,001.19	3,123.75
9	46,405.40	59,250.84	33,594.60	34,497.29	55,079.85	45,502.71	11,908.11	4,170.99
10	40,462.29	63,623.89	39,537.71	26,447.54	58,205.94	53,552.46	14,014.75	5,417.95
11	33,896.84	67,374.60	46,103.16	17,554.90	60,489.14	62,445.10	16,341.94	6,885.46
12	26,643.90	70,437.82	53,356.10	7,731.08	61,841.16	72,268.92	18,912.82	8,596.66
13	18,631.49	72,741.57	61,368.51	DEBT FREE	62,180.48	80,000.00		10,561.09
14	9,780.08	74,206.32	70,219.92					12,025.84
15	854.38	74,744.22	80,000.00					12,563.74

```
        TOTAL INTEREST SAVED:    12,563.74
        TOTAL TERM SAVED:        27.36 (PAYMENTS)  2.28  (YEARS)
```

Table 11–2   Amortization Schedule Re: Table 11–1

```
Names:        MR. & MRS. JOHN ABBOTT
Property:     13467 CAMINO AVENUE, SARASOTA, FL 34732
Telephone:    (803)555-8888
Tax I.D.:     123-45-6789
```

ORIGINAL LOAN AMOUNT: 80,000.00	BIWEEKLY PAYMENT:	429.84
ORIGINAL INTEREST RATE: 10.000	TOTAL BIWEEKLY INTEREST PAID:	62,180.48
ORIGINAL TERM OF LOAN: 15 (YRS)	LAST BIWEEKLY PAYMENT DATE:	08/26/2003
NUMBER OF PREVIOUS PAYMENTS: 0	NEW TERM OF LOAN:	12.72 (YRS)
CURRENT LOAN BALANCE: 80,000.00		

PMT #	PAYMENT DATE	PAYMENT AMOUNT	INTEREST PAID	PRINCIPAL PAID	BALANCE OWED	ACCUMULATED INTEREST	ACCUMULATED PRINCIPAL
1	01/01/1991	429.84	0.00	0.00	80,000.00	0.00	0.00
2	01/15/1991	429.84	666.67	193.01	79,806.99	666.67	193.01
3	01/29/1991	429.84	0.00	0.00	79,806.99	666.67	193.01
4	02/12/1991	429.84	665.06	194.62	79,612.37	1,331.73	387.63
5	02/26/1991	429.84	0.00	0.00	79,612.37	1,331.73	387.63
6	03/12/1991	429.84	663.44	196.24	79,416.13	1,995.17	583.87
7	03/26/1991	429.84	0.00	0.00	79,416.13	1,995.17	583.87
8	04/09/1991	429.84	661.80	197.88	79,218.25	2,656.97	781.75
9	04/23/1991	429.84	0.00	0.00	79,218.25	2,656.97	781.75
10	05/07/1991	429.84	660.15	199.53	79,018.72	3,317.12	981.28
11	05/21/1991	429.84	0.00	0.00	79,018.72	3,317.12	981.28
12	06/04/1991	429.84	658.49	201.19	78,817.53	3,975.61	1,182.47
13	06/18/1991	429.84	0.00	0.00	78,817.53	3,975.61	1,182.47
14	07/02/1991	429.84	656.81	202.87	78,614.66	4,632.42	1,385.34
15	07/16/1991	429.84	0.00	0.00	78,614.66	4,632.42	1,385.34
16	07/30/1991	429.84	655.12	204.56	78,410.10	5,287.54	1,589.90
17	08/13/1991	429.84	0.00	0.00	78,410.10	5,287.54	1,589.90
18	08/27/1991	429.84	653.42	206.26	78,203.84	5,940.96	1,796.16
19	09/10/1991	429.84	0.00	0.00	78,203.84	5,940.96	1,796.16
20	09/24/1991	429.84	651.70	207.98	77,995.86	6,592.66	2,004.14
21	10/08/1991	429.84	0.00	0.00	77,995.86	6,592.66	2,004.14
22	10/22/1991	429.84	649.97	209.71	77,786.15	7,242.63	2,213.85
23	11/05/1991	429.84	0.00	0.00	77,786.15	7,242.63	2,213.85
24	11/19/1991	429.84	648.22	211.46	77,574.69	7,890.85	2,425.31
25	12/03/1991	429.84	0.00	0.00	77,574.69	7,890.85	2,425.31
26	12/17/1991	429.84	0.00	859.68	76,715.01	7,890.85	3,284.99
27	12/31/1991	429.84	0.00	0.00	76,715.01	7,890.85	3,284.99
28	01/14/1992	429.84	639.29	220.39	76,494.62	8,530.14	3,505.38
29	01/28/1992	429.84	0.00	0.00	76,494.62	8,530.14	3,505.38
30	02/11/1992	429.84	637.46	222.22	76,272.40	9,167.60	3,727.60
31	02/25/1992	429.84	0.00	0.00	76,272.40	9,167.60	3,727.60
32	03/10/1992	429.84	635.60	224.08	76,048.32	9,803.20	3,951.68
33	03/24/1992	429.84	0.00	0.00	76,048.32	9,803.20	3,951.68
34	04/07/1992	429.84	633.74	225.94	75,822.38	10,436.94	4,177.62

Table 11–2   Continued

Names: MR. & MRS. JOHN ABBOTT

PMT #	PAYMENT DATE	PAYMENT AMOUNT	INTEREST PAID	PRINCIPAL PAID	BALANCE OWED	ACCUMULATED INTEREST	ACCUMULATED PRINCIPAL
35	04/21/1992	429.84	0.00	0.00	75,822.38	10,436.94	4,177.62
36	05/05/1992	429.84	631.85	227.83	75,594.55	11,068.79	4,405.45
37	05/19/1992	429.84	0.00	0.00	75,594.55	11,068.79	4,405.45
38	06/02/1992	429.84	629.95	229.73	75,364.82	11,698.74	4,635.18
39	06/16/1992	429.84	0.00	0.00	75,364.82	11,698.74	4,635.18
40	06/30/1992	429.84	628.04	231.64	75,133.18	12,326.78	4,866.82
41	07/14/1992	429.84	0.00	0.00	75,133.18	12,326.78	4,866.82
42	07/28/1992	429.84	626.11	233.57	74,899.61	12,952.89	5,100.39
43	08/11/1992	429.84	0.00	0.00	74,899.61	12,952.89	5,100.39
44	08/25/1992	429.84	624.16	235.52	74,664.09	13,577.05	5,335.91
45	09/08/1992	429.84	0.00	0.00	74,664.09	13,577.05	5,335.91
46	09/22/1992	429.84	622.20	237.48	74,426.61	14,199.25	5,573.39
47	10/06/1992	429.84	0.00	0.00	74,426.61	14,199.25	5,573.39
48	10/20/1992	429.84	620.22	239.46	74,187.15	14,819.47	5,812.85
49	11/03/1992	429.84	0.00	0.00	74,187.15	14,819.47	5,812.85
50	11/17/1992	429.84	618.23	241.45	73,945.70	15,437.70	6,054.30
51	12/01/1992	429.84	0.00	0.00	73,945.70	15,437.70	6,054.30
52	12/15/1992	429.84	0.00	859.68	73,086.02	15,437.70	6,913.98
53	12/29/1992	429.84	0.00	0.00	73,086.02	15,437.70	6,913.98
54	01/12/1993	429.84	609.05	250.63	72,835.39	16,046.75	7,164.61
55	01/26/1993	429.84	0.00	0.00	72,835.39	16,046.75	7,164.61
56	02/09/1993	429.84	606.96	252.72	72,582.67	16,653.71	7,417.33
57	02/23/1993	429.84	0.00	0.00	72,582.67	16,653.71	7,417.33
58	03/09/1993	429.84	604.86	254.82	72,327.85	17,258.57	7,672.15
59	03/23/1993	429.84	0.00	0.00	72,327.85	17,258.57	7,672.15
60	04/06/1993	429.84	602.73	256.95	72,070.90	17,861.30	7,929.10
61	04/20/1993	429.84	0.00	0.00	72,070.90	17,861.30	7,929.10
62	05/04/1993	429.84	600.59	259.09	71,811.81	18,461.89	8,188.19
63	05/18/1993	429.84	0.00	0.00	71,811.81	18,461.89	8,188.19
64	06/01/1993	429.84	598.43	261.25	71,550.56	19,060.32	8,449.44
65	06/15/1993	429.84	0.00	0.00	71,550.56	19,060.32	8,449.44
66	06/29/1993	429.84	596.25	263.43	71,287.13	19,656.57	8,712.87
67	07/13/1993	429.84	0.00	0.00	71,287.13	19,656.57	8,712.87
68	07/27/1993	429.84	594.06	265.62	71,021.51	20,250.63	8,978.49
69	08/10/1993	429.84	0.00	0.00	71,021.51	20,250.63	8,978.49
70	08/24/1993	429.84	591.85	267.83	70,753.68	20,842.48	9,246.32
71	09/07/1993	429.84	0.00	0.00	70,753.68	20,842.48	9,246.32
72	09/21/1993	429.84	589.61	270.07	70,483.61	21,432.09	9,516.39
73	10/05/1993	429.84	0.00	0.00	70,483.61	21,432.09	9,516.39
74	10/19/1993	429.84	587.36	272.32	70,211.29	22,019.45	9,788.71
75	11/02/1993	429.84	0.00	0.00	70,211.29	22,019.45	9,788.71
76	11/16/1993	429.84	585.09	274.59	69,936.70	22,604.54	10,063.30
77	11/30/1993	429.84	0.00	0.00	69,936.70	22,604.54	10,063.30
78	12/14/1993	429.84	0.00	859.68	69,077.02	22,604.54	10,922.98
79	12/28/1993	429.84	0.00	0.00	69,077.02	22,604.54	10,922.98

Table 11–2   Continued

Names: MR. & MRS. JOHN ABBOTT

PMT #	PAYMENT DATE	PAYMENT AMOUNT	INTEREST PAID	PRINCIPAL PAID	BALANCE OWED	ACCUMULATED INTEREST	ACCUMULATED PRINCIPAL
80	01/11/1994	429.84	575.64	284.04	68,792.98	23,180.18	11,207.02
81	01/25/1994	429.84	0.00	0.00	68,792.98	23,180.18	11,207.02
82	02/08/1994	429.84	573.27	286.41	68,506.57	23,753.45	11,493.43
83	02/22/1994	429.84	0.00	0.00	68,506.57	23,753.45	11,493.43
84	03/08/1994	429.84	570.89	288.79	68,217.78	24,324.34	11,782.22
85	03/22/1994	429.84	0.00	0.00	68,217.78	24,324.34	11,782.22
86	04/05/1994	429.84	568.48	291.20	67,926.58	24,892.82	12,073.42
87	04/19/1994	429.84	0.00	0.00	67,926.58	24,892.82	12,073.42
88	05/03/1994	429.84	566.05	293.63	67,632.95	25,458.87	12,367.05
89	05/17/1994	429.84	0.00	0.00	67,632.95	25,458.87	12,367.05
90	05/31/1994	429.84	563.61	296.07	67,336.88	26,022.48	12,663.12
91	06/14/1994	429.84	0.00	0.00	67,336.88	26,022.48	12,663.12
92	06/28/1994	429.84	561.14	298.54	67,038.34	26,583.62	12,961.66
93	07/12/1994	429.84	0.00	0.00	67,038.34	26,583.62	12,961.66
94	07/26/1994	429.84	558.65	301.03	66,737.31	27,142.27	13,262.69
95	08/09/1994	429.84	0.00	0.00	66,737.31	27,142.27	13,262.69
96	08/23/1994	429.84	556.14	303.54	66,433.77	27,698.41	13,566.23
97	09/06/1994	429.84	0.00	0.00	66,433.77	27,698.41	13,566.23
98	09/20/1994	429.84	553.61	306.07	66,127.70	28,252.02	13,872.30
99	10/04/1994	429.84	0.00	0.00	66,127.70	28,252.02	13,872.30
100	10/18/1994	429.84	551.06	308.62	65,819.08	28,803.08	14,180.92
101	11/01/1994	429.84	0.00	0.00	65,819.08	28,803.08	14,180.92
102	11/15/1994	429.84	548.49	311.19	65,507.89	29,351.57	14,492.11
103	11/29/1994	429.84	0.00	0.00	65,507.89	29,351.57	14,492.11
104	12/13/1994	429.84	0.00	859.68	64,648.21	29,351.57	15,351.79
105	12/27/1994	429.84	0.00	0.00	64,648.21	29,351.57	15,351.79
106	01/10/1995	429.84	538.74	320.94	64,327.27	29,890.31	15,672.73
107	01/24/1995	429.84	0.00	0.00	64,327.27	29,890.31	15,672.73
108	02/07/1995	429.84	536.06	323.62	64,003.65	30,426.37	15,996.35
109	02/21/1995	429.84	0.00	0.00	64,003.65	30,426.37	15,996.35
110	03/07/1995	429.84	533.36	326.32	63,677.33	30,959.73	16,322.67
111	03/21/1995	429.84	0.00	0.00	63,677.33	30,959.73	16,322.67
112	04/04/1995	429.84	530.64	329.04	63,348.29	31,490.37	16,651.71
113	04/18/1995	429.84	0.00	0.00	63,348.29	31,490.37	16,651.71
114	05/02/1995	429.84	527.90	331.78	63,016.51	32,018.27	16,983.49
115	05/16/1995	429.84	0.00	0.00	63,016.51	32,018.27	16,983.49
116	05/30/1995	429.84	525.14	334.54	62,681.97	32,543.41	17,318.03
117	06/13/1995	429.84	0.00	0.00	62,681.97	32,543.41	17,318.03
118	06/27/1995	429.84	522.35	337.33	62,344.64	33,065.76	17,655.36
119	07/11/1995	429.84	0.00	0.00	62,344.64	33,065.76	17,655.36
120	07/25/1995	429.84	519.54	340.14	62,004.50	33,585.30	17,995.50
121	08/08/1995	429.84	0.00	0.00	62,004.50	33,585.30	17,995.50
122	08/22/1995	429.84	516.70	342.98	61,661.52	34,102.00	18,338.48
123	09/05/1995	429.84	0.00	0.00	61,661.52	34,102.00	18,338.48
124	09/19/1995	429.84	513.85	345.83	61,315.69	34,615.85	18,684.31

Table 11–2   Continued

Names: MR. & MRS. JOHN ABBOTT

PMT #	PAYMENT DATE	PAYMENT AMOUNT	INTEREST PAID	PRINCIPAL PAID	BALANCE OWED	ACCUMULATED INTEREST	ACCUMULATED PRINCIPAL
125	10/03/1995	429.84	0.00	0.00	61,315.69	34,615.85	18,684.31
126	10/17/1995	429.84	510.96	348.72	60,966.97	35,126.81	19,033.03
127	10/31/1995	429.84	0.00	0.00	60,966.97	35,126.81	19,033.03
128	11/14/1995	429.84	508.06	351.62	60,615.35	35,634.87	19,384.65
129	11/28/1995	429.84	0.00	0.00	60,615.35	35,634.87	19,384.65
130	12/12/1995	429.84	0.00	859.68	59,755.67	35,634.87	20,244.33
131	12/26/1995	429.84	0.00	0.00	59,755.67	35,634.87	20,244.33
132	01/09/1996	429.84	497.96	361.72	59,393.95	36,132.83	20,606.05
133	01/23/1996	429.84	0.00	0.00	59,393.95	36,132.83	20,606.05
134	02/06/1996	429.84	494.95	364.73	59,029.22	36,627.78	20,970.78
135	02/20/1996	429.84	0.00	0.00	59,029.22	36,627.78	20,970.78
136	03/05/1996	429.84	491.91	367.77	58,661.45	37,119.69	21,338.55
137	03/19/1996	429.84	0.00	0.00	58,661.45	37,119.69	21,338.55
138	04/02/1996	429.84	488.85	370.83	58,290.62	37,608.54	21,709.38
139	04/16/1996	429.84	0.00	0.00	58,290.62	37,608.54	21,709.38
140	04/30/1996	429.84	485.76	373.92	57,916.70	38,094.30	22,083.30
141	05/14/1996	429.84	0.00	0.00	57,916.70	38,094.30	22,083.30
142	05/28/1996	429.84	482.64	377.04	57,539.66	38,576.94	22,460.34
143	06/11/1996	429.84	0.00	0.00	57,539.66	38,576.94	22,460.34
144	06/25/1996	429.84	479.50	380.18	57,159.48	39,056.44	22,840.52
145	07/09/1996	429.84	0.00	0.00	57,159.48	39,056.44	22,840.52
146	07/23/1996	429.84	476.33	383.35	56,776.13	39,532.77	23,223.87
147	08/06/1996	429.84	0.00	0.00	56,776.13	39,532.77	23,223.87
148	08/20/1996	429.84	473.13	386.55	56,389.58	40,005.90	23,610.42
149	09/03/1996	429.84	0.00	0.00	56,389.58	40,005.90	23,610.42
150	09/17/1996	429.84	469.91	389.77	55,999.81	40,475.81	24,000.19
151	10/01/1996	429.84	0.00	0.00	55,999.81	40,475.81	24,000.19
152	10/15/1996	429.84	466.67	393.01	55,606.80	40,942.48	24,393.20
153	10/29/1996	429.84	0.00	0.00	55,606.80	40,942.48	24,393.20
154	11/12/1996	429.84	463.39	396.29	55,210.51	41,405.87	24,789.49
155	11/26/1996	429.84	0.00	0.00	55,210.51	41,405.87	24,789.49
156	12/10/1996	429.84	0.00	859.68	54,350.83	41,405.87	25,649.17
157	12/24/1996	429.84	0.00	0.00	54,350.83	41,405.87	25,649.17
158	01/07/1997	429.84	452.92	406.76	53,944.07	41,858.79	26,055.93
159	01/21/1997	429.84	0.00	0.00	53,944.07	41,858.79	26,055.93
160	02/04/1997	429.84	449.53	410.15	53,533.92	42,308.32	26,466.08
161	02/18/1997	429.84	0.00	0.00	53,533.92	42,308.32	26,466.08
162	03/04/1997	429.84	446.12	413.56	53,120.36	42,754.44	26,879.64
163	03/18/1997	429.84	0.00	0.00	53,120.36	42,754.44	26,879.64
164	04/01/1997	429.84	442.67	417.01	52,703.35	43,197.11	27,296.65
165	04/15/1997	429.84	0.00	0.00	52,703.35	43,197.11	27,296.65
166	04/29/1997	429.84	439.19	420.49	52,282.86	43,636.30	27,717.14
167	05/13/1997	429.84	0.00	0.00	52,282.86	43,636.30	27,717.14
168	05/27/1997	429.84	435.69	423.99	51,858.87	44,071.99	28,141.13
169	06/10/1997	429.84	0.00	0.00	51,858.87	44,071.99	28,141.13

Table 11–2   Continued

Names: MR. & MRS. JOHN ABBOTT

PMT #	PAYMENT DATE	PAYMENT AMOUNT	INTEREST PAID	PRINCIPAL PAID	BALANCE OWED	ACCUMULATED INTEREST	ACCUMULATED PRINCIPAL
170	06/24/1997	429.84	432.16	427.52	51,431.35	44,504.15	28,568.65
171	07/08/1997	429.84	0.00	0.00	51,431.35	44,504.15	28,568.65
172	07/22/1997	429.84	428.59	431.09	51,000.26	44,932.74	28,999.74
173	08/05/1997	429.84	0.00	0.00	51,000.26	44,932.74	28,999.74
174	08/19/1997	429.84	425.00	434.68	50,565.58	45,357.74	29,434.42
175	09/02/1997	429.84	0.00	0.00	50,565.58	45,357.74	29,434.42
176	09/16/1997	429.84	421.38	438.30	50,127.28	45,779.12	29,872.72
177	09/30/1997	429.84	0.00	0.00	50,127.28	45,779.12	29,872.72
178	10/14/1997	429.84	417.73	441.95	49,685.33	46,196.85	30,314.67
179	10/28/1997	429.84	0.00	0.00	49,685.33	46,196.85	30,314.67
180	11/11/1997	429.84	414.04	445.64	49,239.69	46,610.89	30,760.31
181	11/25/1997	429.84	0.00	0.00	49,239.69	46,610.89	30,760.31
182	12/09/1997	429.84	0.00	859.68	48,380.01	46,610.89	31,619.99
183	12/23/1997	429.84	0.00	0.00	48,380.01	46,610.89	31,619.99
184	01/06/1998	429.84	403.17	456.51	47,923.50	47,014.06	32,076.50
185	01/20/1998	429.84	0.00	0.00	47,923.50	47,014.06	32,076.50
186	02/03/1998	429.84	399.36	460.32	47,463.18	47,413.42	32,536.82
187	02/17/1998	429.84	0.00	0.00	47,463.18	47,413.42	32,536.82
188	03/03/1998	429.84	395.53	464.15	46,999.03	47,808.95	33,000.97
189	03/17/1998	429.84	0.00	0.00	46,999.03	47,808.95	33,000.97
190	03/31/1998	429.84	391.66	468.02	46,531.01	48,200.61	33,468.99
191	04/14/1998	429.84	0.00	0.00	46,531.01	48,200.61	33,468.99
192	04/28/1998	429.84	387.76	471.92	46,059.09	48,588.37	33,940.91
193	05/12/1998	429.84	0.00	0.00	46,059.09	48,588.37	33,940.91
194	05/26/1998	429.84	383.83	475.85	45,583.24	48,972.20	34,416.76
195	06/09/1998	429.84	0.00	0.00	45,583.24	48,972.20	34,416.76
196	06/23/1998	429.84	379.86	479.82	45,103.42	49,352.06	34,896.58
197	07/07/1998	429.84	0.00	0.00	45,103.42	49,352.06	34,896.58
198	07/21/1998	429.84	375.86	483.82	44,619.60	49,727.92	35,380.40
199	08/04/1998	429.84	0.00	0.00	44,619.60	49,727.92	35,380.40
200	08/18/1998	429.84	371.83	487.85	44,131.75	50,099.75	35,868.25
201	09/01/1998	429.84	0.00	0.00	44,131.75	50,099.75	35,868.25
202	09/15/1998	429.84	367.76	491.92	43,639.83	50,467.51	36,360.17
203	09/29/1998	429.84	0.00	0.00	43,639.83	50,467.51	36,360.17
204	10/13/1998	429.84	363.67	496.01	43,143.82	50,831.18	36,856.18
205	10/27/1998	429.84	0.00	0.00	43,143.82	50,831.18	36,856.18
206	11/10/1998	429.84	359.53	500.15	42,643.67	51,190.71	37,356.33
207	11/24/1998	429.84	0.00	0.00	42,643.67	51,190.71	37,356.33
208	12/08/1998	429.84	0.00	859.68	41,783.99	51,190.71	38,216.01
209	12/22/1998	429.84	0.00	0.00	41,783.99	51,190.71	38,216.01
210	01/05/1999	429.84	348.20	511.48	41,272.51	51,538.91	38,727.49
211	01/19/1999	429.84	0.00	0.00	41,272.51	51,538.91	38,727.49
212	02/02/1999	429.84	343.94	515.74	40,756.77	51,882.85	39,243.23
213	02/16/1999	429.84	0.00	0.00	40,756.77	51,882.85	39,243.23
214	03/02/1999	429.84	339.64	520.04	40,236.73	52,222.49	39,763.27

Table 11–2   Continued

Names: MR. & MRS. JOHN ABBOTT

PMT #	PAYMENT DATE	PAYMENT AMOUNT	INTEREST PAID	PRINCIPAL PAID	BALANCE OWED	ACCUMULATED INTEREST	ACCUMULATED PRINCIPAL
215	03/16/1999	429.84	0.00	0.00	40,236.73	52,222.49	39,763.27
216	03/30/1999	429.84	335.31	524.37	39,712.36	52,557.80	40,287.64
217	04/13/1999	429.84	0.00	0.00	39,712.36	52,557.80	40,287.64
218	04/27/1999	429.84	330.94	528.74	39,183.62	52,888.74	40,816.38
219	05/11/1999	429.84	0.00	0.00	39,183.62	52,888.74	40,816.38
220	05/25/1999	429.84	326.53	533.15	38,650.47	53,215.27	41,349.53
221	06/08/1999	429.84	0.00	0.00	38,650.47	53,215.27	41,349.53
222	06/22/1999	429.84	322.09	537.59	38,112.88	53,537.36	41,887.12
223	07/06/1999	429.84	0.00	0.00	38,112.88	53,537.36	41,887.12
224	07/20/1999	429.84	317.61	542.07	37,570.81	53,854.97	42,429.19
225	08/03/1999	429.84	0.00	0.00	37,570.81	53,854.97	42,429.19
226	08/17/1999	429.84	313.09	546.59	37,024.22	54,168.06	42,975.78
227	08/31/1999	429.84	0.00	0.00	37,024.22	54,168.06	42,975.78
228	09/14/1999	429.84	308.54	551.14	36,473.08	54,476.60	43,526.92
229	09/28/1999	429.84	0.00	0.00	36,473.08	54,476.60	43,526.92
230	10/12/1999	429.84	303.94	555.74	35,917.34	54,780.54	44,082.66
231	10/26/1999	429.84	0.00	0.00	35,917.34	54,780.54	44,082.66
232	11/09/1999	429.84	299.31	560.37	35,356.97	55,079.85	44,643.03
233	11/23/1999	429.84	0.00	0.00	35,356.97	55,079.85	44,643.03
234	12/07/1999	429.84	0.00	859.68	34,497.29	55,079.85	45,502.71
235	12/21/1999	429.84	0.00	0.00	34,497.29	55,079.85	45,502.71
236	01/04/2000	429.84	287.48	572.20	33,925.09	55,367.33	46,074.91
237	01/18/2000	429.84	0.00	0.00	33,925.09	55,367.33	46,074.91
238	02/01/2000	429.84	282.71	576.97	33,348.12	55,650.04	46,651.88
239	02/15/2000	429.84	0.00	0.00	33,348.12	55,650.04	46,651.88
240	02/29/2000	429.84	277.90	581.78	32,766.34	55,927.94	47,233.66
241	03/14/2000	429.84	0.00	0.00	32,766.34	55,927.94	47,233.66
242	03/28/2000	429.84	273.05	586.63	32,179.71	56,200.99	47,820.29
243	04/11/2000	429.84	0.00	0.00	32,179.71	56,200.99	47,820.29
244	04/25/2000	429.84	268.16	591.52	31,588.19	56,469.15	48,411.81
245	05/09/2000	429.84	0.00	0.00	31,588.19	56,469.15	48,411.81
246	05/23/2000	429.84	263.23	596.45	30,991.74	56,732.38	49,008.26
247	06/06/2000	429.84	0.00	0.00	30,991.74	56,732.38	49,008.26
248	06/20/2000	429.84	258.26	601.42	30,390.32	56,990.64	49,609.68
249	07/04/2000	429.84	0.00	0.00	30,390.32	56,990.64	49,609.68
250	07/18/2000	429.84	253.25	606.43	29,783.89	57,243.89	50,216.11
251	08/01/2000	429.84	0.00	0.00	29,783.89	57,243.89	50,216.11
252	08/15/2000	429.84	248.20	611.48	29,172.41	57,492.09	50,827.59
253	08/29/2000	429.84	0.00	0.00	29,172.41	57,492.09	50,827.59
254	09/12/2000	429.84	243.10	616.58	28,555.83	57,735.19	51,444.17
255	09/26/2000	429.84	0.00	0.00	28,555.83	57,735.19	51,444.17
256	10/10/2000	429.84	237.97	621.71	27,934.12	57,973.16	52,065.88
257	10/24/2000	429.84	0.00	0.00	27,934.12	57,973.16	52,065.88
258	11/07/2000	429.84	232.78	626.90	27,307.22	58,205.94	52,692.78
259	11/21/2000	429.84	0.00	0.00	27,307.22	58,205.94	52,692.78

Table 11–2   Continued

Names: MR. & MRS. JOHN ABBOTT

PMT #	PAYMENT DATE	PAYMENT AMOUNT	INTEREST PAID	PRINCIPAL PAID	BALANCE OWED	ACCUMULATED INTEREST	ACCUMULATED PRINCIPAL
260	12/05/2000	429.84	0.00	859.68	26,447.54	58,205.94	53,552.46
261	12/19/2000	429.84	0.00	0.00	26,447.54	58,205.94	53,552.46
262	01/02/2001	429.84	220.40	639.28	25,808.26	58,426.34	54,191.74
263	01/16/2001	429.84	0.00	0.00	25,808.26	58,426.34	54,191.74
264	01/30/2001	429.84	215.07	644.61	25,163.65	58,641.41	54,836.35
265	02/13/2001	429.84	0.00	0.00	25,163.65	58,641.41	54,836.35
266	02/27/2001	429.84	209.70	649.98	24,513.67	58,851.11	55,486.33
267	03/13/2001	429.84	0.00	0.00	24,513.67	58,851.11	55,486.33
268	03/27/2001	429.84	204.28	655.40	23,858.27	59,055.39	56,141.73
269	04/10/2001	429.84	0.00	0.00	23,858.27	59,055.39	56,141.73
270	04/24/2001	429.84	198.82	660.86	23,197.41	59,254.21	56,802.59
271	05/08/2001	429.84	0.00	0.00	23,197.41	59,254.21	56,802.59
272	05/22/2001	429.84	193.31	666.37	22,531.04	59,447.52	57,468.96
273	06/05/2001	429.84	0.00	0.00	22,531.04	59,447.52	57,468.96
274	06/19/2001	429.84	187.76	671.92	21,859.12	59,635.28	58,140.88
275	07/03/2001	429.84	0.00	0.00	21,859.12	59,635.28	58,140.88
276	07/17/2001	429.84	182.16	677.52	21,181.60	59,817.44	58,818.40
277	07/31/2001	429.84	0.00	0.00	21,181.60	59,817.44	58,818.40
278	08/14/2001	429.84	176.51	683.17	20,498.43	59,993.95	59,501.57
279	08/28/2001	429.84	0.00	0.00	20,498.43	59,993.95	59,501.57
280	09/11/2001	429.84	170.82	688.86	19,809.57	60,164.77	60,190.43
281	09/25/2001	429.84	0.00	0.00	19,809.57	60,164.77	60,190.43
282	10/09/2001	429.84	165.08	694.60	19,114.97	60,329.85	60,885.03
283	10/23/2001	429.84	0.00	0.00	19,114.97	60,329.85	60,885.03
284	11/06/2001	429.84	159.29	700.39	18,414.58	60,489.14	61,585.42
285	11/20/2001	429.84	0.00	0.00	18,414.58	60,489.14	61,585.42
286	12/04/2001	429.84	0.00	859.68	17,554.90	60,489.14	62,445.10
287	12/18/2001	429.84	0.00	0.00	17,554.90	60,489.14	62,445.10
288	01/01/2002	429.84	146.29	713.39	16,841.51	60,635.43	63,158.49
289	01/15/2002	429.84	0.00	0.00	16,841.51	60,635.43	63,158.49
290	01/29/2002	429.84	140.35	719.33	16,122.18	60,775.78	63,877.82
291	02/12/2002	429.84	0.00	0.00	16,122.18	60,775.78	63,877.82
292	02/26/2002	429.84	134.35	725.33	15,396.85	60,910.13	64,603.15
293	03/12/2002	429.84	0.00	0.00	15,396.85	60,910.13	64,603.15
294	03/26/2002	429.84	128.31	731.37	14,665.48	61,038.44	65,334.52
295	04/09/2002	429.84	0.00	0.00	14,665.48	61,038.44	65,334.52
296	04/23/2002	429.84	122.21	737.47	13,928.01	61,160.65	66,071.99
297	05/07/2002	429.84	0.00	0.00	13,928.01	61,160.65	66,071.99
298	05/21/2002	429.84	116.07	743.61	13,184.40	61,276.72	66,815.60
299	06/04/2002	429.84	0.00	0.00	13,184.40	61,276.72	66,815.60
300	06/18/2002	429.84	109.87	749.81	12,434.59	61,386.59	67,565.41
301	07/02/2002	429.84	0.00	0.00	12,434.59	61,386.59	67,565.41
302	07/16/2002	429.84	103.62	756.06	11,678.53	61,490.21	68,321.47
303	07/30/2002	429.84	0.00	0.00	11,678.53	61,490.21	68,321.47
304	08/13/2002	429.84	97.32	762.36	10,916.17	61,587.53	69,083.83

Table 11-2   Continued

Names: MR. & MRS. JOHN ABBOTT

PMT #	PAYMENT DATE	PAYMENT AMOUNT	INTEREST PAID	PRINCIPAL PAID	BALANCE OWED	ACCUMULATED INTEREST	ACCUMULATED PRINCIPAL
305	08/27/2002	429.84	0.00	0.00	10,916.17	61,587.53	69,083.83
306	09/10/2002	429.84	90.97	768.71	10,147.46	61,678.50	69,852.54
307	09/24/2002	429.84	0.00	0.00	10,147.46	61,678.50	69,852.54
308	10/08/2002	429.84	84.56	775.12	9,372.34	61,763.06	70,627.66
309	10/22/2002	429.84	0.00	0.00	9,372.34	61,763.06	70,627.66
310	11/05/2002	429.84	78.10	781.58	8,590.76	61,841.16	71,409.24
311	11/19/2002	429.84	0.00	0.00	8,590.76	61,841.16	71,409.24
312	12/03/2002	429.84	0.00	859.68	7,731.08	61,841.16	72,268.92
313	12/17/2002	429.84	0.00	0.00	7,731.08	61,841.16	72,268.92
314	12/31/2002	429.84	64.43	795.25	6,935.83	61,905.59	73,064.17
315	01/14/2003	429.84	0.00	0.00	6,935.83	61,905.59	73,064.17
316	01/28/2003	429.84	57.80	801.88	6,133.95	61,963.39	73,866.05
317	02/11/2003	429.84	0.00	0.00	6,133.95	61,963.39	73,866.05
318	02/25/2003	429.84	51.12	808.56	5,325.39	62,014.51	74,674.61
319	03/11/2003	429.84	0.00	0.00	5,325.39	62,014.51	74,674.61
320	03/25/2003	429.84	44.38	815.30	4,510.09	62,058.89	75,489.91
321	04/08/2003	429.84	0.00	0.00	4,510.09	62,058.89	75,489.91
322	04/22/2003	429.84	37.58	822.10	3,687.99	62,096.47	76,312.01
323	05/06/2003	429.84	0.00	0.00	3,687.99	62,096.47	76,312.01
324	05/20/2003	429.84	30.73	828.95	2,859.04	62,127.20	77,140.96
325	06/03/2003	429.84	0.00	0.00	2,859.04	62,127.20	77,140.96
326	06/17/2003	429.84	23.83	835.85	2,023.19	62,151.03	77,976.81
327	07/01/2003	429.84	0.00	0.00	2,023.19	62,151.03	77,976.81
328	07/15/2003	429.84	16.86	842.82	1,180.37	62,167.89	78,819.63
329	07/29/2003	429.84	0.00	0.00	1,180.37	62,167.89	78,819.63
330	08/12/2003	429.84	9.84	849.84	330.53	62,177.73	79,669.47
331	08/26/2003	333.28	2.75	330.53	0.00	62,180.48	80,000.00

**Table 11–3   Comparison of Costs and Savings for
Mr. & Mrs. Carl Williams—Homeowners
Conventional vs. Biweekly Programs
Summary**

```
===========================================================================================
| ORIGINAL LOAN AMOUNT:        80,000.00          ANNUAL INTEREST RATE:        10.000 % |
| ORIGINAL LOAN TERM:          30 (YEARS)         CURRENT MONTHLY PAYMENT:      702.06  |
| NUMBER OF PREVIOUS PAYMENTS: 0                  'NEW' BIWEEKLY PAYMENT:       351.03  |
| CURRENT LOAN BALANCE:        80,000.00                                                |
===========================================================================================
```

	CURRENT MONTHLY			'NEW' BIWEEKLY			DIFFERENCE	
END OF YEAR	REMAINING BALANCE	INTEREST PAID TO-DATE	(EQUITY) PRINCIPAL PAID TO-DATE	REMAINING BALANCE	INTEREST PAID TO-DATE	(EQUITY) PRINCIPAL PAID TO-DATE	EQUTIY GROWTH TO-DATE	INTEREST SAVED TO-DATE
1	79,555.25	7,979.97	444.75	78,853.19	7,979.97	1,146.81	702.06	0.00
2	79,063.93	15,913.37	936.07	77,586.31	15,839.87	2,413.69	1,477.62	73.50
3	78,521.19	23,795.35	1,478.81	76,186.76	23,567.10	3,813.24	2,334.43	228.25
4	77,921.59	31,620.47	2,078.41	74,640.67	31,147.79	5,359.33	3,280.92	472.68
5	77,259.23	39,382.83	2,740.77	72,932.69	38,566.59	7,067.31	4,326.54	816.24
6	76,527.49	47,075.81	3,472.51	71,045.85	45,806.53	8,954.15	5,481.64	1,269.28
7	75,719.12	54,692.16	4,280.88	68,961.45	52,848.91	11,038.55	6,757.67	1,843.25
8	74,826.09	62,223.85	5,173.91	66,658.78	59,673.02	13,341.22	8,167.31	2,550.83
9	73,839.57	69,662.05	6,160.43	64,114.99	66,256.01	15,885.01	9,724.58	3,406.04
10	72,749.76	76,996.96	7,250.24	61,304.82	72,572.62	18,695.18	11,444.94	4,424.34
11	71,545.83	84,217.75	8,454.17	58,200.38	78,594.96	21,799.62	13,345.45	5,622.79
12	70,215.83	91,312.47	9,784.17	54,770.87	84,292.23	25,229.13	15,444.96	7,020.24
13	68,746.57	98,267.93	11,253.43	50,982.24	89,630.38	29,017.76	17,764.33	8,637.55
14	67,123.45	105,069.53	12,876.55	46,796.90	94,571.82	33,203.10	20,326.55	10,497.71
15	65,330.37	111,701.17	14,669.63	42,173.29	99,074.99	37,826.71	23,157.08	12,626.18
16	63,349.53	118,145.05	16,650.47	37,065.54	103,094.02	42,934.46	26,283.99	15,051.03
17	61,161.26	124,381.50	18,838.74	31,422.95	106,578.21	48,577.05	29,738.31	17,803.29
18	58,743.87	130,388.83	21,256.13	25,189.50	109,471.54	54,810.50	33,554.37	20,917.29
19	56,073.33	136,143.01	23,926.67	18,303.34	111,712.16	61,696.66	37,769.99	24,430.85
20	53,123.15	141,617.55	26,876.85	10,696.10	113,231.70	69,303.90	42,427.05	28,385.85
21	49,864.04	146,783.16	30,135.96	2,292.28	113,954.66	77,707.72	47,571.76	32,828.50
22	46,263.68	151,607.52	33,736.32	DEBT FREE	113,996.73	80,000.00		37,610.79
23	42,286.30	156,054.86	37,713.70					42,058.13
24	37,892.43	160,085.71	42,107.57					46,088.98
25	33,038.48	163,656.48	46,961.52					49,659.75
26	27,676.26	166,718.98	52,323.74					52,722.25
27	21,752.56	169,220.00	58,247.44					55,223.27
28	15,208.54	171,100.70	64,791.46					57,103.97
29	7,979.30	172,296.18	72,020.70					58,299.45
30	689.38	172,734.66	80,000.00					58,737.93

```
        TOTAL INTEREST SAVED:    58,737.93
        TOTAL TERM SAVED:       104.88 (PAYMENTS)   8.74 (YEARS)
```

Table 11–4   Amortization Schedule Re: Table 3

Names: MR. & MRS. CARL WILLIAMS
Property: 305 MAIN STREET, ALBRIGHT CITY , MO 48764
Telephone: (287)555-8888
Tax I.D.:   123-45-6789

ORIGINAL LOAN AMOUNT:	80,000.00	BIWEEKLY PAYMENT:	351.03
ORIGINAL INTEREST RATE:	10.000	TOTAL BIWEEKLY INTEREST PAID:	113,996.73
ORIGINAL TERM OF LOAN:	30 (YRS)	LAST BIWEEKLY PAYMENT DATE:	02/28/2012
NUMBER OF PREVIOUS PAYMENTS:	0	NEW TERM OF LOAN:	21.26 (YRS)
CURRENT LOAN BALANCE:	80,000.00		

PMT #	PAYMENT DATE	PAYMENT AMOUNT	INTEREST PAID	PRINCIPAL PAID	BALANCE OWED	ACCUMULATED INTEREST	ACCUMULATED PRINCIPAL
1	01/01/1991	351.03	0.00	0.00	80,000.00	0.00	0.00
2	01/15/1991	351.03	666.67	35.39	79,964.61	666.67	35.39
3	01/29/1991	351.03	0.00	0.00	79,964.61	666.67	35.39
4	02/12/1991	351.03	666.37	35.69	79,928.92	1,333.04	71.08
5	02/26/1991	351.03	0.00	0.00	79,928.92	1,333.04	71.08
6	03/12/1991	351.03	666.07	35.99	79,892.93	1,999.11	107.07
7	03/26/1991	351.03	0.00	0.00	79,892.93	1,999.11	107.07
8	04/09/1991	351.03	665.77	36.29	79,856.64	2,664.88	143.36
9	04/23/1991	351.03	0.00	0.00	79,856.64	2,664.88	143.36
10	05/07/1991	351.03	665.47	36.59	79,820.05	3,330.35	179.95
11	05/21/1991	351.03	0.00	0.00	79,820.05	3,330.35	179.95
12	06/04/1991	351.03	665.17	36.89	79,783.16	3,995.52	216.84
13	06/18/1991	351.03	0.00	0.00	79,783.16	3,995.52	216.84
14	07/02/1991	351.03	664.86	37.20	79,745.96	4,660.38	254.04
15	07/16/1991	351.03	0.00	0.00	79,745.96	4,660.38	254.04
16	07/30/1991	351.03	664.55	37.51	79,708.45	5,324.93	291.55
17	08/13/1991	351.03	0.00	0.00	79,708.45	5,324.93	291.55
18	08/27/1991	351.03	664.24	37.82	79,670.63	5,989.17	329.37
19	09/10/1991	351.03	0.00	0.00	79,670.63	5,989.17	329.37
20	09/24/1991	351.03	663.92	38.14	79,632.49	6,653.09	367.51
21	10/08/1991	351.03	0.00	0.00	79,632.49	6,653.09	367.51
22	10/22/1991	351.03	663.60	38.46	79,594.03	7,316.69	405.97
23	11/05/1991	351.03	0.00	0.00	79,594.03	7,316.69	405.97
24	11/19/1991	351.03	663.28	38.78	79,555.25	7,979.97	444.75
25	12/03/1991	351.03	0.00	0.00	79,555.25	7,979.97	444.75
26	12/17/1991	351.03	0.00	702.06	78,853.19	7,979.97	1,146.81
27	12/31/1991	351.03	0.00	0.00	78,853.19	7,979.97	1,146.81
28	01/14/1992	351.03	657.11	44.95	78,808.24	8,637.08	1,191.76
29	01/28/1992	351.03	0.00	0.00	78,808.24	8,637.08	1,191.76
30	02/11/1992	351.03	656.74	45.32	78,762.92	9,293.82	1,237.08
31	02/25/1992	351.03	0.00	0.00	78,762.92	9,293.82	1,237.08
32	03/10/1992	351.03	656.36	45.70	78,717.22	9,950.18	1,282.78
33	03/24/1992	351.03	0.00	0.00	78,717.22	9,950.18	1,282.78
34	04/07/1992	351.03	655.98	46.08	78,671.14	10,606.16	1,328.86

Table 11–4   Continued

Names: MR. & MRS. CARL WILLIAMS

PMT #	PAYMENT DATE	PAYMENT AMOUNT	INTEREST PAID	PRINCIPAL PAID	BALANCE OWED	ACCUMULATED INTEREST	ACCUMULATED PRINCIPAL
35	04/21/1992	351.03	0.00	0.00	78,671.14	10,606.16	1,328.86
36	05/05/1992	351.03	655.59	46.47	78,624.67	11,261.75	1,375.33
37	05/19/1992	351.03	0.00	0.00	78,624.67	11,261.75	1,375.33
38	06/02/1992	351.03	655.21	46.85	78,577.82	11,916.96	1,422.18
39	06/16/1992	351.03	0.00	0.00	78,577.82	11,916.96	1,422.18
40	06/30/1992	351.03	654.82	47.24	78,530.58	12,571.78	1,469.42
41	07/14/1992	351.03	0.00	0.00	78,530.58	12,571.78	1,469.42
42	07/28/1992	351.03	654.42	47.64	78,482.94	13,226.20	1,517.06
43	08/11/1992	351.03	0.00	0.00	78,482.94	13,226.20	1,517.06
44	08/25/1992	351.03	654.02	48.04	78,434.90	13,880.22	1,565.10
45	09/08/1992	351.03	0.00	0.00	78,434.90	13,880.22	1,565.10
46	09/22/1992	351.03	653.62	48.44	78,386.46	14,533.84	1,613.54
47	10/06/1992	351.03	0.00	0.00	78,386.46	14,533.84	1,613.54
48	10/20/1992	351.03	653.22	48.84	78,337.62	15,187.06	1,662.38
49	11/03/1992	351.03	0.00	0.00	78,337.62	15,187.06	1,662.38
50	11/17/1992	351.03	652.81	49.25	78,288.37	15,839.87	1,711.63
51	12/01/1992	351.03	0.00	0.00	78,288.37	15,839.87	1,711.63
52	12/15/1992	351.03	0.00	702.06	77,586.31	15,839.87	2,413.69
53	12/29/1992	351.03	0.00	0.00	77,586.31	15,839.87	2,413.69
54	01/12/1993	351.03	646.55	55.51	77,530.80	16,486.42	2,469.20
55	01/26/1993	351.03	0.00	0.00	77,530.80	16,486.42	2,469.20
56	02/09/1993	351.03	646.09	55.97	77,474.83	17,132.51	2,525.17
57	02/23/1993	351.03	0.00	0.00	77,474.83	17,132.51	2,525.17
58	03/09/1993	351.03	645.62	56.44	77,418.39	17,778.13	2,581.61
59	03/23/1993	351.03	0.00	0.00	77,418.39	17,778.13	2,581.61
60	04/06/1993	351.03	645.15	56.91	77,361.48	18,423.28	2,638.52
61	04/20/1993	351.03	0.00	0.00	77,361.48	18,423.28	2,638.52
62	05/04/1993	351.03	644.68	57.38	77,304.10	19,067.96	2,695.90
63	05/18/1993	351.03	0.00	0.00	77,304.10	19,067.96	2,695.90
64	06/01/1993	351.03	644.20	57.86	77,246.24	19,712.16	2,753.76
65	06/15/1993	351.03	0.00	0.00	77,246.24	19,712.16	2,753.76
66	06/29/1993	351.03	643.72	58.34	77,187.90	20,355.88	2,812.10
67	07/13/1993	351.03	0.00	0.00	77,187.90	20,355.88	2,812.10
68	07/27/1993	351.03	643.23	58.83	77,129.07	20,999.11	2,870.93
69	08/10/1993	351.03	0.00	0.00	77,129.07	20,999.11	2,870.93
70	08/24/1993	351.03	642.74	59.32	77,069.75	21,641.85	2,930.25
71	09/07/1993	351.03	0.00	0.00	77,069.75	21,641.85	2,930.25
72	09/21/1993	351.03	642.25	59.81	77,009.94	22,284.10	2,990.06
73	10/05/1993	351.03	0.00	0.00	77,009.94	22,284.10	2,990.06
74	10/19/1993	351.03	641.75	60.31	76,949.63	22,925.85	3,050.37
75	11/02/1993	351.03	0.00	0.00	76,949.63	22,925.85	3,050.37
76	11/16/1993	351.03	641.25	60.81	76,888.82	23,567.10	3,111.18
77	11/30/1993	351.03	0.00	0.00	76,888.82	23,567.10	3,111.18
78	12/14/1993	351.03	0.00	702.06	76,186.76	23,567.10	3,813.24
79	12/28/1993	351.03	0.00	0.00	76,186.76	23,567.10	3,813.24

Table 11-4   Continued

Names: MR. & MRS. CARL WILLIAMS

PMT #	PAYMENT DATE	PAYMENT AMOUNT	INTEREST PAID	PRINCIPAL PAID	BALANCE OWED	ACCUMULATED INTEREST	ACCUMULATED PRINCIPAL
80	01/11/1994	351.03	634.89	67.17	76,119.59	24,201.99	3,880.41
81	01/25/1994	351.03	0.00	0.00	76,119.59	24,201.99	3,880.41
82	02/08/1994	351.03	634.33	67.73	76,051.86	24,836.32	3,948.14
83	02/22/1994	351.03	0.00	0.00	76,051.86	24,836.32	3,948.14
84	03/08/1994	351.03	633.77	68.29	75,983.57	25,470.09	4,016.43
85	03/22/1994	351.03	0.00	0.00	75,983.57	25,470.09	4,016.43
86	04/05/1994	351.03	633.20	68.86	75,914.71	26,103.29	4,085.29
87	04/19/1994	351.03	0.00	0.00	75,914.71	26,103.29	4,085.29
88	05/03/1994	351.03	632.62	69.44	75,845.27	26,735.91	4,154.73
89	05/17/1994	351.03	0.00	0.00	75,845.27	26,735.91	4,154.73
90	05/31/1994	351.03	632.04	70.02	75,775.25	27,367.95	4,224.75
91	06/14/1994	351.03	0.00	0.00	75,775.25	27,367.95	4,224.75
92	06/28/1994	351.03	631.46	70.60	75,704.65	27,999.41	4,295.35
93	07/12/1994	351.03	0.00	0.00	75,704.65	27,999.41	4,295.35
94	07/26/1994	351.03	630.87	71.19	75,633.46	28,630.28	4,366.54
95	08/09/1994	351.03	0.00	0.00	75,633.46	28,630.28	4,366.54
96	08/23/1994	351.03	630.28	71.78	75,561.68	29,260.56	4,438.32
97	09/06/1994	351.03	0.00	0.00	75,561.68	29,260.56	4,438.32
98	09/20/1994	351.03	629.68	72.38	75,489.30	29,890.24	4,510.70
99	10/04/1994	351.03	0.00	0.00	75,489.30	29,890.24	4,510.70
100	10/18/1994	351.03	629.08	72.98	75,416.32	30,519.32	4,583.68
101	11/01/1994	351.03	0.00	0.00	75,416.32	30,519.32	4,583.68
102	11/15/1994	351.03	628.47	73.59.	75,342.73	31,147.79	4,657.27
103	11/29/1994	351.03	0.00	0.00	75,342.73	31,147.79	4,657.27
104	12/13/1994	351.03	0.00	702.06	74,640.67	31,147.79	5,359.33
105	12/27/1994	351.03	0.00	0.00	74,640.67	31,147.79	5,359.33
106	01/10/1995	351.03	622.01	80.05	74,560.62	31,769.80	5,439.38
107	01/24/1995	351.03	0.00	0.00	74,560.62	31,769.80	5,439.38
108	02/07/1995	351.03	621.34	80.72	74,479.90	32,391.14	5,520.10
109	02/21/1995	351.03	0.00	0.00	74,479.90	32,391.14	5,520.10
110	03/07/1995	351.03	620.67	81.39	74,398.51	33,011.81	5,601.49
111	03/21/1995	351.03	0.00	0.00	74,398.51	33,011.81	5,601.49
112	04/04/1995	351.03	619.99	82.07	74,316.44	33,631.80	5,683.56
113	04/18/1995	351.03	0.00	0.00	74,316.44	33,631.80	5,683.56
114	05/02/1995	351.03	619.30	82.76	74,233.68	34,251.10	5,766.32
115	05/16/1995	351.03	0.00	0.00	74,233.68	34,251.10	5,766.32
116	05/30/1995	351.03	618.61	83.45	74,150.23	34,869.71	5,849.77
117	06/13/1995	351.03	0.00	0.00	74,150.23	34,869.71	5,849.77
118	06/27/1995	351.03	617.92	84.14	74,066.09	35,487.63	5,933.91
119	07/11/1995	351.03	0.00	0.00	74,066.09	35,487.63	5,933.91
120	07/25/1995	351.03	617.22	84.84	73,981.25	36,104.85	6,018.75
121	08/08/1995	351.03	0.00	0.00	73,981.25	36,104.85	6,018.75
122	08/22/1995	351.03	616.51	85.55	73,895.70	36,721.36	6,104.30
123	09/05/1995	351.03	0.00	0.00	73,895.70	36,721.36	6,104.30
124	09/19/1995	351.03	615.80	86.26	73,809.44	37,337.16	6,190.56

Table 11–4   Continued

Names: MR. & MRS. CARL WILLIAMS

PMT #	PAYMENT DATE	PAYMENT AMOUNT	INTEREST PAID	PRINCIPAL PAID	BALANCE OWED	ACCUMULATED INTEREST	ACCUMULATED PRINCIPAL
125	10/03/1995	351.03	0.00	0.00	73,809.44	37,337.16	6,190.56
126	10/17/1995	351.03	615.08	86.98	73,722.46	37,952.24	6,277.54
127	10/31/1995	351.03	0.00	0.00	73,722.46	37,952.24	6,277.54
128	11/14/1995	351.03	614.35	87.71	73,634.75	38,566.59	6,365.25
129	11/28/1995	351.03	0.00	0.00	73,634.75	38,566.59	6,365.25
130	12/12/1995	351.03	0.00	702.06	72,932.69	38,566.59	7,067.31
131	12/26/1995	351.03	0.00	0.00	72,932.69	38,566.59	7,067.31
132	01/09/1996	351.03	607.77	94.29	72,838.40	39,174.36	7,161.60
133	01/23/1996	351.03	0.00	0.00	72,838.40	39,174.36	7,161.60
134	02/06/1996	351.03	606.99	95.07	72,743.33	39,781.35	7,256.67
135	02/20/1996	351.03	0.00	0.00	72,743.33	39,781.35	7,256.67
136	03/05/1996	351.03	606.19	95.87	72,647.46	40,387.54	7,352.54
137	03/19/1996	351.03	0.00	0.00	72,647.46	40,387.54	7,352.54
138	04/02/1996	351.03	605.40	96.66	72,550.80	40,992.94	7,449.20
139	04/16/1996	351.03	0.00	0.00	72,550.80	40,992.94	7,449.20
140	04/30/1996	351.03	604.59	97.47	72,453.33	41,597.53	7,546.67
141	05/14/1996	351.03	0.00	0.00	72,453.33	41,597.53	7,546.67
142	05/28/1996	351.03	603.78	98.28	72,355.05	42,201.31	7,644.95
143	06/11/1996	351.03	0.00	0.00	72,355.05	42,201.31	7,644.95
144	06/25/1996	351.03	602.96	99.10	72,255.95	42,804.27	7,744.05
145	07/09/1996	351.03	0.00	0.00	72,255.95	42,804.27	7,744.05
146	07/23/1996	351.03	602.13	99.93	72,156.02	43,406.40	7,843.98
147	08/06/1996	351.03	0.00	0.00	72,156.02	43,406.40	7,843.98
148	08/20/1996	351.03	601.30	100.76	72,055.26	44,007.70	7,944.74
149	09/03/1996	351.03	0.00	0.00	72,055.26	44,007.70	7,944.74
150	09/17/1996	351.03	600.46	101.60	71,953.66	44,608.16	8,046.34
151	10/01/1996	351.03	0.00	0.00	71,953.66	44,608.16	8,046.34
152	10/15/1996	351.03	599.61	102.45	71,851.21	45,207.77	8,148.79
153	10/29/1996	351.03	0.00	0.00	71,851.21	45,207.77	8,148.79
154	11/12/1996	351.03	598.76	103.30	71,747.91	45,806.53	8,252.09
155	11/26/1996	351.03	0.00	0.00	71,747.91	45,806.53	8,252.09
156	12/10/1996	351.03	0.00	702.06	71,045.85	45,806.53	8,954.15
157	12/24/1996	351.03	0.00	0.00	71,045.85	45,806.53	8,954.15
158	01/07/1997	351.03	592.05	110.01	70,935.84	46,398.58	9,064.16
159	01/21/1997	351.03	0.00	0.00	70,935.84	46,398.58	9,064.16
160	02/04/1997	351.03	591.13	110.93	70,824.91	46,989.71	9,175.09
161	02/18/1997	351.03	0.00	0.00	70,824.91	46,989.71	9,175.09
162	03/04/1997	351.03	590.21	111.85	70,713.06	47,579.92	9,286.94
163	03/18/1997	351.03	0.00	0.00	70,713.06	47,579.92	9,286.94
164	04/01/1997	351.03	589.28	112.78	70,600.28	48,169.20	9,399.72
165	04/15/1997	351.03	0.00	0.00	70,600.28	48,169.20	9,399.72
166	04/29/1997	351.03	588.34	113.72	70,486.56	48,757.54	9,513.44
167	05/13/1997	351.03	0.00	0.00	70,486.56	48,757.54	9,513.44
168	05/27/1997	351.03	587.39	114.67	70,371.89	49,344.93	9,628.11
169	06/10/1997	351.03	0.00	0.00	70,371.89	49,344.93	9,628.11

Table 11–4   Continued

Names: MR. & MRS. CARL WILLIAMS

PMT #	PAYMENT DATE	PAYMENT AMOUNT	INTEREST PAID	PRINCIPAL PAID	BALANCE OWED	ACCUMULATED INTEREST	ACCUMULATED PRINCIPAL
170	06/24/1997	351.03	586.43	115.63	70,256.26	49,931.36	9,743.74
171	07/08/1997	351.03	0.00	0.00	70,256.26	49,931.36	9,743.74
172	07/22/1997	351.03	585.47	116.59	70,139.67	50,516.83	9,860.33
173	08/05/1997	351.03	0.00	0.00	70,139.67	50,516.83	9,860.33
174	08/19/1997	351.03	584.50	117.56	70,022.11	51,101.33	9,977.89
175	09/02/1997	351.03	0.00	0.00	70,022.11	51,101.33	9,977.89
176	09/16/1997	351.03	583.52	118.54	69,903.57	51,684.85	10,096.43
177	09/30/1997	351.03	0.00	0.00	69,903.57	51,684.85	10,096.43
178	10/14/1997	351.03	582.53	119.53	69,784.04	52,267.38	10,215.96
179	10/28/1997	351.03	0.00	0.00	69,784.04	52,267.38	10,215.96
180	11/11/1997	351.03	581.53	120.53	69,663.51	52,848.91	10,336.49
181	11/25/1997	351.03	0.00	0.00	69,663.51	52,848.91	10,336.49
182	12/09/1997	351.03	0.00	702.06	68,961.45	52,848.91	11,038.55
183	12/23/1997	351.03	0.00	0.00	68,961.45	52,848.91	11,038.55
184	01/06/1998	351.03	574.68	127.38	68,834.07	53,423.59	11,165.93
185	01/20/1998	351.03	0.00	0.00	68,834.07	53,423.59	11,165.93
186	02/03/1998	351.03	573.62	128.44	68,705.63	53,997.21	11,294.37
187	02/17/1998	351.03	0.00	0.00	68,705.63	53,997.21	11,294.37
188	03/03/1998	351.03	572.55	129.51	68,576.12	54,569.76	11,423.88
189	03/17/1998	351.03	0.00	0.00	68,576.12	54,569.76	11,423.88
190	03/31/1998	351.03	571.47	130.59	68,445.53	55,141.23	11,554.47
191	04/14/1998	351.03	0.00	0.00	68,445.53	55,141.23	11,554.47
192	04/28/1998	351.03	570.38	131.68	68,313.85	55,711.61	11,686.15
193	05/12/1998	351.03	0.00	0.00	68,313.85	55,711.61	11,686.15
194	05/26/1998	351.03	569.28	132.78	68,181.07	56,280.89	11,818.93
195	06/09/1998	351.03	0.00	0.00	68,181.07	56,280.89	11,818.93
196	06/23/1998	351.03	568.18	133.88	68,047.19	56,849.07	11,952.81
197	07/07/1998	351.03	0.00	0.00	68,047.19	56,849.07	11,952.81
198	07/21/1998	351.03	567.06	135.00	67,912.19	57,416.13	12,087.81
199	08/04/1998	351.03	0.00	0.00	67,912.19	57,416.13	12,087.81
200	08/18/1998	351.03	565.93	136.13	67,776.06	57,982.06	12,223.94
201	09/01/1998	351.03	0.00	0.00	67,776.06	57,982.06	12,223.94
202	09/15/1998	351.03	564.80	137.26	67,638.80	58,546.86	12,361.20
203	09/29/1998	351.03	0.00	0.00	67,638.80	58,546.86	12,361.20
204	10/13/1998	351.03	563.66	138.40	67,500.40	59,110.52	12,499.60
205	10/27/1998	351.03	0.00	0.00	67,500.40	59,110.52	12,499.60
206	11/10/1998	351.03	562.50	139.56	67,360.84	59,673.02	12,639.16
207	11/24/1998	351.03	0.00	0.00	67,360.84	59,673.02	12,639.16
208	12/08/1998	351.03	0.00	702.06	66,658.78	59,673.02	13,341.22
209	12/22/1998	351.03	0.00	0.00	66,658.78	59,673.02	13,341.22
210	01/05/1999	351.03	555.49	146.57	66,512.21	60,228.51	13,487.79
211	01/19/1999	351.03	0.00	0.00	66,512.21	60,228.51	13,487.79
212	02/02/1999	351.03	554.27	147.79	66,364.42	60,782.78	13,635.58
213	02/16/1999	351.03	0.00	0.00	66,364.42	60,782.78	13,635.58
214	03/02/1999	351.03	553.04	149.02	66,215.40	61,335.82	13,784.60

Table 11–4   Continued

Names: MR. & MRS. CARL WILLIAMS

PMT #	PAYMENT DATE	PAYMENT AMOUNT	INTEREST PAID	PRINCIPAL PAID	BALANCE OWED	ACCUMULATED INTEREST	ACCUMULATED PRINCIPAL
215	03/16/1999	351.03	0.00	0.00	66,215.40	61,335.82	13,784.60
216	03/30/1999	351.03	551.80	150.26	66,065.14	61,887.62	13,934.86
217	04/13/1999	351.03	0.00	0.00	66,065.14	61,887.62	13,934.86
218	04/27/1999	351.03	550.54	151.52	65,913.62	62,438.16	14,086.38
219	05/11/1999	351.03	0.00	0.00	65,913.62	62,438.16	14,086.38
220	05/25/1999	351.03	549.28	152.78	65,760.84	62,987.44	14,239.16
221	06/08/1999	351.03	0.00	0.00	65,760.84	62,987.44	14,239.16
222	06/22/1999	351.03	548.01	154.05	65,606.79	63,535.45	14,393.21
223	07/06/1999	351.03	0.00	0.00	65,606.79	63,535.45	14,393.21
224	07/20/1999	351.03	546.72	155.34	65,451.45	64,082.17	14,548.55
225	08/03/1999	351.03	0.00	0.00	65,451.45	64,082.17	14,548.55
226	08/17/1999	351.03	545.43	156.63	65,294.82	64,627.60	14,705.18
227	08/31/1999	351.03	0.00	0.00	65,294.82	64,627.60	14,705.18
228	09/14/1999	351.03	544.12	157.94	65,136.88	65,171.72	14,863.12
229	09/28/1999	351.03	0.00	0.00	65,136.88	65,171.72	14,863.12
230	10/12/1999	351.03	542.81	159.25	64,977.63	65,714.53	15,022.37
231	10/26/1999	351.03	0.00	0.00	64,977.63	65,714.53	15,022.37
232	11/09/1999	351.03	541.48	160.58	64,817.05	66,256.01	15,182.95
233	11/23/1999	351.03	0.00	0.00	64,817.05	66,256.01	15,182.95
234	12/07/1999	351.03	0.00	702.06	64,114.99	66,256.01	15,885.01
235	12/21/1999	351.03	0.00	0.00	64,114.99	66,256.01	15,885.01
236	01/04/2000	351.03	534.29	167.77	63,947.22	66,790.30	16,052.78
237	01/18/2000	351.03	0.00	0.00	63,947.22	66,790.30	16,052.78
238	02/01/2000	351.03	532.89	169.17	63,778.05	67,323.19	16,221.95
239	02/15/2000	351.03	0.00	0.00	63,778.05	67,323.19	16,221.95
240	02/29/2000	351.03	531.48	170.58	63,607.47	67,854.67	16,392.53
241	03/14/2000	351.03	0.00	0.00	63,607.47	67,854.67	16,392.53
242	03/28/2000	351.03	530.06	172.00	63,435.47	68,384.73	16,564.53
243	04/11/2000	351.03	0.00	0.00	63,435.47	68,384.73	16,564.53
244	04/25/2000	351.03	528.63	173.43	63,262.04	68,913.36	16,737.96
245	05/09/2000	351.03	0.00	0.00	63,262.04	68,913.36	16,737.96
246	05/23/2000	351.03	527.18	174.88	63,087.16	69,440.54	16,912.84
247	06/06/2000	351.03	0.00	0.00	63,087.16	69,440.54	16,912.84
248	06/20/2000	351.03	525.73	176.33	62,910.83	69,966.27	17,089.17
249	07/04/2000	351.03	0.00	0.00	62,910.83	69,966.27	17,089.17
250	07/18/2000	351.03	524.26	177.80	62,733.03	70,490.53	17,266.97
251	08/01/2000	351.03	0.00	0.00	62,733.03	70,490.53	17,266.97
252	08/15/2000	351.03	522.78	179.28	62,553.75	71,013.31	17,446.25
253	08/29/2000	351.03	0.00	0.00	62,553.75	71,013.31	17,446.25
254	09/12/2000	351.03	521.28	180.78	62,372.97	71,534.59	17,627.03
255	09/26/2000	351.03	0.00	0.00	62,372.97	71,534.59	17,627.03
256	10/10/2000	351.03	519.77	182.29	62,190.68	72,054.36	17,809.32
257	10/24/2000	351.03	0.00	0.00	62,190.68	72,054.36	17,809.32
258	11/07/2000	351.03	518.26	183.80	62,006.88	72,572.62	17,993.12
259	11/21/2000	351.03	0.00	0.00	62,006.88	72,572.62	17,993.12

Table 11-4 Continued

Names: MR. & MRS. CARL WILLIAMS

PMT #	PAYMENT DATE	PAYMENT AMOUNT	INTEREST PAID	PRINCIPAL PAID	BALANCE OWED	ACCUMULATED INTEREST	ACCUMULATED PRINCIPAL
260	12/05/2000	351.03	0.00	702.06	61,304.82	72,572.62	18,695.18
261	12/19/2000	351.03	0.00	0.00	61,304.82	72,572.62	18,695.18
262	01/02/2001	351.03	510.87	191.19	61,113.63	73,083.49	18,886.37
263	01/16/2001	351.03	0.00	0.00	61,113.63	73,083.49	18,886.37
264	01/30/2001	351.03	509.28	192.78	60,920.85	73,592.77	19,079.15
265	02/13/2001	351.03	0.00	0.00	60,920.85	73,592.77	19,079.15
266	02/27/2001	351.03	507.67	194.39	60,726.46	74,100.44	19,273.54
267	03/13/2001	351.03	0.00	0.00	60,726.46	74,100.44	19,273.54
268	03/27/2001	351.03	506.05	196.01	60,530.45	74,606.49	19,469.55
269	04/10/2001	351.03	0.00	0.00	60,530.45	74,606.49	19,469.55
270	04/24/2001	351.03	504.42	197.64	60,332.81	75,110.91	19,667.19
271	05/08/2001	351.03	0.00	0.00	60,332.81	75,110.91	19,667.19
272	05/22/2001	351.03	502.77	199.29	60,133.52	75,613.68	19,866.48
273	06/05/2001	351.03	0.00	0.00	60,133.52	75,613.68	19,866.48
274	06/19/2001	351.03	501.11	200.95	59,932.57	76,114.79	20,067.43
275	07/03/2001	351.03	0.00	0.00	59,932.57	76,114.79	20,067.43
276	07/17/2001	351.03	499.44	202.62	59,729.95	76,614.23	20,270.05
277	07/31/2001	351.03	0.00	0.00	59,729.95	76,614.23	20,270.05
278	08/14/2001	351.03	497.75	204.31	59,525.64	77,111.98	20,474.36
279	08/28/2001	351.03	0.00	0.00	59,525.64	77,111.98	20,474.36
280	09/11/2001	351.03	496.05	206.01	59,319.63	77,608.03	20,680.37
281	09/25/2001	351.03	0.00	0.00	59,319.63	77,608.03	20,680.37
282	10/09/2001	351.03	494.33	207.73	59,111.90	78,102.36	20,888.10
283	10/23/2001	351.03	0.00	0.00	59,111.90	78,102.36	20,888.10
284	11/06/2001	351.03	492.60	209.46	58,902.44	78,594.96	21,097.56
285	11/20/2001	351.03	0.00	0.00	58,902.44	78,594.96	21,097.56
286	12/04/2001	351.03	0.00	702.06	58,200.38	78,594.96	21,799.62
287	12/18/2001	351.03	0.00	0.00	58,200.38	78,594.96	21,799.62
288	01/01/2002	351.03	485.00	217.06	57,983.32	79,079.96	22,016.68
289	01/15/2002	351.03	0.00	0.00	57,983.32	79,079.96	22,016.68
290	01/29/2002	351.03	483.19	218.87	57,764.45	79,563.15	22,235.55
291	02/12/2002	351.03	0.00	0.00	57,764.45	79,563.15	22,235.55
292	02/26/2002	351.03	481.37	220.69	57,543.76	80,044.52	22,456.24
293	03/12/2002	351.03	0.00	0.00	57,543.76	80,044.52	22,456.24
294	03/26/2002	351.03	479.53	222.53	57,321.23	80,524.05	22,678.77
295	04/09/2002	351.03	0.00	0.00	57,321.23	80,524.05	22,678.77
296	04/23/2002	351.03	477.68	224.38	57,096.85	81,001.73	22,903.15
297	05/07/2002	351.03	0.00	0.00	57,096.85	81,001.73	22,903.15
298	05/21/2002	351.03	475.81	226.25	56,870.60	81,477.54	23,129.40
299	06/04/2002	351.03	0.00	0.00	56,870.60	81,477.54	23,129.40
300	06/18/2002	351.03	473.92	228.14	56,642.46	81,951.46	23,357.54
301	07/02/2002	351.03	0.00	0.00	56,642.46	81,951.46	23,357.54
302	07/16/2002	351.03	472.02	230.04	56,412.42	82,423.48	23,587.58
303	07/30/2002	351.03	0.00	0.00	56,412.42	82,423.48	23,587.58
304	08/13/2002	351.03	470.10	231.96	56,180.46	82,893.58	23,819.54

Table 11–4 Continued

Names: MR. & MRS. CARL WILLIAMS

PMT #	PAYMENT DATE	PAYMENT AMOUNT	INTEREST PAID	PRINCIPAL PAID	BALANCE OWED	ACCUMULATED INTEREST	ACCUMULATED PRINCIPAL
305	08/27/2002	351.03	0.00	0.00	56,180.46	82,893.58	23,819.54
306	09/10/2002	351.03	468.17	233.89	55,946.57	83,361.75	24,053.43
307	09/24/2002	351.03	0.00	0.00	55,946.57	83,361.75	24,053.43
308	10/08/2002	351.03	466.22	235.84	55,710.73	83,827.97	24,289.27
309	10/22/2002	351.03	0.00	0.00	55,710.73	83,827.97	24,289.27
310	11/05/2002	351.03	464.26	237.80	55,472.93	84,292.23	24,527.07
311	11/19/2002	351.03	0.00	0.00	55,472.93	84,292.23	24,527.07
312	12/03/2002	351.03	0.00	702.06	54,770.87	84,292.23	25,229.13
313	12/17/2002	351.03	0.00	0.00	54,770.87	84,292.23	25,229.13
314	12/31/2002	351.03	456.42	245.64	54,525.23	84,748.65	25,474.77
315	01/14/2003	351.03	0.00	0.00	54,525.23	84,748.65	25,474.77
316	01/28/2003	351.03	454.38	247.68	54,277.55	85,203.03	25,722.45
317	02/11/2003	351.03	0.00	0.00	54,277.55	85,203.03	25,722.45
318	02/25/2003	351.03	452.31	249.75	54,027.80	85,655.34	25,972.20
319	03/11/2003	351.03	0.00	0.00	54,027.80	85,655.34	25,972.20
320	03/25/2003	351.03	450.23	251.83	53,775.97	86,105.57	26,224.03
321	04/08/2003	351.03	0.00	0.00	53,775.97	86,105.57	26,224.03
322	04/22/2003	351.03	448.13	253.93	53,522.04	86,553.70	26,477.96
323	05/06/2003	351.03	0.00	0.00	53,522.04	86,553.70	26,477.96
324	05/20/2003	351.03	446.02	256.04	53,266.00	86,999.72	26,734.00
325	06/03/2003	351.03	0.00	0.00	53,266.00	86,999.72	26,734.00
326	06/17/2003	351.03	443.88	258.18	53,007.82	87,443.60	26,992.18
327	07/01/2003	351.03	0.00	0.00	53,007.82	87,443.60	26,992.18
328	07/15/2003	351.03	441.73	260.33	52,747.49	87,885.33	27,252.51
329	07/29/2003	351.03	0.00	0.00	52,747.49	87,885.33	27,252.51
330	08/12/2003	351.03	439.56	262.50	52,484.99	88,324.89	27,515.01
331	08/26/2003	351.03	0.00	0.00	52,484.99	88,324.89	27,515.01
332	09/09/2003	351.03	437.37	264.69	52,220.30	88,762.26	27,779.70
333	09/23/2003	351.03	0.00	0.00	52,220.30	88,762.26	27,779.70
334	10/07/2003	351.03	435.17	266.89	51,953.41	89,197.43	28,046.59
335	10/21/2003	351.03	0.00	0.00	51,953.41	89,197.43	28,046.59
336	11/04/2003	351.03	432.95	269.11	51,684.30	89,630.38	28,315.70
337	11/18/2003	351.03	0.00	0.00	51,684.30	89,630.38	28,315.70
338	12/02/2003	351.03	0.00	702.06	50,982.24	89,630.38	29,017.76
339	12/16/2003	351.03	0.00	0.00	50,982.24	89,630.38	29,017.76
340	12/30/2003	351.03	424.85	277.21	50,705.03	90,055.23	29,294.97
341	01/13/2004	351.03	0.00	0.00	50,705.03	90,055.23	29,294.97
342	01/27/2004	351.03	422.54	279.52	50,425.51	90,477.77	29,574.49
343	02/10/2004	351.03	0.00	0.00	50,425.51	90,477.77	29,574.49
344	02/24/2004	351.03	420.21	281.85	50,143.66	90,897.98	29,856.34
345	03/09/2004	351.03	0.00	0.00	50,143.66	90,897.98	29,856.34
346	03/23/2004	351.03	417.86	284.20	49,859.46	91,315.84	30,140.54
347	04/06/2004	351.03	0.00	0.00	49,859.46	91,315.84	30,140.54
348	04/20/2004	351.03	415.50	286.56	49,572.90	91,731.34	30,427.10
349	05/04/2004	351.03	0.00	0.00	49,572.90	91,731.34	30,427.10

Table 11–4   Continued

Names: MR. & MRS. CARL WILLIAMS

PMT #	PAYMENT DATE	PAYMENT AMOUNT	INTEREST PAID	PRINCIPAL PAID	BALANCE OWED	ACCUMULATED INTEREST	ACCUMULATED PRINCIPAL
350	05/18/2004	351.03	413.11	288.95	49,283.95	92,144.45	30,716.05
351	06/01/2004	351.03	0.00	0.00	49,283.95	92,144.45	30,716.05
352	06/15/2004	351.03	410.70	291.36	48,992.59	92,555.15	31,007.41
353	06/29/2004	351.03	0.00	0.00	48,992.59	92,555.15	31,007.41
354	07/13/2004	351.03	408.27	293.79	48,698.80	92,963.42	31,301.20
355	07/27/2004	351.03	0.00	0.00	48,698.80	92,963.42	31,301.20
356	08/10/2004	351.03	405.82	296.24	48,402.56	93,369.24	31,597.44
357	08/24/2004	351.03	0.00	0.00	48,402.56	93,369.24	31,597.44
358	09/07/2004	351.03	403.35	298.71	48,103.85	93,772.59	31,896.15
359	09/21/2004	351.03	0.00	0.00	48,103.85	93,772.59	31,896.15
360	10/05/2004	351.03	400.87	301.19	47,802.66	94,173.46	32,197.34
361	10/19/2004	351.03	0.00	0.00	47,802.66	94,173.46	32,197.34
362	11/02/2004	351.03	398.36	303.70	47,498.96	94,571.82	32,501.04
363	11/16/2004	351.03	0.00	0.00	47,498.96	94,571.82	32,501.04
364	11/30/2004	351.03	0.00	702.06	46,796.90	94,571.82	33,203.10
365	12/14/2004	351.03	0.00	0.00	46,796.90	94,571.82	33,203.10
366	12/28/2004	351.03	389.97	312.09	46,484.81	94,961.79	33,515.19
367	01/11/2005	351.03	0.00	0.00	46,484.81	94,961.79	33,515.19
368	01/25/2005	351.03	387.37	314.69	46,170.12	95,349.16	33,829.88
369	02/08/2005	351.03	0.00	0.00	46,170.12	95,349.16	33,829.88
370	02/22/2005	351.03	384.75	317.31	45,852.81	95,733.91	34,147.19
371	03/08/2005	351.03	0.00	0.00	45,852.81	95,733.91	34,147.19
372	03/22/2005	351.03	382.11	319.95	45,532.86	96,116.02	34,467.14
373	04/05/2005	351.03	0.00	0.00	45,532.86	96,116.02	34,467.14
374	04/19/2005	351.03	379.44	322.62	45,210.24	96,495.46	34,789.76
375	05/03/2005	351.03	0.00	0.00	45,210.24	96,495.46	34,789.76
376	05/17/2005	351.03	376.75	325.31	44,884.93	96,872.21	35,115.07
377	05/31/2005	351.03	0.00	0.00	44,884.93	96,872.21	35,115.07
378	06/14/2005	351.03	374.04	328.02	44,556.91	97,246.25	35,443.09
379	06/28/2005	351.03	0.00	0.00	44,556.91	97,246.25	35,443.09
380	07/12/2005	351.03	371.31	330.75	44,226.16	97,617.56	35,773.84
381	07/26/2005	351.03	0.00	0.00	44,226.16	97,617.56	35,773.84
382	08/09/2005	351.03	368.55	333.51	43,892.65	97,986.11	36,107.35
383	08/23/2005	351.03	0.00	0.00	43,892.65	97,986.11	36,107.35
384	09/06/2005	351.03	365.77	336.29	43,556.36	98,351.88	36,443.64
385	09/20/2005	351.03	0.00	0.00	43,556.36	98,351.88	36,443.64
386	10/04/2005	351.03	362.97	339.09	43,217.27	98,714.85	36,782.73
387	10/18/2005	351.03	0.00	0.00	43,217.27	98,714.85	36,782.73
388	11/01/2005	351.03	360.14	341.92	42,875.35	99,074.99	37,124.65
389	11/15/2005	351.03	0.00	0.00	42,875.35	99,074.99	37,124.65
390	11/29/2005	351.03	0.00	702.06	42,173.29	99,074.99	37,826.71
391	12/13/2005	351.03	0.00	0.00	42,173.29	99,074.99	37,826.71
392	12/27/2005	351.03	351.44	350.62	41,822.67	99,426.43	38,177.33
393	01/10/2006	351.03	0.00	0.00	41,822.67	99,426.43	38,177.33
394	01/24/2006	351.03	348.52	353.54	41,469.13	99,774.95	38,530.87

Table 11–4 Continued

Names: MR. & MRS. CARL WILLIAMS

PMT #	PAYMENT DATE	PAYMENT AMOUNT	INTEREST PAID	PRINCIPAL PAID	BALANCE OWED	ACCUMULATED INTEREST	ACCUMULATED PRINCIPAL
395	02/07/2006	351.03	0.00	0.00	41,469.13	99,774.95	38,530.87
396	02/21/2006	351.03	345.58	356.48	41,112.65	100,120.53	38,887.35
397	03/07/2006	351.03	0.00	0.00	41,112.65	100,120.53	38,887.35
398	03/21/2006	351.03	342.61	359.45	40,753.20	100,463.14	39,246.80
399	04/04/2006	351.03	0.00	0.00	40,753.20	100,463.14	39,246.80
400	04/18/2006	351.03	339.61	362.45	40,390.75	100,802.75	39,609.25
401	05/02/2006	351.03	0.00	0.00	40,390.75	100,802.75	39,609.25
402	05/16/2006	351.03	336.59	365.47	40,025.28	101,139.34	39,974.72
403	05/30/2006	351.03	0.00	0.00	40,025.28	101,139.34	39,974.72
404	06/13/2006	351.03	333.54	368.52	39,656.76	101,472.88	40,343.24
405	06/27/2006	351.03	0.00	0.00	39,656.76	101,472.88	40,343.24
406	07/11/2006	351.03	330.47	371.59	39,285.17	101,803.35	40,714.83
407	07/25/2006	351.03	0.00	0.00	39,285.17	101,803.35	40,714.83
408	08/08/2006	351.03	327.38	374.68	38,910.49	102,130.73	41,089.51
409	08/22/2006	351.03	0.00	0.00	38,910.49	102,130.73	41,089.51
410	09/05/2006	351.03	324.25	377.81	38,532.68	102,454.98	41,467.32
411	09/19/2006	351.03	0.00	0.00	38,532.68	102,454.98	41,467.32
412	10/03/2006	351.03	321.11	380.95	38,151.73	102,776.09	41,848.27
413	10/17/2006	351.03	0.00	0.00	38,151.73	102,776.09	41,848.27
414	10/31/2006	351.03	317.93	384.13	37,767.60	103,094.02	42,232.40
415	11/14/2006	351.03	0.00	0.00	37,767.60	103,094.02	42,232.40
416	11/28/2006	351.03	0.00	702.06	37,065.54	103,094.02	42,934.46
417	12/12/2006	351.03	0.00	0.00	37,065.54	103,094.02	42,934.46
418	12/26/2006	351.03	308.88	393.18	36,672.36	103,402.90	43,327.64
419	01/09/2007	351.03	0.00	0.00	36,672.36	103,402.90	43,327.64
420	01/23/2007	351.03	305.60	396.46	36,275.90	103,708.50	43,724.10
421	02/06/2007	351.03	0.00	0.00	36,275.90	103,708.50	43,724.10
422	02/20/2007	351.03	302.30	399.76	35,876.14	104,010.80	44,123.86
423	03/06/2007	351.03	0.00	0.00	35,876.14	104,010.80	44,123.86
424	03/20/2007	351.03	298.97	403.09	35,473.05	104,309.77	44,526.95
425	04/03/2007	351.03	0.00	0.00	35,473.05	104,309.77	44,526.95
426	04/17/2007	351.03	295.61	406.45	35,066.60	104,605.38	44,933.40
427	05/01/2007	351.03	0.00	0.00	35,066.60	104,605.38	44,933.40
428	05/15/2007	351.03	292.22	409.84	34,656.76	104,897.60	45,343.24
429	05/29/2007	351.03	0.00	0.00	34,656.76	104,897.60	45,343.24
430	06/12/2007	351.03	288.81	413.25	34,243.51	105,186.41	45,756.49
431	06/26/2007	351.03	0.00	0.00	34,243.51	105,186.41	45,756.49
432	07/10/2007	351.03	285.36	416.70	33,826.81	105,471.77	46,173.19
433	07/24/2007	351.03	0.00	0.00	33,826.81	105,471.77	46,173.19
434	08/07/2007	351.03	281.89	420.17	33,406.64	105,753.66	46,593.36
435	08/21/2007	351.03	0.00	0.00	33,406.64	105,753.66	46,593.36
436	09/04/2007	351.03	278.39	423.67	32,982.97	106,032.05	47,017.03
437	09/18/2007	351.03	0.00	0.00	32,982.97	106,032.05	47,017.03
438	10/02/2007	351.03	274.86	427.20	32,555.77	106,306.91	47,444.23
439	10/16/2007	351.03	0.00	0.00	32,555.77	106,306.91	47,444.23

Table 11-4   Continued

Names: MR. & MRS. CARL WILLIAMS

PMT #	PAYMENT DATE	PAYMENT AMOUNT	INTEREST PAID	PRINCIPAL PAID	BALANCE OWED	ACCUMULATED INTEREST	ACCUMULATED PRINCIPAL
440	10/30/2007	351.03	271.30	430.76	32,125.01	106,578.21	47,874.99
441	11/13/2007	351.03	0.00	0.00	32,125.01	106,578.21	47,874.99
442	11/27/2007	351.03	0.00	702.06	31,422.95	106,578.21	48,577.05
443	12/11/2007	351.03	0.00	0.00	31,422.95	106,578.21	48,577.05
444	12/25/2007	351.03	261.86	440.20	30,982.75	106,840.07	49,017.25
445	01/08/2008	351.03	0.00	0.00	30,982.75	106,840.07	49,017.25
446	01/22/2008	351.03	258.19	443.87	30,538.88	107,098.26	49,461.12
447	02/05/2008	351.03	0.00	0.00	30,538.88	107,098.26	49,461.12
448	02/19/2008	351.03	254.49	447.57	30,091.31	107,352.75	49,908.69
449	03/04/2008	351.03	0.00	0.00	30,091.31	107,352.75	49,908.69
450	03/18/2008	351.03	250.76	451.30	29,640.01	107,603.51	50,359.99
451	04/01/2008	351.03	0.00	0.00	29,640.01	107,603.51	50,359.99
452	04/15/2008	351.03	247.00	455.06	29,184.95	107,850.51	50,815.05
453	04/29/2008	351.03	0.00	0.00	29,184.95	107,850.51	50,815.05
454	05/13/2008	351.03	243.21	458.85	28,726.10	108,093.72	51,273.90
455	05/27/2008	351.03	0.00	0.00	28,726.10	108,093.72	51,273.90
456	06/10/2008	351.03	239.38	462.68	28,263.42	108,333.10	51,736.58
457	06/24/2008	351.03	0.00	0.00	28,263.42	108,333.10	51,736.58
458	07/08/2008	351.03	235.53	466.53	27,796.89	108,568.63	52,203.11
459	07/22/2008	351.03	0.00	0.00	27,796.89	108,568.63	52,203.11
460	08/05/2008	351.03	231.64	470.42	27,326.47	108,800.27	52,673.53
461	08/19/2008	351.03	0.00	0.00	27,326.47	108,800.27	52,673.53
462	09/02/2008	351.03	227.72	474.34	26,852.13	109,027.99	53,147.87
463	09/16/2008	351.03	0.00	0.00	26,852.13	109,027.99	53,147.87
464	09/30/2008	351.03	223.77	478.29	26,373.84	109,251.76	53,626.16
465	10/14/2008	351.03	0.00	0.00	26,373.84	109,251.76	53,626.16
466	10/28/2008	351.03	219.78	482.28	25,891.56	109,471.54	54,108.44
467	11/11/2008	351.03	0.00	0.00	25,891.56	109,471.54	54,108.44
468	11/25/2008	351.03	0.00	702.06	25,189.50	109,471.54	54,810.50
469	12/09/2008	351.03	0.00	0.00	25,189.50	109,471.54	54,810.50
470	12/23/2008	351.03	209.91	492.15	24,697.35	109,681.45	55,302.65
471	01/06/2009	351.03	0.00	0.00	24,697.35	109,681.45	55,302.65
472	01/20/2009	351.03	205.81	496.25	24,201.10	109,887.26	55,798.90
473	02/03/2009	351.03	0.00	0.00	24,201.10	109,887.26	55,798.90
474	02/17/2009	351.03	201.68	500.38	23,700.72	110,088.94	56,299.28
475	03/03/2009	351.03	0.00	0.00	23,700.72	110,088.94	56,299.28
476	03/17/2009	351.03	197.51	504.55	23,196.17	110,286.45	56,803.83
477	03/31/2009	351.03	0.00	0.00	23,196.17	110,286.45	56,803.83
478	04/14/2009	351.03	193.30	508.76	22,687.41	110,479.75	57,312.59
479	04/28/2009	351.03	0.00	0.00	22,687.41	110,479.75	57,312.59
480	05/12/2009	351.03	189.06	513.00	22,174.41	110,668.81	57,825.59
481	05/26/2009	351.03	0.00	0.00	22,174.41	110,668.81	57,825.59
482	06/09/2009	351.03	184.79	517.27	21,657.14	110,853.60	58,342.86
483	06/23/2009	351.03	0.00	0.00	21,657.14	110,853.60	58,342.86
484	07/07/2009	351.03	180.48	521.58	21,135.56	111,034.08	58,864.44

Table 11–4   Continued

Names: MR. & MRS. CARL WILLIAMS

PMT #	PAYMENT DATE	PAYMENT AMOUNT	INTEREST PAID	PRINCIPAL PAID	BALANCE OWED	ACCUMULATED INTEREST	ACCUMULATED PRINCIPAL
485	07/21/2009	351.03	0.00	0.00	21,135.56	111,034.08	58,864.44
486	08/04/2009	351.03	176.13	525.93	20,609.63	111,210.21	59,390.37
487	08/18/2009	351.03	0.00	0.00	20,609.63	111,210.21	59,390.37
488	09/01/2009	351.03	171.75	530.31	20,079.32	111,381.96	59,920.68
489	09/15/2009	351.03	0.00	0.00	20,079.32	111,381.96	59,920.68
490	09/29/2009	351.03	167.33	534.73	19,544.59	111,549.29	60,455.41
491	10/13/2009	351.03	0.00	0.00	19,544.59	111,549.29	60,455.41
492	10/27/2009	351.03	162.87	539.19	19,005.40	111,712.16	60,994.60
493	11/10/2009	351.03	0.00	0.00	19,005.40	111,712.16	60,994.60
494	11/24/2009	351.03	0.00	702.06	18,303.34	111,712.16	61,696.66
495	12/08/2009	351.03	0.00	0.00	18,303.34	111,712.16	61,696.66
496	12/22/2009	351.03	152.53	549.53	17,753.81	111,864.69	62,246.19
497	01/05/2010	351.03	0.00	0.00	17,753.81	111,864.69	62,246.19
498	01/19/2010	351.03	147.95	554.11	17,199.70	112,012.64	62,800.30
499	02/02/2010	351.03	0.00	0.00	17,199.70	112,012.64	62,800.30
500	02/16/2010	351.03	143.33	558.73	16,640.97	112,155.97	63,359.03
501	03/02/2010	351.03	0.00	0.00	16,640.97	112,155.97	63,359.03
502	03/16/2010	351.03	138.67	563.39	16,077.58	112,294.64	63,922.42
503	03/30/2010	351.03	0.00	0.00	16,077.58	112,294.64	63,922.42
504	04/13/2010	351.03	133.98	568.08	15,509.50	112,428.62	64,490.50
505	04/27/2010	351.03	0.00	0.00	15,509.50	112,428.62	64,490.50
506	05/11/2010	351.03	129.25	572.81	14,936.69	112,557.87	65,063.31
507	05/25/2010	351.03	0.00	0.00	14,936.69	112,557.87	65,063.31
508	06/08/2010	351.03	124.47	577.59	14,359.10	112,682.34	65,640.90
509	06/22/2010	351.03	0.00	0.00	14,359.10	112,682.34	65,640.90
510	07/06/2010	351.03	119.66	582.40	13,776.70	112,802.00	66,223.30
511	07/20/2010	351.03	0.00	0.00	13,776.70	112,802.00	66,223.30
512	08/03/2010	351.03	114.81	587.25	13,189.45	112,916.81	66,810.55
513	08/17/2010	351.03	0.00	0.00	13,189.45	112,916.81	66,810.55
514	08/31/2010	351.03	109.91	592.15	12,597.30	113,026.72	67,402.70
515	09/14/2010	351.03	0.00	0.00	12,597.30	113,026.72	67,402.70
516	09/28/2010	351.03	104.98	597.08	12,000.22	113,131.70	67,999.78
517	10/12/2010	351.03	0.00	0.00	12,000.22	113,131.70	67,999.78
518	10/26/2010	351.03	100.00	602.06	11,398.16	113,231.70	68,601.84
519	11/09/2010	351.03	0.00	0.00	11,398.16	113,231.70	68,601.84
520	11/23/2010	351.03	0.00	702.06	10,696.10	113,231.70	69,303.90
521	12/07/2010	351.03	0.00	0.00	10,696.10	113,231.70	69,303.90
522	12/21/2010	351.03	89.13	612.93	10,083.17	113,320.83	69,916.83
523	01/04/2011	351.03	0.00	0.00	10,083.17	113,320.83	69,916.83
524	01/18/2011	351.03	84.03	618.03	9,465.14	113,404.86	70,534.86
525	02/01/2011	351.03	0.00	0.00	9,465.14	113,404.86	70,534.86
526	02/15/2011	351.03	78.88	623.18	8,841.96	113,483.74	71,158.04
527	03/01/2011	351.03	0.00	0.00	8,841.96	113,483.74	71,158.04
528	03/15/2011	351.03	73.68	628.38	8,213.58	113,557.42	71,786.42
529	03/29/2011	351.03	0.00	0.00	8,213.58	113,557.42	71,786.42

Table 11–4   Continued

Names: MR. & MRS. CARL WILLIAMS

PMT #	PAYMENT DATE	PAYMENT AMOUNT	INTEREST PAID	PRINCIPAL PAID	BALANCE OWED	ACCUMULATED INTEREST	ACCUMULATED PRINCIPAL
530	04/12/2011	351.03	68.45	633.61	7,579.97	113,625.87	72,420.03
531	04/26/2011	351.03	0.00	0.00	7,579.97	113,625.87	72,420.03
532	05/10/2011	351.03	63.17	638.89	6,941.08	113,689.04	73,058.92
533	05/24/2011	351.03	0.00	0.00	6,941.08	113,689.04	73,058.92
534	06/07/2011	351.03	57.84	644.22	6,296.86	113,746.88	73,703.14
535	06/21/2011	351.03	0.00	0.00	6,296.86	113,746.88	73,703.14
536	07/05/2011	351.03	52.47	649.59	5,647.27	113,799.35	74,352.73
537	07/19/2011	351.03	0.00	0.00	5,647.27	113,799.35	74,352.73
538	08/02/2011	351.03	47.06	655.00	4,992.27	113,846.41	75,007.73
539	08/16/2011	351.03	0.00	0.00	4,992.27	113,846.41	75,007.73
540	08/30/2011	351.03	41.60	660.46	4,331.81	113,888.01	75,668.19
541	09/13/2011	351.03	0.00	0.00	4,331.81	113,888.01	75,668.19
542	09/27/2011	351.03	36.10	665.96	3,665.85	113,924.11	76,334.15
543	10/11/2011	351.03	0.00	0.00	3,665.85	113,924.11	76,334.15
544	10/25/2011	351.03	30.55	671.51	2,994.34	113,954.66	77,005.66
545	11/08/2011	351.03	0.00	0.00	2,994.34	113,954.66	77,005.66
546	11/22/2011	351.03	0.00	702.06	2,292.28	113,954.66	77,707.72
547	12/06/2011	351.03	0.00	0.00	2,292.28	113,954.66	77,707.72
548	12/20/2011	351.03	19.10	682.96	1,609.32	113,973.76	78,390.68
549	01/03/2012	351.03	0.00	0.00	1,609.32	113,973.76	78,390.68
550	01/17/2012	351.03	13.41	688.65	920.67	113,987.17	79,079.33
551	01/31/2012	351.03	0.00	0.00	920.67	113,987.17	79,079.33
552	02/14/2012	351.03	7.67	694.39	226.28	113,994.84	79,773.72
553	02/28/2012	228.17	1.89	226.28	0.00	113,996.73	80,000.00

Table 11–5   Comparison of Costs and Savings for Ms. Elizabeth Raines—Homeowner Conventional vs. Biweekly Programs

ORIGINAL LOAN AMOUNT:	110,000.00		ANNUAL INTEREST RATE:	12.000 %
ORIGINAL LOAN TERM:	15 (YEARS)		CURRENT MONTHLY PAYMENT:	1,320.18
NUMBER OF PREVIOUS PAYMENTS:	0		'NEW' BIWEEKLY PAYMENT:	660.09
CURRENT LOAN BALANCE:	110,000.00			

	CURRENT MONTHLY			'NEW' BIWEEKLY			DIFFERENCE	
END OF YEAR	REMAINING BALANCE	INTEREST PAID TO-DATE	(EQUITY) PRINCIPAL PAID TO-DATE	REMAINING BALANCE	INTEREST PAID TO-DATE	(EQUITY) PRINCIPAL PAID TO-DATE	EQUTIY GROWTH TO-DATE	INTEREST SAVED TO-DATE
1	107,207.56	13,049.72	2,792.44	105,887.38	13,049.72	4,112.62	1,320.18	0.00
2	104,060.98	25,745.30	5,939.02	101,253.17	25,577.85	8,746.83	2,807.81	167.45
3	100,515.33	38,041.81	9,484.67	96,031.26	37,518.28	13,968.74	4,484.07	523.53
4	96,519.98	49,888.62	13,480.02	90,147.06	48,796.42	19,852.94	6,372.92	1,092.20
5	92,017.93	61,228.73	17,982.07	83,516.58	59,328.28	26,483.42	8,501.35	1,900.45
6	86,944.94	71,997.90	23,055.06	76,045.23	69,019.27	33,954.77	10,899.71	2,978.63
7	81,228.54	82,123.66	28,771.46	67,626.31	77,762.69	42,373.69	13,602.23	4,360.97
8	74,787.18	91,524.46	35,212.82	58,139.65	85,438.37	51,860.35	16,647.53	6,086.09
9	67,528.87	100,108.31	42,471.13	47,449.84	91,910.90	62,550.16	20,079.03	8,197.41
10	59,350.04	107,771.64	50,649.96	35,404.29	97,027.69	74,595.71	23,945.75	10,743.95
11	50,133.90	114,397.66	59,866.10	21,831.06	100,616.80	88,168.94	28,302.84	13,780.86
12	39,748.95	119,854.87	70,251.05	6,536.40	102,484.48	103,463.60	33,212.55	17,370.39
13	28,046.92	123,995.00	81,953.08	DEBT FREE	102,685.91	110,000.00		21,309.09
14	14,860.77	126,651.01	95,139.23					23,965.10
15	1,309.41	127,634.72	110,000.00					24,948.81

TOTAL INTEREST SAVED: 24,948.81
TOTAL TERM SAVED: 31.32 (PAYMENTS)   2.61 (YEARS)

Table 11-6   Amortization Schedule Re: Table 5

Names:	MS. ELIZABETH RAINES
Property:	613 RIVER ROAD, RIVERVIEW, PA 71486
Telephone:	(406)555-8888
Tax I.D.:	123-45-6789

```
=====================================================================================================
| ORIGINAL LOAN AMOUNT:          110,000.00       BIWEEKLY PAYMENT:                        660.09 |
| ORIGINAL INTEREST RATE:            12.000       TOTAL BIWEEKLY INTEREST PAID:        102,685.91 |
| ORIGINAL TERM OF LOAN:         15 (YRS)         LAST BIWEEKLY PAYMENT DATE:          05/06/2003 |
| NUMBER OF PREVIOUS PAYMENTS:             0      NEW TERM OF LOAN:                    12.39 (YRS) |
| CURRENT LOAN BALANCE:          110,000.00                                                         |
=====================================================================================================
```

PMT #	PAYMENT DATE	PAYMENT AMOUNT	INTEREST PAID	PRINCIPAL PAID	BALANCE OWED	ACCUMULATED INTEREST	ACCUMULATED PRINCIPAL
1	01/01/1991	660.09	0.00	0.00	110,000.00	0.00	0.00
2	01/15/1991	660.09	1,100.00	220.18	109,779.82	1,100.00	220.18
3	01/29/1991	660.09	0.00	0.00	109,779.82	1,100.00	220.18
4	02/12/1991	660.09	1,097.80	222.38	109,557.44	2,197.80	442.56
5	02/26/1991	660.09	0.00	0.00	109,557.44	2,197.80	442.56
6	03/12/1991	660.09	1,095.57	224.61	109,332.83	3,293.37	667.17
7	03/26/1991	660.09	0.00	0.00	109,332.83	3,293.37	667.17
8	04/09/1991	660.09	1,093.33	226.85	109,105.98	4,386.70	894.02
9	04/23/1991	660.09	0.00	0.00	109,105.98	4,386.70	894.02
10	05/07/1991	660.09	1,091.06	229.12	108,876.86	5,477.76	1,123.14
11	05/21/1991	660.09	0.00	0.00	108,876.86	5,477.76	1,123.14
12	06/04/1991	660.09	1,088.77	231.41	108,645.45	6,566.53	1,354.55
13	06/18/1991	660.09	0.00	0.00	108,645.45	6,566.53	1,354.55
14	07/02/1991	660.09	1,086.45	233.73	108,411.72	7,652.98	1,588.28
15	07/16/1991	660.09	0.00	0.00	108,411.72	7,652.98	1,588.28
16	07/30/1991	660.09	1,084.12	236.06	108,175.66	8,737.10	1,824.34
17	08/13/1991	660.09	0.00	0.CO	108,175.66	8,737.10	1,824.34
18	08/27/1991	660.09	1,081.76	238.42	107,937.24	9,818.86	2,062.76
19	09/10/1991	660.09	0.00	0.00	107,937.24	9,818.86	2,062.76
20	09/24/1991	660.09	1,079.37	240.81	107,696.43	10,898.23	2,303.57
21	10/08/1991	660.09	0.00	0.00	107,696.43	10,898.23	2,303.57
22	10/22/1991	660.09	1,076.96	243.22	107,453.21	11,975.19	2,546.79
23	11/05/1991	660.09	0.00	0.00	107,453.21	11,975.19	2,546.79
24	11/19/1991	660.09	1,074.53	245.65	107,207.56	13,049.72	2,792.44
25	12/03/1991	660.09	0.00	0.00	107,207.56	13,049.72	2,792.44
26	12/17/1991	660.09	0.00	1,320.18	105,887.38	13,049.72	4,112.62
27	12/31/1991	660.09	0.00	0.00	105,887.38	13,049.72	4,112.62
28	01/14/1992	660.09	1,058.87	261.31	105,626.07	14,108.59	4,373.93
29	01/28/1992	660.09	0.00	0.00	105,626.07	14,108.59	4,373.93
30	02/11/1992	660.09	1,056.26	263.92	105,362.15	15,164.85	4,637.85
31	02/25/1992	660.09	0.00	0.00	105,362.15	15,164.85	4,637.85
32	03/10/1992	660.09	1,053.62	266.56	105,095.59	16,218.47	4,904.41
33	03/24/1992	660.09	0.00	0.00	105,095.59	16,218.47	4,904.41
34	04/07/1992	660.09	1,050.96	269.22	104,826.37	17,269.43	5,173.63

Table 11-6   Continued

Names: MS. ELIZABETH RAINES

PMT #	PAYMENT DATE	PAYMENT AMOUNT	INTEREST PAID	PRINCIPAL PAID	BALANCE OWED	ACCUMULATED INTEREST	ACCUMULATED PRINCIPAL
35	04/21/1992	660.09	0.00	0.00	104,826.37	17,269.43	5,173.63
36	05/05/1992	660.09	1,048.26	271.92	104,554.45	18,317.69	5,445.55
37	05/19/1992	660.09	0.00	0.00	104,554.45	18,317.69	5,445.55
38	06/02/1992	660.09	1,045.54	274.64	104,279.81	19,363.23	5,720.19
39	06/16/1992	660.09	0.00	0.00	104,279.81	19,363.23	5,720.19
40	06/30/1992	660.09	1,042.80	277.38	104,002.43	20,406.03	5,997.57
41	07/14/1992	660.09	0.00	0.00	104,002.43	20,406.03	5,997.57
42	07/28/1992	660.09	1,040.02	280.16	103,722.27	21,446.05	6,277.73
43	08/11/1992	660.09	0.00	0.00	103,722.27	21,446.05	6,277.73
44	08/25/1992	660.09	1,037.22	282.96	103,439.31	22,483.27	6,560.69
45	09/08/1992	660.09	0.00	0.00	103,439.31	22,483.27	6,560.69
46	09/22/1992	660.09	1,034.39	285.79	103,153.52	23,517.66	6,846.48
47	10/06/1992	660.09	0.00	0.00	103,153.52	23,517.66	6,846.48
48	10/20/1992	660.09	1,031.54	288.64	102,864.88	24,549.20	7,135.12
49	11/03/1992	660.09	0.00	0.00	102,864.88	24,549.20	7,135.12
50	11/17/1992	660.09	1,028.65	291.53	102,573.35	25,577.85	7,426.65
51	12/01/1992	660.09	0.00	0.00	102,573.35	25,577.85	7,426.65
52	12/15/1992	660.09	0.00	1,320.18	101,253.17	25,577.85	8,746.83
53	12/29/1992	660.09	0.00	0.00	101,253.17	25,577.85	8,746.83
54	01/12/1993	660.09	1,012.53	307.65	100,945.52	26,590.38	9,054.48
55	01/26/1993	660.09	0.00	0.00	100,945.52	26,590.38	9,054.48
56	02/09/1993	660.09	1,009.46	310.72	100,634.80	27,599.84	9,365.20
57	02/23/1993	660.09	0.00	0.00	100,634.80	27,599.84	9,365.20
58	03/09/1993	660.09	1,006.35	313.83	100,320.97	28,606.19	9,679.03
59	03/23/1993	660.09	0.00	0.00	100,320.97	28,606.19	9,679.03
60	04/06/1993	660.09	1,003.21	316.97	100,004.00	29,609.40	9,996.00
61	04/20/1993	660.09	0.00	0.00	100,004.00	29,609.40	9,996.00
62	05/04/1993	660.09	1,000.04	320.14	99,683.86	30,609.44	10,316.14
63	05/18/1993	660.09	0.00	0.00	99,683.86	30,609.44	10,316.14
64	06/01/1993	660.09	996.84	323.34	99,360.52	31,606.28	10,639.48
65	06/15/1993	660.09	0.00	0.00	99,360.52	31,606.28	10,639.48
66	06/29/1993	660.09	993.61	326.57	99,033.95	32,599.89	10,966.05
67	07/13/1993	660.09	0.00	0.00	99,033.95	32,599.89	10,966.05
68	07/27/1993	660.09	990.34	329.84	98,704.11	33,590.23	11,295.89
69	08/10/1993	660.09	0.00	0.00	98,704.11	33,590.23	11,295.89
70	08/24/1993	660.09	987.04	333.14	98,370.97	34,577.27	11,629.03
71	09/07/1993	660.09	0.00	0.00	98,370.97	34,577.27	11,629.03
72	09/21/1993	660.09	983.71	336.47	98,034.50	35,560.98	11,965.50
73	10/05/1993	660.09	0.00	0.00	98,034.50	35,560.98	11,965.50
74	10/19/1993	660.09	980.35	339.83	97,694.67	36,541.33	12,305.33
75	11/02/1993	660.09	0.00	0.00	97,694.67	36,541.33	12,305.33
76	11/16/1993	660.09	976.95	343.23	97,351.44	37,518.28	12,648.56
77	11/30/1993	660.09	0.00	0.00	97,351.44	37,518.28	12,648.56
78	12/14/1993	660.09	0.00	1,320.18	96,031.26	37,518.28	13,968.74
79	12/28/1993	660.09	0.00	0.00	96,031.26	37,518.28	13,968.74

Table 11–6   Continued

Names: MS. ELIZABETH RAINES

PMT #	PAYMENT DATE	PAYMENT AMOUNT	INTEREST PAID	PRINCIPAL PAID	BALANCE OWED	ACCUMULATED INTEREST	ACCUMULATED PRINCIPAL
80	01/11/1994	660.09	960.31	359.87	95,671.39	38,478.59	14,328.61
81	01/25/1994	660.09	0.00	0.00	95,671.39	38,478.59	14,328.61
82	02/08/1994	660.09	956.71	363.47	95,307.92	39,435.30	14,692.08
83	02/22/1994	660.09	0.00	0.00	95,307.92	39,435.30	14,692.08
84	03/08/1994	660.09	953.08	367.10	94,940.82	40,388.38	15,059.18
85	03/22/1994	660.09	0.00	0.00	94,940.82	40,388.38	15,059.18
86	04/05/1994	660.09	949.41	370.77	94,570.05	41,337.79	15,429.95
87	04/19/1994	660.09	0.00	0.00	94,570.05	41,337.79	15,429.95
88	05/03/1994	660.09	945.70	374.48	94,195.57	42,283.49	15,804.43
89	05/17/1994	660.09	0.00	0.00	94,195.57	42,283.49	15,804.43
90	05/31/1994	660.09	941.96	378.22	93,817.35	43,225.45	16,182.65
91	06/14/1994	660.09	0.00	0.00	93,817.35	43,225.45	16,182.65
92	06/28/1994	660.09	938.17	382.01	93,435.34	44,163.62	16,564.66
93	07/12/1994	660.09	0.00	0.00	93,435.34	44,163.62	16,564.66
94	07/26/1994	660.09	934.35	385.83	93,049.51	45,097.97	16,950.49
95	08/09/1994	660.09	0.00	0.00	93,049.51	45,097.97	16,950.49
96	08/23/1994	660.09	930.50	389.68	92,659.83	46,028.47	17,340.17
97	09/06/1994	660.09	0.00	0.00	92,659.83	46,028.47	17,340.17
98	09/20/1994	660.09	926.60	393.58	92,266.25	46,955.07	17,733.75
99	10/04/1994	660.09	0.00	0.00	92,266.25	46,955.07	17,733.75
100	10/18/1994	660.09	922.66	397.52	91,868.73	47,877.73	18,131.27
101	11/01/1994	660.09	0.00	0.00	91,868.73	47,877.73	18,131.27
102	11/15/1994	660.09	918.69	401.49	91,467.24	48,796.42	18,532.76
103	11/29/1994	660.09	0.00	0.00	91,467.24	48,796.42	18,532.76
104	12/13/1994	660.09	0.00	1,320.18	90,147.06	48,796.42	19,852.94
105	12/27/1994	660.09	0.00	0.00	90,147.06	48,796.42	19,852.94
106	01/10/1995	660.09	901.47	418.71	89,728.35	49,697.89	20,271.65
107	01/24/1995	660.09	0.00	0.00	89,728.35	49,697.89	20,271.65
108	02/07/1995	660.09	897.28	422.90	89,305.45	50,595.17	20,694.55
109	02/21/1995	660.09	0.00	0.00	89,305.45	50,595.17	20,694.55
110	03/07/1995	660.09	893.05	427.13	88,878.32	51,488.22	21,121.68
111	03/21/1995	660.09	0.00	0.00	88,878.32	51,488.22	21,121.68
112	04/04/1995	660.09	888.78	431.40	88,446.92	52,377.00	21,553.08
113	04/18/1995	660.09	0.00	0.00	88,446.92	52,377.00	21,553.08
114	05/02/1995	660.09	884.47	435.71	88,011.21	53,261.47	21,988.79
115	05/16/1995	660.09	0.00	0.00	88,011.21	53,261.47	21,988.79
116	05/30/1995	660.09	880.11	440.07	87,571.14	54,141.58	22,428.86
117	06/13/1995	660.09	0.00	0.00	87,571.14	54,141.58	22,428.86
118	06/27/1995	660.09	875.71	444.47	87,126.67	55,017.29	22,873.33
119	07/11/1995	660.09	0.00	0.00	87,126.67	55,017.29	22,873.33
120	07/25/1995	660.09	871.27	448.91	86,677.76	55,888.56	23,322.24
121	08/08/1995	660.09	0.00	0.00	86,677.76	55,888.56	23,322.24
122	08/22/1995	660.09	866.78	453.40	86,224.36	56,755.34	23,775.64
123	09/05/1995	660.09	0.00	0.00	86,224.36	56,755.34	23,775.64
124	09/19/1995	660.09	862.24	457.94	85,766.42	57,617.58	24,233.58

Table 11–6   Continued

Names: MS. ELIZABETH RAINES

PMT #	PAYMENT DATE	PAYMENT AMOUNT	INTEREST PAID	PRINCIPAL PAID	BALANCE OWED	ACCUMULATED INTEREST	ACCUMULATED PRINCIPAL
125	10/03/1995	660.09	0.00	0.00	85,766.42	57,617.58	24,233.58
126	10/17/1995	660.09	857.66	462.52	85,303.90	58,475.24	24,696.10
127	10/31/1995	660.09	0.00	0.00	85,303.90	58,475.24	24,696.10
128	11/14/1995	660.09	853.04	467.14	84,836.76	59,328.28	25,163.24
129	11/28/1995	660.09	0.00	0.00	84,836.76	59,328.28	25,163.24
130	12/12/1995	660.09	0.00	1,320.18	83,516.58	59,328.28	26,483.42
131	12/26/1995	660.09	0.00	0.00	83,516.58	59,328.28	26,483.42
132	01/09/1996	660.09	835.17	485.01	83,031.57	60,163.45	26,968.43
133	01/23/1996	660.09	0.00	0.00	83,031.57	60,163.45	26,968.43
134	02/06/1996	660.09	830.32	489.86	82,541.71	60,993.77	27,458.29
135	02/20/1996	660.09	0.00	0.00	82,541.71	60,993.77	27,458.29
136	03/05/1996	660.09	825.42	494.76	82,046.95	61,819.19	27,953.05
137	03/19/1996	660.09	0.00	0.00	82,046.95	61,819.19	27,953.05
138	04/02/1996	660.09	820.47	499.71	81,547.24	62,639.66	28,452.76
139	04/16/1996	660.09	0.00	0.00	81,547.24	62,639.66	28,452.76
140	04/30/1996	660.09	815.47	504.71	81,042.53	63,455.13	28,957.47
141	05/14/1996	660.09	0.00	0.00	81,042.53	63,455.13	28,957.47
142	05/28/1996	660.09	810.43	509.75	80,532.78	64,265.56	29,467.22
143	06/11/1996	660.09	0.00	0.00	80,532.78	64,265.56	29,467.22
144	06/25/1996	660.09	805.33	514.85	80,017.93	65,070.89	29,982.07
145	07/09/1996	660.09	0.00	0.00	80,017.93	65,070.89	29,982.07
146	07/23/1996	660.09	800.18	520.00	79,497.93	65,871.07	30,502.07
147	08/06/1996	660.09	0.00	0.00	79,497.93	65,871.07	30,502.07
148	08/20/1996	660.09	794.98	525.20	78,972.73	66,666.05	31,027.27
149	09/03/1996	660.09	0.00	0.00	78,972.73	66,666.05	31,027.27
150	09/17/1996	660.09	789.73	530.45	78,442.28	67,455.78	31,557.72
151	10/01/1996	660.09	0.00	0.00	78,442.28	67,455.78	31,557.72
152	10/15/1996	660.09	784.42	535.76	77,906.52	68,240.20	32,093.48
153	10/29/1996	660.09	0.00	0.00	77,906.52	68,240.20	32,093.48
154	11/12/1996	660.09	779.07	541.11	77,365.41	69,019.27	32,634.59
155	11/26/1996	660.09	0.00	0.00	77,365.41	69,019.27	32,634.59
156	12/10/1996	660.09	0.00	1,320.18	76,045.23	69,019.27	33,954.77
157	12/24/1996	660.09	0.00	0.00	76,045.23	69,019.27	33,954.77
158	01/07/1997	660.09	760.45	559.73	75,485.50	69,779.72	34,514.50
159	01/21/1997	660.09	0.00	0.00	75,485.50	69,779.72	34,514.50
160	02/04/1997	660.09	754.86	565.32	74,920.18	70,534.58	35,079.82
161	02/18/1997	660.09	0.00	0.00	74,920.18	70,534.58	35,079.82
162	03/04/1997	660.09	749.20	570.98	74,349.20	71,283.78	35,650.80
163	03/18/1997	660.09	0.00	0.00	74,349.20	71,283.78	35,650.80
164	04/01/1997	660.09	743.49	576.69	73,772.51	72,027.27	36,227.49
165	04/15/1997	660.09	0.00	0.00	73,772.51	72,027.27	36,227.49
166	04/29/1997	660.09	737.73	582.45	73,190.06	72,765.00	36,809.94
167	05/13/1997	660.09	0.00	0.00	73,190.06	72,765.00	36,809.94
168	05/27/1997	660.09	731.90	588.28	72,601.78	73,496.90	37,398.22
169	06/10/1997	660.09	0.00	0.00	72,601.78	73,496.90	37,398.22

Table 11–6   Continued

Names: MS. ELIZABETH RAINES

PMT #	PAYMENT DATE	PAYMENT AMOUNT	INTEREST PAID	PRINCIPAL PAID	BALANCE OWED	ACCUMULATED INTEREST	ACCUMULATED PRINCIPAL
170	06/24/1997	660.09	726.02	594.16	72,007.62	74,222.92	37,992.38
171	07/08/1997	660.09	0.00	0.00	72,007.62	74,222.92	37,992.38
172	07/22/1997	660.09	720.08	600.10	71,407.52	74,943.00	38,592.48
173	08/05/1997	660.09	0.00	0.00	71,407.52	74,943.00	38,592.48
174	08/19/1997	660.09	714.08	606.10	70,801.42	75,657.08	39,198.58
175	09/02/1997	660.09	0.00	0.00	70,801.42	75,657.08	39,198.58
176	09/16/1997	660.09	708.01	612.17	70,189.25	76,365.09	39,810.75
177	09/30/1997	660.09	0.00	0.00	70,189.25	76,365.09	39,810.75
178	10/14/1997	660.09	701.89	618.29	69,570.96	77,066.98	40,429.04
179	10/28/1997	660.09	0.00	0.00	69,570.96	77,066.98	40,429.04
180	11/11/1997	660.09	695.71	624.47	68,946.49	77,762.69	41,053.51
181	11/25/1997	660.09	0.00	0.00	68,946.49	77,762.69	41,053.51
182	12/09/1997	660.09	0.00	1,320.18	67,626.31	77,762.69	42,373.69
183	12/23/1997	660.09	0.00	0.00	67,626.31	77,762.69	42,373.69
184	01/06/1998	660.09	676.26	643.92	66,982.39	78,438.95	43,017.61
185	01/20/1998	660.09	0.00	0.00	66,982.39	78,438.95	43,017.61
186	02/03/1998	660.09	669.82	650.36	66,332.03	79,108.77	43,667.97
187	02/17/1998	660.09	0.00	0.00	66,332.03	79,108.77	43,667.97
188	03/03/1998	660.09	663.32	656.86	65,675.17	79,772.09	44,324.83
189	03/17/1998	660.09	0.00	0.00	65,675.17	79,772.09	44,324.83
190	03/31/1998	660.09	656.75	663.43	65,011.74	80,428.84	44,988.26
191	04/14/1998	660.09	0.00	0.00	65,011.74	80,428.84	44,988.26
192	04/28/1998	660.09	650.12	670.06	64,341.68	81,078.96	45,658.32
193	05/12/1998	660.09	0.00	0.00	64,341.68	81,078.96	45,658.32
194	05/26/1998	660.09	643.42	676.76	63,664.92	81,722.38	46,335.08
195	06/09/1998	660.09	0.00	0.00	63,664.92	81,722.38	46,335.08
196	06/23/1998	660.09	636.65	683.53	62,981.39	82,359.03	47,018.61
197	07/07/1998	660.09	0.00	0.00	62,981.39	82,359.03	47,018.61
198	07/21/1998	660.09	629.81	690.37	62,291.02	82,988.84	47,708.98
199	08/04/1998	660.09	0.00	0.00	62,291.02	82,988.84	47,708.98
200	08/18/1998	660.09	622.91	697.27	61,593.75	83,611.75	48,406.25
201	09/01/1998	660.09	0.00	0.00	61,593.75	83,611.75	48,406.25
202	09/15/1998	660.09	615.94	704.24	60,889.51	84,227.69	49,110.49
203	09/29/1998	660.09	0.00	0.00	60,889.51	84,227.69	49,110.49
204	10/13/1998	660.09	608.90	711.28	60,178.23	84,836.59	49,821.77
205	10/27/1998	660.09	0.00	0.00	60,178.23	84,836.59	49,821.77
206	11/10/1998	660.09	601.78	718.40	59,459.83	85,438.37	50,540.17
207	11/24/1998	660.09	0.00	0.00	59,459.83	85,438.37	50,540.17
208	12/08/1998	660.09	0.00	1,320.18	58,139.65	85,438.37	51,860.35
209	12/22/1998	660.09	0.00	0.00	58,139.65	85,438.37	51,860.35
210	01/05/1999	660.09	581.40	738.78	57,400.87	86,019.77	52,599.13
211	01/19/1999	660.09	0.00	0.00	57,400.87	86,019.77	52,599.13
212	02/02/1999	660.09	574.01	746.17	56,654.70	86,593.78	53,345.30
213	02/16/1999	660.09	0.00	0.00	56,654.70	86,593.78	53,345.30
214	03/02/1999	660.09	566.55	753.63	55,901.07	87,160.33	54,098.93

Table 11–6   Continued

Names: MS. ELIZABETH RAINES

PMT #	PAYMENT DATE	PAYMENT AMOUNT	INTEREST PAID	PRINCIPAL PAID	BALANCE OWED	ACCUMULATED INTEREST	ACCUMULATED PRINCIPAL
215	03/16/1999	660.09	0.00	0.00	55,901.07	87,160.33	54,098.93
216	03/30/1999	660.09	559.01	761.17	55,139.90	87,719.34	54,860.10
217	04/13/1999	660.09	0.00	0.00	55,139.90	87,719.34	54,860.10
218	04/27/1999	660.09	551.40	768.78	54,371.12	88,270.74	55,628.88
219	05/11/1999	660.09	0.00	0.00	54,371.12	88,270.74	55,628.88
220	05/25/1999	660.09	543.71	776.47	53,594.65	88,814.45	56,405.35
221	06/08/1999	660.09	0.00	0.00	53,594.65	88,814.45	56,405.35
222	06/22/1999	660.09	535.95	784.23	52,810.42	89,350.40	57,189.58
223	07/06/1999	660.09	0.00	0.00	52,810.42	89,350.40	57,189.58
224	07/20/1999	660.09	528.10	792.08	52,018.34	89,878.50	57,981.66
225	08/03/1999	660.09	0.00	0.00	52,018.34	89,878.50	57,981.66
226	08/17/1999	660.09	520.18	800.00	51,218.34	90,398.68	58,781.66
227	08/31/1999	660.09	0.00	0.00	51,218.34	90,398.68	58,781.66
228	09/14/1999	660.09	512.18	808.00	50,410.34	90,910.86	59,589.66
229	09/28/1999	660.09	0.00	0.00	50,410.34	90,910.86	59,589.66
230	10/12/1999	660.09	504.10	816.08	49,594.26	91,414.96	60,405.74
231	10/26/1999	660.09	0.00	0.00	49,594.26	91,414.96	60,405.74
232	11/09/1999	660.09	495.94	824.24	48,770.02	91,910.90	61,229.98
233	11/23/1999	660.09	0.00	0.00	48,770.02	91,910.90	61,229.98
234	12/07/1999	660.09	0.00	1,320.18	47,449.84	91,910.90	62,550.16
235	12/21/1999	660.09	0.00	0.00	47,449.84	91,910.90	62,550.16
236	01/04/2000	660.09	474.50	845.68	46,604.16	92,385.40	63,395.84
237	01/18/2000	660.09	0.00	0.00	46,604.16	92,385.40	63,395.84
238	02/01/2000	660.09	466.04	854.14	45,750.02	92,851.44	64,249.98
239	02/15/2000	660.09	0.00	0.00	45,750.02	92,851.44	64,249.98
240	02/29/2000	660.09	457.50	862.68	44,887.34	93,308.94	65,112.66
241	03/14/2000	660.09	0.00	0.00	44,887.34	93,308.94	65,112.66
242	03/28/2000	660.09	448.87	871.31	44,016.03	93,757.81	65,983.97
243	04/11/2000	660.09	0.00	0.00	44,016.03	93,757.81	65,983.97
244	04/25/2000	660.09	440.16	880.02	43,136.01	94,197.97	66,863.99
245	05/09/2000	660.09	0.00	0.00	43,136.01	94,197.97	66,863.99
246	05/23/2000	660.09	431.36	888.82	42,247.19	94,629.33	67,752.81
247	06/06/2000	660.09	0.00	0.00	42,247.19	94,629.33	67,752.81
248	06/20/2000	660.09	422.47	897.71	41,349.48	95,051.80	68,650.52
249	07/04/2000	660.09	0.00	0.00	41,349.48	95,051.80	68,650.52
250	07/18/2000	660.09	413.49	906.69	40,442.79	95,465.29	69,557.21
251	08/01/2000	660.09	0.00	0.00	40,442.79	95,465.29	69,557.21
252	08/15/2000	660.09	404.43	915.75	39,527.04	95,869.72	70,472.96
253	08/29/2000	660.09	0.00	0.00	39,527.04	95,869.72	70,472.96
254	09/12/2000	660.09	395.27	924.91	38,602.13	96,264.99	71,397.87
255	09/26/2000	660.09	0.00	0.00	38,602.13	96,264.99	71,397.87
256	10/10/2000	660.09	386.02	934.16	37,667.97	96,651.01	72,332.03
257	10/24/2000	660.09	0.00	0.00	37,667.97	96,651.01	72,332.03
258	11/07/2000	660.09	376.68	943.50	36,724.47	97,027.69	73,275.53
259	11/21/2000	660.09	0.00	0.00	36,724.47	97,027.69	73,275.53

Table 11–6   Continued

Names: MS. ELIZABETH RAINES

PMT #	PAYMENT DATE	PAYMENT AMOUNT	INTEREST PAID	PRINCIPAL PAID	BALANCE OWED	ACCUMULATED INTEREST	ACCUMULATED PRINCIPAL
260	12/05/2000	660.09	0.00	1,320.18	35,404.29	97,027.69	74,595.71
261	12/19/2000	660.09	0.00	0.00	35,404.29	97,027.69	74,595.71
262	01/02/2001	660.09	354.04	966.14	34,438.15	97,381.73	75,561.85
263	01/16/2001	660.09	0.00	0.00	34,438.15	97,381.73	75,561.85
264	01/30/2001	660.09	344.38	975.80	33,462.35	97,726.11	76,537.65
265	02/13/2001	660.09	0.00	0.00	33,462.35	97,726.11	76,537.65
266	02/27/2001	660.09	334.62	985.56	32,476.79	98,060.73	77,523.21
267	03/13/2001	660.09	0.00	0.00	32,476.79	98,060.73	77,523.21
268	03/27/2001	660.09	324.77	995.41	31,481.38	98,385.50	78,518.62
269	04/10/2001	660.09	0.00	0.00	31,481.38	98,385.50	78,518.62
270	04/24/2001	660.09	314.81	1,005.37	30,476.01	98,700.31	79,523.99
271	05/08/2001	660.09	0.00	0.00	30,476.01	98,700.31	79,523.99
272	05/22/2001	660.09	304.76	1,015.42	29,460.59	99,005.07	80,539.41
273	06/05/2001	660.09	0.00	0.00	29,460.59	99,005.07	80,539.41
274	06/19/2001	660.09	294.61	1,025.57	28,435.02	99,299.68	81,564.98
275	07/03/2001	660.09	0.00	0.00	28,435.02	99,299.68	81,564.98
276	07/17/2001	660.09	284.35	1,035.83	27,399.19	99,584.03	82,600.81
277	07/31/2001	660.09	0.00	0.00	27,399.19	99,584.03	82,600.81
278	08/14/2001	660.09	273.99	1,046.19	26,353.00	99,858.02	83,647.00
279	08/28/2001	660.09	0.00	0.00	26,353.00	99,858.02	83,647.00
280	09/11/2001	660.09	263.53	1,056.65	25,296.35	100,121.55	84,703.65
281	09/25/2001	660.09	0.00	0.00	25,296.35	100,121.55	84,703.65
282	10/09/2001	660.09	252.96	1,067.22	24,229.13	100,374.51	85,770.87
283	10/23/2001	660.09	0.00	0.00	24,229.13	100,374.51	85,770.87
284	11/06/2001	660.09	242.29	1,077.89	23,151.24	100,616.80	86,848.76
285	11/20/2001	660.09	0.00	0.00	23,151.24	100,616.80	86,848.76
286	12/04/2001	660.09	0.00	1,320.18	21,831.06	100,616.80	88,168.94
287	12/18/2001	660.09	0.00	0.00	21,831.06	100,616.80	88,168.94
288	01/01/2002	660.09	218.31	1,101.87	20,729.19	100,835.11	89,270.81
289	01/15/2002	660.09	0.00	0.00	20,729.19	100,835.11	89,270.81
290	01/29/2002	660.09	207.29	1,112.89	19,616.30	101,042.40	90,383.70
291	02/12/2002	660.09	0.00	0.00	19,616.30	101,042.40	90,383.70
292	02/26/2002	660.09	196.16	1,124.02	18,492.28	101,238.56	91,507.72
293	03/12/2002	660.09	0.00	0.00	18,492.28	101,238.56	91,507.72
294	03/26/2002	660.09	184.92	1,135.26	17,357.02	101,423.48	92,642.98
295	04/09/2002	660.09	0.00	0.00	17,357.02	101,423.48	92,642.98
296	04/23/2002	660.09	173.57	1,146.61	16,210.41	101,597.05	93,789.59
297	05/07/2002	660.09	0.00	0.00	16,210.41	101,597.05	93,789.59
298	05/21/2002	660.09	162.10	1,158.08	15,052.33	101,759.15	94,947.67
299	06/04/2002	660.09	0.00	0.00	15,052.33	101,759.15	94,947.67
300	06/18/2002	660.09	150.52	1,169.66	13,882.67	101,909.67	96,117.33
301	07/02/2002	660.09	0.00	0.00	13,882.67	101,909.67	96,117.33
302	07/16/2002	660.09	138.83	1,181.35	12,701.32	102,048.50	97,298.68
303	07/30/2002	660.09	0.00	0.00	12,701.32	102,048.50	97,298.68
304	08/13/2002	660.09	127.01	1,193.17	11,508.15	102,175.51	98,491.85

Table 11–6   Continued

Names: MS. ELIZABETH RAINES

PMT #	PAYMENT DATE	PAYMENT AMOUNT	INTEREST PAID	PRINCIPAL PAID	BALANCE OWED	ACCUMULATED INTEREST	ACCUMULATED PRINCIPAL
305	08/27/2002	660.09	0.00	0.00	11,508.15	102,175.51	98,491.85
306	09/10/2002	660.09	115.08	1,205.10	10,303.05	102,290.59	99,696.95
307	09/24/2002	660.09	0.00	0.00	10,303.05	102,290.59	99,696.95
308	10/08/2002	660.09	103.03	1,217.15	9,085.90	102,393.62	100,914.10
309	10/22/2002	660.09	0.00	0.00	9,085.90	102,393.62	100,914.10
310	11/05/2002	660.09	90.86	1,229.32	7,856.58	102,484.48	102,143.42
311	11/19/2002	660.09	0.00	0.00	7,856.58	102,484.48	102,143.42
312	12/03/2002	660.09	0.00	1,320.18	6,536.40	102,484.48	103,463.60
313	12/17/2002	660.09	0.00	0.00	6,536.40	102,484.48	103,463.60
314	12/31/2002	660.09	65.36	1,254.82	5,281.58	102,549.84	104,718.42
315	01/14/2003	660.09	0.00	0.00	5,281.58	102,549.84	104,718.42
316	01/28/2003	660.09	52.82	1,267.36	4,014.22	102,602.66	105,985.78
317	02/11/2003	660.09	0.00	0.00	4,014.22	102,602.66	105,985.78
318	02/25/2003	660.09	40.14	1,280.04	2,734.18	102,642.80	107,265.82
319	03/11/2003	660.09	0.00	0.00	2,734.18	102,642.80	107,265.82
320	03/25/2003	660.09	27.34	1,292.84	1,441.34	102,670.14	108,558.66
321	04/08/2003	660.09	0.00	0.00	1,441.34	102,670.14	108,558.66
322	04/22/2003	660.09	14.41	1,305.77	135.57	102,684.55	109,864.43
323	05/06/2003	136.93	1.36	135.57	0.00	102,685.91	110,000.00

Table 11-7 Comparison of Costs and Savings for Mr. Alan Spalding—Homeowner Summary

```
=======================================================================================================
| ORIGINAL LOAN AMOUNT:          110,000.00                    ANNUAL INTEREST RATE:        12.000 % |
| ORIGINAL LOAN TERM:              30 (YEARS)                   CURRENT MONTHLY PAYMENT:     1,131.47  |
| NUMBER OF PREVIOUS PAYMENTS:      0                           'NEW' BIWEEKLY PAYMENT:        565.74  |
| CURRENT LOAN BALANCE:          110,000.00                                                            |
=======================================================================================================
```

	CURRENT MONTHLY			'NEW' BIWEEKLY			DIFFERENCE	
END OF YEAR	REMAINING BALANCE	INTEREST PAID TO-DATE	(EQUITY) PRINCIPAL PAID TO-DATE	REMAINING BALANCE	INTEREST PAID TO-DATE	(EQUITY) PRINCIPAL PAID TO-DATE	EQUITY GROWTH TO-DATE	INTEREST SAVED TO-DATE
1	109,600.88	13,178.52	399.12	108,469.28	13,178.52	1,530.72	1,131.60	0.00
2	109,151.15	26,306.43	848.85	106,744.42	26,162.90	3,255.58	2,406.73	143.53
3	108,644.37	39,377.29	1,355.63	104,800.78	38,928.50	5,199.22	3,843.59	448.79
4	108,073.33	52,383.89	1,926.67	102,610.66	51,447.62	7,389.34	5,462.67	936.27
5	107,429.86	65,318.06	2,570.14	100,142.78	63,688.98	9,857.22	7,287.08	1,629.08
6	106,704.79	78,170.63	3,295.21	97,361.91	75,617.35	12,638.09	9,342.88	2,553.28
7	105,887.75	90,931.23	4,112.25	94,228.37	87,193.05	15,771.63	11,659.38	3,738.18
8	104,967.09	103,588.21	5,032.91	90,697.40	98,371.32	19,302.60	14,269.69	5,216.89
9	103,929.67	116,128.43	6,070.33	86,718.62	109,101.78	23,281.38	17,211.05	7,026.65
10	102,760.68	128,537.08	7,239.32	82,235.24	119,327.64	27,764.76	20,525.44	9,209.44
11	101,443.44	140,797.48	8,556.56	77,183.24	128,984.88	32,816.76	24,260.20	11,812.60
12	99,959.12	152,890.80	10,040.88	71,490.53	138,001.41	38,509.47	28,468.59	14,889.39
13	98,286.57	164,795.89	11,713.43	65,075.85	146,295.97	44,924.15	33,210.72	18,499.92
14	96,401.90	176,488.86	13,598.10	57,847.61	153,776.97	52,152.39	38,554.29	22,711.89
15	94,278.20	187,942.80	15,721.80	49,702.68	160,341.28	60,297.32	44,575.52	27,601.52
16	91,885.16	199,127.40	18,114.84	40,524.75	165,872.59	69,475.25	51,360.41	33,254.81
17	89,188.63	210,008.51	20,811.37	30,182.83	170,239.91	79,817.17	59,005.80	39,768.60
18	86,150.12	220,547.64	23,849.88	18,529.29	173,295.61	91,470.71	67,620.83	47,252.03
19	82,726.23	230,701.39	27,273.77	5,397.77	174,873.33	104,602.23	77,328.46	55,828.06
20	78,868.12	240,420.92	31,131.88	DEBT FREE	175,034.39	110,000.00		65,386.53
21	74,520.69	249,651.13	35,479.31					74,616.74
22	69,621.89	258,329.97	40,378.11					83,295.58
23	64,101.82	266,387.54	45,898.18					91,353.15
24	57,881.67	273,745.03	52,118.33					98,710.64
25	50,872.66	280,313.66	59,127.34					105,279.27
26	42,974.71	285,993.35	67,025.29					110,958.96
27	34,075.10	290,671.38	75,924.90					115,636.99
28	24,046.79	294,220.71	85,953.21					119,186.32
29	12,746.66	296,498.22	97,253.34					121,463.83
30	13.40	297,342.73	110,000.00					122,308.34

```
TOTAL INTEREST SAVED:    122,308.34
TOTAL TERM SAVED:        127.44 (PAYMENTS)  10.62  (YEARS)
```

Table 11–8   Amortization Schedule Re: Table 7

Names:	MR. ALAN SPALDING
Property:	1647 TOWERS BLVD., SPRINGFIELD, IL 60468
Telephone:	(309)555-8888
Tax I.D.:	123-45-6789

ORIGINAL LOAN AMOUNT:	110,000.00	BIWEEKLY PAYMENT:	565.74
ORIGINAL INTEREST RATE:	12.000	TOTAL BIWEEKLY INTEREST PAID:	175,034.39
ORIGINAL TERM OF LOAN:	30 (YRS)	LAST BIWEEKLY PAYMENT DATE:	04/13/2010
NUMBER OF PREVIOUS PAYMENTS:	0	NEW TERM OF LOAN:	19.38 (YRS)
CURRENT LOAN BALANCE:	110,000.00		

PMT #	PAYMENT DATE	PAYMENT AMOUNT	INTEREST PAID	PRINCIPAL PAID	BALANCE OWED	ACCUMULATED INTEREST	ACCUMULATED PRINCIPAL
1	01/01/1991	565.74	0.00	0.00	110,000.00	0.00	0.00
2	01/15/1991	565.74	1,100.00	31.48	109,968.52	1,100.00	31.48
3	01/29/1991	565.74	0.00	0.00	109,968.52	1,100.00	31.48
4	02/12/1991	565.74	1,099.69	31.79	109,936.73	2,199.69	63.27
5	02/26/1991	565.74	0.00	0.00	109,936.73	2,199.69	63.27
6	03/12/1991	565.74	1,099.37	32.11	109,904.62	3,299.06	95.38
7	03/26/1991	565.74	0.00	0.00	109,904.62	3,299.06	95.38
8	04/09/1991	565.74	1,099.05	32.43	109,872.19	4,398.11	127.81
9	04/23/1991	565.74	0.00	0.00	109,872.19	4,398.11	127.81
10	05/07/1991	565.74	1,098.72	32.76	109,839.43	5,496.83	160.57
11	05/21/1991	565.74	0.00	0.00	109,839.43	5,496.83	160.57
12	06/04/1991	565.74	1,098.39	33.09	109,806.34	6,595.22	193.66
13	06/18/1991	565.74	0.00	0.00	109,806.34	6,595.22	193.66
14	07/02/1991	565.74	1,098.06	33.42	109,772.92	7,693.28	227.08
15	07/16/1991	565.74	0.00	0.00	109,772.92	7,693.28	227.08
16	07/30/1991	565.74	1,097.73	33.75	109,739.17	8,791.01	260.83
17	08/13/1991	565.74	0.00	0.00	109,739.17	8,791.01	260.83
18	08/27/1991	565.74	1,097.39	34.09	109,705.08	9,888.40	294.92
19	09/10/1991	565.74	0.00	0.00	109,705.08	9,888.40	294.92
20	09/24/1991	565.74	1,097.05	34.43	109,670.65	10,985.45	329.35
21	10/08/1991	565.74	0.00	0.00	109,670.65	10,985.45	329.35
22	10/22/1991	565.74	1,096.71	34.77	109,635.88	12,082.16	364.12
23	11/05/1991	565.74	0.00	0.00	109,635.88	12,082.16	364.12
24	11/19/1991	565.74	1,096.36	35.12	109,600.76	13,178.52	399.24
25	12/03/1991	565.74	0.00	0.00	109,600.76	13,178.52	399.24
26	12/17/1991	565.74	0.00	1,131.48	108,469.28	13,178.52	1,530.72
27	12/31/1991	565.74	0.00	0.00	108,469.28	13,178.52	1,530.72
28	01/14/1992	565.74	1,084.69	46.79	108,422.49	14,263.21	1,577.51
29	01/28/1992	565.74	0.00	0.00	108,422.49	14,263.21	1,577.51
30	02/11/1992	565.74	1,084.22	47.26	108,375.23	15,347.43	1,624.77
31	02/25/1992	565.74	0.00	0.00	108,375.23	15,347.43	1,624.77
32	03/10/1992	565.74	1,083.75	47.73	108,327.50	16,431.18	1,672.50
33	03/24/1992	565.74	0.00	0.00	108,327.50	16,431.18	1,672.50
34	04/07/1992	565.74	1,083.28	48.20	108,279.30	17,514.46	1,720.70

Table 11–8   Continued

Names: MR. ALAN SPALDING

PMT #	PAYMENT DATE	PAYMENT AMOUNT	INTEREST PAID	PRINCIPAL PAID	BALANCE OWED	ACCUMULATED INTEREST	ACCUMULATED PRINCIPAL
35	04/21/1992	565.74	0.00	0.00	108,279.30	17,514.46	1,720.70
36	05/05/1992	565.74	1,082.79	48.69	108,230.61	18,597.25	1,769.39
37	05/19/1992	565.74	0.00	0.00	108,230.61	18,597.25	1,769.39
38	06/02/1992	565.74	1,082.31	49.17	108,181.44	19,679.56	1,818.56
39	06/16/1992	565.74	0.00	0.00	108,181.44	19,679.56	1,818.56
40	06/30/1992	565.74	1,081.81	49.67	108,131.77	20,761.37	1,868.23
41	07/14/1992	565.74	0.00	0.00	108,131.77	20,761.37	1,868.23
42	07/28/1992	565.74	1,081.32	50.16	108,081.61	21,842.69	1,918.39
43	08/11/1992	565.74	0.00	0.00	108,081.61	21,842.69	1,918.39
44	08/25/1992	565.74	1,080.82	50.66	108,030.95	22,923.51	1,969.05
45	09/08/1992	565.74	0.00	0.00	108,030.95	22,923.51	1,969.05
46	09/22/1992	565.74	1,080.31	51.17	107,979.78	24,003.82	2,020.22
47	10/06/1992	565.74	0.00	0.00	107,979.78	24,003.82	2,020.22
48	10/20/1992	565.74	1,079.80	51.68	107,928.10	25,083.62	2,071.90
49	11/03/1992	565.74	0.00	0.00	107,928.10	25,083.62	2,071.90
50	11/17/1992	565.74	1,079.28	52.20	107,875.90	26,162.90	2,124.10
51	12/01/1992	565.74	0.00	0.00	107,875.90	26,162.90	2,124.10
52	12/15/1992	565.74	0.00	1,131.48	106,744.42	26,162.90	3,255.58
53	12/29/1992	565.74	0.00	0.00	106,744.42	26,162.90	3,255.58
54	01/12/1993	565.74	1,067.44	64.04	106,680.38	27,230.34	3,319.62
55	01/26/1993	565.74	0.00	0.00	106,680.38	27,230.34	3,319.62
56	02/09/1993	565.74	1,066.80	64.68	106,615.70	28,297.14	3,384.30
57	02/23/1993	565.74	0.00	0.00	106,615.70	28,297.14	3,384.30
58	03/09/1993	565.74	1,066.16	65.32	106,550.38	29,363.30	3,449.62
59	03/23/1993	565.74	0.00	0.00	106,550.38	29,363.30	3,449.62
60	04/06/1993	565.74	1,065.50	65.98	106,484.40	30,428.80	3,515.60
61	04/20/1993	565.74	0.00	0.00	106,484.40	30,428.80	3,515.60
62	05/04/1993	565.74	1,064.84	66.64	106,417.76	31,493.64	3,582.24
63	05/18/1993	565.74	0.00	0.00	106,417.76	31,493.64	3,582.24
64	06/01/1993	565.74	1,064.18	67.30	106,350.46	32,557.82	3,649.54
65	06/15/1993	565.74	0.00	0.00	106,350.46	32,557.82	3,649.54
66	06/29/1993	565.74	1,063.50	67.98	106,282.48	33,621.32	3,717.52
67	07/13/1993	565.74	0.00	0.00	106,282.48	33,621.32	3,717.52
68	07/27/1993	565.74	1,062.82	68.66	106,213.82	34,684.14	3,786.18
69	08/10/1993	565.74	0.00	0.00	106,213.82	34,684.14	3,786.18
70	08/24/1993	565.74	1,062.14	69.34	106,144.48	35,746.28	3,855.52
71	09/07/1993	565.74	0.00	0.00	106,144.48	35,746.28	3,855.52
72	09/21/1993	565.74	1,061.44	70.04	106,074.44	36,807.72	3,925.56
73	10/05/1993	565.74	0.00	0.00	106,074.44	36,807.72	3,925.56
74	10/19/1993	565.74	1,060.74	70.74	106,003.70	37,868.46	3,996.30
75	11/02/1993	565.74	0.00	0.00	106,003.70	37,868.46	3,996.30
76	11/16/1993	565.74	1,060.04	71.44	105,932.26	38,928.50	4,067.74
77	11/30/1993	565.74	0.00	0.00	105,932.26	38,928.50	4,067.74
78	12/14/1993	565.74	0.00	1,131.48	104,800.78	38,928.50	5,199.22
79	12/28/1993	565.74	0.00	0.00	104,800.78	38,928.50	5,199.22

Table 11–8 Continued

Names: MR. ALAN SPALDING

PMT #	PAYMENT DATE	PAYMENT AMOUNT	INTEREST PAID	PRINCIPAL PAID	BALANCE OWED	ACCUMULATED INTEREST	ACCUMULATED PRINCIPAL
80	01/11/1994	565.74	1,048.01	83.47	104,717.31	39,976.51	5,282.69
81	01/25/1994	565.74	0.00	0.00	104,717.31	39,976.51	5,282.69
82	02/08/1994	565.74	1,047.17	84.31	104,633.00	41,023.68	5,367.00
83	02/22/1994	565.74	0.00	0.00	104,633.00	41,023.68	5,367.00
84	03/08/1994	565.74	1,046.33	85.15	104,547.85	42,070.01	5,452.15
85	03/22/1994	565.74	0.00	0.00	104,547.85	42,070.01	5,452.15
86	04/05/1994	565.74	1,045.48	86.00	104,461.85	43,115.49	5,538.15
87	04/19/1994	565.74	0.00	0.00	104,461.85	43,115.49	5,538.15
88	05/03/1994	565.74	1,044.62	86.86	104,374.99	44,160.11	5,625.01
89	05/17/1994	565.74	0.00	0.00	104,374.99	44,160.11	5,625.01
90	05/31/1994	565.74	1,043.75	87.73	104,287.26	45,203.86	5,712.74
91	06/14/1994	565.74	0.00	0.00	104,287.26	45,203.86	5,712.74
92	06/28/1994	565.74	1,042.87	88.61	104,198.65	46,246.73	5,801.35
93	07/12/1994	565.74	0.00	0.00	104,198.65	46,246.73	5,801.35
94	07/26/1994	565.74	1,041.99	89.49	104,109.16	47,288.72	5,890.84
95	08/09/1994	565.74	0.00	0.00	104,109.16	47,288.72	5,890.84
96	08/23/1994	565.74	1,041.09	90.39	104,018.77	48,329.81	5,981.23
97	09/06/1994	565.74	0.00	0.00	104,018.77	48,329.81	5,981.23
98	09/20/1994	565.74	1,040.19	91.29	103,927.48	49,370.00	6,072.52
99	10/04/1994	565.74	0.00	0.00	103,927.48	49,370.00	6,072.52
100	10/18/1994	565.74	1,039.27	92.21	103,835.27	50,409.27	6,164.73
101	11/01/1994	565.74	0.00	0.00	103,835.27	50,409.27	6,164.73
102	11/15/1994	565.74	1,038.35	93.13	103,742.14	51,447.62	6,257.86
103	11/29/1994	565.74	0.00	0.00	103,742.14	51,447.62	6,257.86
104	12/13/1994	565.74	0.00	1,131.48	102,610.66	51,447.62	7,389.34
105	12/27/1994	565.74	0.00	0.00	102,610.66	51,447.62	7,389.34
106	01/10/1995	565.74	1,026.11	105.37	102,505.29	52,473.73	7,494.71
107	01/24/1995	565.74	0.00	0.00	102,505.29	52,473.73	7,494.71
108	02/07/1995	565.74	1,025.05	106.43	102,398.86	53,498.78	7,601.14
109	02/21/1995	565.74	0.00	0.00	102,398.86	53,498.78	7,601.14
110	03/07/1995	565.74	1,023.99	107.49	102,291.37	54,522.77	7,708.63
111	03/21/1995	565.74	0.00	0.00	102,291.37	54,522.77	7,708.63
112	04/04/1995	565.74	1,022.91	108.57	102,182.80	55,545.68	7,817.20
113	04/18/1995	565.74	0.00	0.00	102,182.80	55,545.68	7,817.20
114	05/02/1995	565.74	1,021.83	109.65	102,073.15	56,567.51	7,926.85
115	05/16/1995	565.74	0.00	0.00	102,073.15	56,567.51	7,926.85
116	05/30/1995	565.74	1,020.73	110.75	101,962.40	57,588.24	8,037.60
117	06/13/1995	565.74	0.00	0.00	101,962.40	57,588.24	8,037.60
118	06/27/1995	565.74	1,019.62	111.86	101,850.54	58,607.86	8,149.46
119	07/11/1995	565.74	0.00	0.00	101,850.54	58,607.86	8,149.46
120	07/25/1995	565.74	1,018.51	112.97	101,737.57	59,626.37	8,262.43
121	08/08/1995	565.74	0.00	0.00	101,737.57	59,626.37	8,262.43
122	08/22/1995	565.74	1,017.38	114.10	101,623.47	60,643.75	8,376.53
123	09/05/1995	565.74	0.00	0.00	101,623.47	60,643.75	8,376.53
124	09/19/1995	565.74	1,016.23	115.25	101,508.22	61,659.98	8,491.78

Table 11-8   Continued

Names: MR. ALAN SPALDING

PMT #	PAYMENT DATE	PAYMENT AMOUNT	INTEREST PAID	PRINCIPAL PAID	BALANCE OWED	ACCUMULATED INTEREST	ACCUMULATED PRINCIPAL
125	10/03/1995	565.74	0.00	0.00	101,508.22	61,659.98	8,491.78
126	10/17/1995	565.74	1,015.08	116.40	101,391.82	62,675.06	8,608.18
127	10/31/1995	565.74	0.00	0.00	101,391.82	62,675.06	8,608.18
128	11/14/1995	565.74	1,013.92	117.56	101,274.26	63,688.98	8,725.74
129	11/28/1995	565.74	0.00	0.00	101,274.26	63,688.98	8,725.74
130	12/12/1995	565.74	0.00	1,131.48	100,142.78	63,688.98	9,857.22
131	12/26/1995	565.74	0.00	0.00	100,142.78	63,688.98	9,857.22
132	01/09/1996	565.74	1,001.43	130.05	100,012.73	64,690.41	9,987.27
133	01/23/1996	565.74	0.00	0.00	100,012.73	64,690.41	9,987.27
134	02/06/1996	565.74	1,000.13	131.35	99,881.38	65,690.54	10,118.62
135	02/20/1996	565.74	0.00	0.00	99,881.38	65,690.54	10,118.62
136	03/05/1996	565.74	998.81	132.67	99,748.71	66,689.35	10,251.29
137	03/19/1996	565.74	0.00	0.00	99,748.71	66,689.35	10,251.29
138	04/02/1996	565.74	997.49	133.99	99,614.72	67,686.84	10,385.28
139	04/16/1996	565.74	0.00	0.00	99,614.72	67,686.84	10,385.28
140	04/30/1996	565.74	996.15	135.33	99,479.39	68,682.99	10,520.61
141	05/14/1996	565.74	0.00	0.00	99,479.39	68,682.99	10,520.61
142	05/28/1996	565.74	994.79	136.69	99,342.70	69,677.78	10,657.30
143	06/11/1996	565.74	0.00	0.00	99,342.70	69,677.78	10,657.30
144	06/25/1996	565.74	993.43	138.05	99,204.65	70,671.21	10,795.35
145	07/09/1996	565.74	0.00	0.00	99,204.65	70,671.21	10,795.35
146	07/23/1996	565.74	992.05	139.43	99,065.22	71,663.26	10,934.78
147	08/06/1996	565.74	0.00	0.00	99,065.22	71,663.26	10,934.78
148	08/20/1996	565.74	990.65	140.83	98,924.39	72,653.91	11,075.61
149	09/03/1996	565.74	0.00	0.00	98,924.39	72,653.91	11,075.61
150	09/17/1996	565.74	989.24	142.24	98,782.15	73,643.15	11,217.85
151	10/01/1996	565.74	0.00	0.00	98,782.15	73,643.15	11,217.85
152	10/15/1996	565.74	987.82	143.66	98,638.49	74,630.97	11,361.51
153	10/29/1996	565.74	0.00	0.00	98,638.49	74,630.97	11,361.51
154	11/12/1996	565.74	986.38	145.10	98,493.39	75,617.35	11,506.61
155	11/26/1996	565.74	0.00	0.00	98,493.39	75,617.35	11,506.61
156	12/10/1996	565.74	0.00	1,131.48	97,361.91	75,617.35	12,638.09
157	12/24/1996	565.74	0.00	0.00	97,361.91	75,617.35	12,638.09
158	01/07/1997	565.74	973.62	157.86	97,204.05	76,590.97	12,795.95
159	01/21/1997	565.74	0.00	0.00	97,204.05	76,590.97	12,795.95
160	02/04/1997	565.74	972.04	159.44	97,044.61	77,563.01	12,955.39
161	02/18/1997	565.74	0.00	0.00	97,044.61	77,563.01	12,955.39
162	03/04/1997	565.74	970.45	161.03	96,883.58	78,533.46	13,116.42
163	03/18/1997	565.74	0.00	0.00	96,883.58	78,533.46	13,116.42
164	04/01/1997	565.74	968.84	162.64	96,720.94	79,502.30	13,279.06
165	04/15/1997	565.74	0.00	0.00	96,720.94	79,502.30	13,279.06
166	04/29/1997	565.74	967.21	164.27	96,556.67	80,469.51	13,443.33
167	05/13/1997	565.74	0.00	0.00	96,556.67	80,469.51	13,443.33
168	05/27/1997	565.74	965.57	165.91	96,390.76	81,435.08	13,609.24
169	06/10/1997	565.74	0.00	0.00	96,390.76	81,435.08	13,609.24

Table 11-8   Continued

Names: MR. ALAN SPALDING

PMT #	PAYMENT DATE	PAYMENT AMOUNT	INTEREST PAID	PRINCIPAL PAID	BALANCE OWED	ACCUMULATED INTEREST	ACCUMULATED PRINCIPAL
170	06/24/1997	565.74	963.91	167.57	96,223.19	82,398.99	13,776.81
171	07/08/1997	565.74	0.00	0.00	96,223.19	82,398.99	13,776.81
172	07/22/1997	565.74	962.23	169.25	96,053.94	83,361.22	13,946.06
173	08/05/1997	565.74	0.00	0.00	96,053.94	83,361.22	13,946.06
174	08/19/1997	565.74	960.54	170.94	95,883.00	84,321.76	14,117.00
175	09/02/1997	565.74	0.00	0.00	95,883.00	84,321.76	14,117.00
176	09/16/1997	565.74	958.83	172.65	95,710.35	85,280.59	14,289.65
177	09/30/1997	565.74	0.00	0.00	95,710.35	85,280.59	14,289.65
178	10/14/1997	565.74	957.10	174.38	95,535.97	86,237.69	14,464.03
179	10/28/1997	565.74	0.00	0.00	95,535.97	86,237.69	14,464.03
180	11/11/1997	565.74	955.36	176.12	95,359.85	87,193.05	14,640.15
181	11/25/1997	565.74	0.00	0.00	95,359.85	87,193.05	14,640.15
182	12/09/1997	565.74	0.00	1,131.48	94,228.37	87,193.05	15,771.63
183	12/23/1997	565.74	0.00	0.00	94,228.37	87,193.05	15,771.63
184	01/06/1998	565.74	942.28	189.20	94,039.17	88,135.33	15,960.83
185	01/20/1998	565.74	0.00	0.00	94,039.17	88,135.33	15,960.83
186	02/03/1998	565.74	940.39	191.09	93,848.08	89,075.72	16,151.92
187	02/17/1998	565.74	0.00	0.00	93,848.08	89,075.72	16,151.92
188	03/03/1998	565.74	938.48	193.00	93,655.08	90,014.20	16,344.92
189	03/17/1998	565.74	0.00	0.00	93,655.08	90,014.20	16,344.92
190	03/31/1998	565.74	936.55	194.93	93,460.15	90,950.75	16,539.85
191	04/14/1998	565.74	0.00	0.00	93,460.15	90,950.75	16,539.85
192	04/28/1998	565.74	934.60	196.88	93,263.27	91,885.35	16,736.73
193	05/12/1998	565.74	0.00	0.00	93,263.27	91,885.35	16,736.73
194	05/26/1998	565.74	932.63	198.85	93,064.42	92,817.98	16,935.58
195	06/09/1998	565.74	0.00	0.00	93,064.42	92,817.98	16,935.58
196	06/23/1998	565.74	930.64	200.84	92,863.58	93,748.62	17,136.42
197	07/07/1998	565.74	0.00	0.00	92,863.58	93,748.62	17,136.42
198	07/21/1998	565.74	928.64	202.84	92,660.74	94,677.26	17,339.26
199	08/04/1998	565.74	0.00	0.00	92,660.74	94,677.26	17,339.26
200	08/18/1998	565.74	926.61	204.87	92,455.87	95,603.87	17,544.13
201	09/01/1998	565.74	0.00	0.00	92,455.87	95,603.87	17,544.13
202	09/15/1998	565.74	924.56	206.92	92,248.95	96,528.43	17,751.05
203	09/29/1998	565.74	0.00	0.00	92,248.95	96,528.43	17,751.05
204	10/13/1998	565.74	922.49	208.99	92,039.96	97,450.92	17,960.04
205	10/27/1998	565.74	0.00	0.00	92,039.96	97,450.92	17,960.04
206	11/10/1998	565.74	920.40	211.08	91,828.88	98,371.32	18,171.12
207	11/24/1998	565.74	0.00	0.00	91,828.88	98,371.32	18,171.12
208	12/08/1998	565.74	0.00	1,131.48	90,697.40	98,371.32	19,302.60
209	12/22/1998	565.74	0.00	0.00	90,697.40	98,371.32	19,302.60
210	01/05/1999	565.74	906.97	224.51	90,472.89	99,278.29	19,527.11
211	01/19/1999	565.74	0.00	0.00	90,472.89	99,278.29	19,527.11
212	02/02/1999	565.74	904.73	226.75	90,246.14	100,183.02	19,753.86
213	02/16/1999	565.74	0.00	0.00	90,246.14	100,183.02	19,753.86
214	03/02/1999	565.74	902.46	229.02	90,017.12	101,085.48	19,982.88

Table 11–8   Continued

Names: MR. ALAN SPALDING

PMT #	PAYMENT DATE	PAYMENT AMOUNT	INTEREST PAID	PRINCIPAL PAID	BALANCE OWED	ACCUMULATED INTEREST	ACCUMULATED PRINCIPAL
215	03/16/1999	565.74	0.00	0.00	90,017.12	101,085.48	19,982.88
216	03/30/1999	565.74	900.17	231.31	89,785.81	101,985.65	20,214.19
217	04/13/1999	565.74	0.00	0.00	89,785.81	101,985.65	20,214.19
218	04/27/1999	565.74	897.86	233.62	89,552.19	102,883.51	20,447.81
219	05/11/1999	565.74	0.00	0.00	89,552.19	102,883.51	20,447.81
220	05/25/1999	565.74	895.52	235.96	89,316.23	103,779.03	20,683.77
221	06/08/1999	565.74	0.00	0.00	89,316.23	103,779.03	20,683.77
222	06/22/1999	565.74	893.16	238.32	89,077.91	104,672.19	20,922.09
223	07/06/1999	565.74	0.00	0.00	89,077.91	104,672.19	20,922.09
224	07/20/1999	565.74	890.78	240.70	88,837.21	105,562.97	21,162.79
225	08/03/1999	565.74	0.00	0.00	88,837.21	105,562.97	21,162.79
226	08/17/1999	565.74	888.37	243.11	88,594.10	106,451.34	21,405.90
227	08/31/1999	565.74	0.00	0.00	88,594.10	106,451.34	21,405.90
228	09/14/1999	565.74	885.94	245.54	88,348.56	107,337.28	21,651.44
229	09/28/1999	565.74	0.00	0.00	88,348.56	107,337.28	21,651.44
230	10/12/1999	565.74	883.49	247.99	88,100.57	108,220.77	21,899.43
231	10/26/1999	565.74	0.00	0.00	88,100.57	108,220.77	21,899.43
232	11/09/1999	565.74	881.01	250.47	87,850.10	109,101.78	22,149.90
233	11/23/1999	565.74	0.00	0.00	87,850.10	109,101.78	22,149.90
234	12/07/1999	565.74	0.00	1,131.48	86,718.62	109,101.78	23,281.38
235	12/21/1999	565.74	0.00	0.00	86,718.62	109,101.78	23,281.38
236	01/04/2000	565.74	867.19	264.29	86,454.33	109,968.97	23,545.67
237	01/18/2000	565.74	0.00	0.00	86,454.33	109,968.97	23,545.67
238	02/01/2000	565.74	864.54	266.94	86,187.39	110,833.51	23,812.61
239	02/15/2000	565.74	0.00	0.00	86,187.39	110,833.51	23,812.61
240	02/29/2000	565.74	861.87	269.61	85,917.78	111,695.38	24,082.22
241	03/14/2000	565.74	0.00	0.00	85,917.78	111,695.38	24,082.22
242	03/28/2000	565.74	859.18	272.30	85,645.48	112,554.56	24,354.52
243	04/11/2000	565.74	0.00	0.00	85,645.48	112,554.56	24,354.52
244	04/25/2000	565.74	856.45	275.03	85,370.45	113,411.01	24,629.55
245	05/09/2000	565.74	0.00	0.00	85,370.45	113,411.01	24,629.55
246	05/23/2000	565.74	853.70	277.78	85,092.67	114,264.71	24,907.33
247	06/06/2000	565.74	0.00	0.00	85,092.67	114,264.71	24,907.33
248	06/20/2000	565.74	850.93	280.55	84,812.12	115,115.64	25,187.88
249	07/04/2000	565.74	0.00	0.00	84,812.12	115,115.64	25,187.88
250	07/18/2000	565.74	848.12	283.36	84,528.76	115,963.76	25,471.24
251	08/01/2000	565.74	0.00	0.00	84,528.76	115,963.76	25,471.24
252	08/15/2000	565.74	845.29	286.19	84,242.57	116,809.05	25,757.43
253	08/29/2000	565.74	0.00	0.00	84,242.57	116,809.05	25,757.43
254	09/12/2000	565.74	842.43	289.05	83,953.52	117,651.48	26,046.48
255	09/26/2000	565.74	0.00	0.00	83,953.52	117,651.48	26,046.48
256	10/10/2000	565.74	839.54	291.94	83,661.58	118,491.02	26,338.42
257	10/24/2000	565.74	0.00	0.00	83,661.58	118,491.02	26,338.42
258	11/07/2000	565.74	836.62	294.86	83,366.72	119,327.64	26,633.28
259	11/21/2000	565.74	0.00	0.00	83,366.72	119,327.64	26,633.28

Table 11–8   Continued

Names: MR. ALAN SPALDING

PMT #	PAYMENT DATE	PAYMENT AMOUNT	INTEREST PAID	PRINCIPAL PAID	BALANCE OWED	ACCUMULATED INTEREST	ACCUMULATED PRINCIPAL
260	12/05/2000	565.74	0.00	1,131.48	82,235.24	119,327.64	27,764.76
261	12/19/2000	565.74	0.00	0.00	82,235.24	119,327.64	27,764.76
262	01/02/2001	565.74	822.35	309.13	81,926.11	120,149.99	28,073.89
263	01/16/2001	565.74	0.00	0.00	81,926.11	120,149.99	28,073.89
264	01/30/2001	565.74	819.26	312.22	81,613.89	120,969.25	28,386.11
265	02/13/2001	565.74	0.00	0.00	81,613.89	120,969.25	28,386.11
266	02/27/2001	565.74	816.14	315.34	81,298.55	121,785.39	28,701.45
267	03/13/2001	565.74	0.00	0.00	81,298.55	121,785.39	28,701.45
268	03/27/2001	565.74	812.99	318.49	80,980.06	122,598.38	29,019.94
269	04/10/2001	565.74	0.00	0.00	80,980.06	122,598.38	29,019.94
270	04/24/2001	565.74	809.80	321.68	80,658.38	123,408.18	29,341.62
271	05/08/2001	565.74	0.00	0.00	80,658.38	123,408.18	29,341.62
272	05/22/2001	565.74	806.58	324.90	80,333.48	124,214.76	29,666.52
273	06/05/2001	565.74	0.00	0.00	80,333.48	124,214.76	29,666.52
274	06/19/2001	565.74	803.33	328.15	80,005.33	125,018.09	29,994.67
275	07/03/2001	565.74	0.00	0.00	80,005.33	125,018.09	29,994.67
276	07/17/2001	565.74	800.05	331.43	79,673.90	125,818.14	30,326.10
277	07/31/2001	565.74	0.00	0.00	79,673.90	125,818.14	30,326.10
278	08/14/2001	565.74	796.74	334.74	79,339.16	126,614.88	30,660.84
279	08/28/2001	565.74	0.00	0.00	79,339.16	126,614.88	30,660.84
280	09/11/2001	565.74	793.39	338.09	79,001.07	127,408.27	30,998.93
281	09/25/2001	565.74	0.00	0.00	79,001.07	127,408.27	30,998.93
282	10/09/2001	565.74	790.01	341.47	78,659.60	128,198.28	31,340.40
283	10/23/2001	565.74	0.00	0.00	78,659.60	128,198.28	31,340.40
284	11/06/2001	565.74	786.60	344.88	78,314.72	128,984.88	31,685.28
285	11/20/2001	565.74	0.00	0.00	78,314.72	128,984.88	31,685.28
286	12/04/2001	565.74	0.00	1,131.48	77,183.24	128,984.88	32,816.76
287	12/18/2001	565.74	0.00	0.00	77,183.24	128,984.88	32,816.76
288	01/01/2002	565.74	771.83	359.65	76,823.59	129,756.71	33,176.41
289	01/15/2002	565.74	0.00	0.00	76,823.59	129,756.71	33,176.41
290	01/29/2002	565.74	768.24	363.24	76,460.35	130,524.95	33,539.65
291	02/12/2002	565.74	0.00	0.00	76,460.35	130,524.95	33,539.65
292	02/26/2002	565.74	764.60	366.88	76,093.47	131,289.55	33,906.53
293	03/12/2002	565.74	0.00	0.00	76,093.47	131,289.55	33,906.53
294	03/26/2002	565.74	760.93	370.55	75,722.92	132,050.48	34,277.08
295	04/09/2002	565.74	0.00	0.00	75,722.92	132,050.48	34,277.08
296	04/23/2002	565.74	757.23	374.25	75,348.67	132,807.71	34,651.33
297	05/07/2002	565.74	0.00	0.00	75,348.67	132,807.71	34,651.33
298	05/21/2002	565.74	753.49	377.99	74,970.68	133,561.20	35,029.32
299	06/04/2002	565.74	0.00	0.00	74,970.68	133,561.20	35,029.32
300	06/18/2002	565.74	749.71	381.77	74,588.91	134,310.91	35,411.09
301	07/02/2002	565.74	0.00	0.00	74,588.91	134,310.91	35,411.09
302	07/16/2002	565.74	745.89	385.59	74,203.32	135,056.80	35,796.68
303	07/30/2002	565.74	0.00	0.00	74,203.32	135,056.80	35,796.68
304	08/13/2002	565.74	742.03	389.45	73,813.87	135,798.83	36,186.13

Table 11–8   Continued

Names: MR. ALAN SPALDING

PMT #	PAYMENT DATE	PAYMENT AMOUNT	INTEREST PAID	PRINCIPAL PAID	BALANCE OWED	ACCUMULATED INTEREST	ACCUMULATED PRINCIPAL
305	08/27/2002	565.74	0.00	0.00	73,813.87	135,798.83	36,186.13
306	09/10/2002	565.74	738.14	393.34	73,420.53	136,536.97	36,579.47
307	09/24/2002	565.74	0.00	0.00	73,420.53	136,536.97	36,579.47
308	10/08/2002	565.74	734.21	397.27	73,023.26	137,271.18	36,976.74
309	10/22/2002	565.74	0.00	0.00	73,023.26	137,271.18	36,976.74
310	11/05/2002	565.74	730.23	401.25	72,622.01	138,001.41	37,377.99
311	11/19/2002	565.74	0.00	0.00	72,622.01	138,001.41	37,377.99
312	12/03/2002	565.74	0.00	1,131.48	71,490.53	138,001.41	38,509.47
313	12/17/2002	565.74	0.00	0.00	71,490.53	138,001.41	38,509.47
314	12/31/2002	565.74	714.91	416.57	71,073.96	138,716.32	38,926.04
315	01/14/2003	565.74	0.00	0.00	71,073.96	138,716.32	38,926.04
316	01/28/2003	565.74	710.74	420.74	70,653.22	139,427.06	39,346.78
317	02/11/2003	565.74	0.00	0.00	70,653.22	139,427.06	39,346.78
318	02/25/2003	565.74	706.53	424.95	70,228.27	140,133.59	39,771.73
319	03/11/2003	565.74	0.00	0.00	70,228.27	140,133.59	39,771.73
320	03/25/2003	565.74	702.28	429.20	69,799.07	140,835.87	40,200.93
321	04/08/2003	565.74	0.00	0.00	69,799.07	140,835.87	40,200.93
322	04/22/2003	565.74	697.99	433.49	69,365.58	141,533.86	40,634.42
323	05/06/2003	565.74	0.00	0.00	69,365.58	141,533.86	40,634.42
324	05/20/2003	565.74	693.66	437.82	68,927.76	142,227.52	41,072.24
325	06/03/2003	565.74	0.00	0.00	68,927.76	142,227.52	41,072.24
326	06/17/2003	565.74	689.28	442.20	68,485.56	142,916.80	41,514.44
327	07/01/2003	565.74	0.00	0.00	68,485.56	142,916.80	41,514.44
328	07/15/2003	565.74	684.86	446.62	68,038.94	143,601.66	41,961.06
329	07/29/2003	565.74	0.00	0.00	68,038.94	143,601.66	41,961.06
330	08/12/2003	565.74	680.39	451.09	67,587.85	144,282.05	42,412.15
331	08/26/2003	565.74	0.00	0.00	67,587.85	144,282.05	42,412.15
332	09/09/2003	565.74	675.88	455.60	67,132.25	144,957.93	42,867.75
333	09/23/2003	565.74	0.00	0.00	67,132.25	144,957.93	42,867.75
334	10/07/2003	565.74	671.32	460.16	66,672.09	145,629.25	43,327.91
335	10/21/2003	565.74	0.00	0.00	66,672.09	145,629.25	43,327.91
336	11/04/2003	565.74	666.72	464.76	66,207.33	146,295.97	43,792.67
337	11/18/2003	565.74	0.00	0.00	66,207.33	146,295.97	43,792.67
338	12/02/2003	565.74	0.00	1,131.48	65,075.85	146,295.97	44,924.15
339	12/16/2003	565.74	0.00	0.00	65,075.85	146,295.97	44,924.15
340	12/30/2003	565.74	650.76	480.72	64,595.13	146,946.73	45,404.87
341	01/13/2004	565.74	0.00	0.00	64,595.13	146,946.73	45,404.87
342	01/27/2004	565.74	645.95	485.53	64,109.60	147,592.68	45,890.40
343	02/10/2004	565.74	0.00	0.00	64,109.60	147,592.68	45,890.40
344	02/24/2004	565.74	641.10	490.38	63,619.22	148,233.78	46,380.78
345	03/09/2004	565.74	0.00	0.00	63,619.22	148,233.78	46,380.78
346	03/23/2004	565.74	636.19	495.29	63,123.93	148,869.97	46,876.07
347	04/06/2004	565.74	0.00	0.00	63,123.93	148,869.97	46,876.07
348	04/20/2004	565.74	631.24	500.24	62,623.69	149,501.21	47,376.31
349	05/04/2004	565.74	0.00	0.00	62,623.69	149,501.21	47,376.31

Table 11–8   Continued

Names: MR. ALAN SPALDING

PMT #	PAYMENT DATE	PAYMENT AMOUNT	INTEREST PAID	PRINCIPAL PAID	BALANCE OWED	ACCUMULATED INTEREST	ACCUMULATED PRINCIPAL
350	05/18/2004	565.74	626.24	505.24	62,118.45	150,127.45	47,881.55
351	06/01/2004	565.74	0.00	0.00	62,118.45	150,127.45	47,881.55
352	06/15/2004	565.74	621.18	510.30	61,608.15	150,748.63	48,391.85
353	06/29/2004	565.74	0.00	0.00	61,608.15	150,748.63	48,391.85
354	07/13/2004	565.74	616.08	515.40	61,092.75	151,364.71	48,907.25
355	07/27/2004	565.74	0.00	0.00	61,092.75	151,364.71	48,907.25
356	08/10/2004	565.74	610.93	520.55	60,572.20	151,975.64	49,427.80
357	08/24/2004	565.74	0.00	0.00	60,572.20	151,975.64	49,427.80
358	09/07/2004	565.74	605.72	525.76	60,046.44	152,581.36	49,953.56
359	09/21/2004	565.74	0.00	0.00	60,046.44	152,581.36	49,953.56
360	10/05/2004	565.74	600.46	531.02	59,515.42	153,181.82	50,484.58
361	10/19/2004	565.74	0.00	0.00	59,515.42	153,181.82	50,484.58
362	11/02/2004	565.74	595.15	536.33	58,979.09	153,776.97	51,020.91
363	11/16/2004	565.74	0.00	0.00	58,979.09	153,776.97	51,020.91
364	11/30/2004	565.74	0.00	1,131.48	57,847.61	153,776.97	52,152.39
365	12/14/2004	565.74	0.00	0.00	57,847.61	153,776.97	52,152.39
366	12/28/2004	565.74	578.48	553.00	57,294.61	154,355.45	52,705.39
367	01/11/2005	565.74	0.00	0.00	57,294.61	154,355.45	52,705.39
368	01/25/2005	565.74	572.95	558.53	56,736.08	154,928.40	53,263.92
369	02/08/2005	565.74	0.00	0.00	56,736.08	154,928.40	53,263.92
370	02/22/2005	565.74	567.36	564.12	56,171.96	155,495.76	53,828.04
371	03/08/2005	565.74	0.00	0.00	56,171.96	155,495.76	53,828.04
372	03/22/2005	565.74	561.72	569.76	55,602.20	156,057.48	54,397.80
373	04/05/2005	565.74	0.00	0.00	55,602.20	156,057.48	54,397.80
374	04/19/2005	565.74	556.02	575.46	55,026.74	156,613.50	54,973.26
375	05/03/2005	565.74	0.00	0.00	55,026.74	156,613.50	54,973.26
376	05/17/2005	565.74	550.27	581.21	54,445.53	157,163.77	55,554.47
377	05/31/2005	565.74	0.00	0.00	54,445.53	157,163.77	55,554.47
378	06/14/2005	565.74	544.46	587.02	53,858.51	157,708.23	56,141.49
379	06/28/2005	565.74	0.00	0.00	53,858.51	157,708.23	56,141.49
380	07/12/2005	565.74	538.59	592.89	53,265.62	158,246.82	56,734.38
381	07/26/2005	565.74	0.00	0.00	53,265.62	158,246.82	56,734.38
382	08/09/2005	565.74	532.66	598.82	52,666.80	158,779.48	57,333.20
383	08/23/2005	565.74	0.00	0.00	52,666.80	158,779.48	57,333.20
384	09/06/2005	565.74	526.67	604.81	52,061.99	159,306.15	57,938.01
385	09/20/2005	565.74	0.00	0.00	52,061.99	159,306.15	57,938.01
386	10/04/2005	565.74	520.62	610.86	51,451.13	159,826.77	58,548.87
387	10/18/2005	565.74	0.00	0.00	51,451.13	159,826.77	58,548.87
388	11/01/2005	565.74	514.51	616.97	50,834.16	160,341.28	59,165.84
389	11/15/2005	565.74	0.00	0.00	50,834.16	160,341.28	59,165.84
390	11/29/2005	565.74	0.00	1,131.48	49,702.68	160,341.28	60,297.32
391	12/13/2005	565.74	0.00	0.00	49,702.68	160,341.28	60,297.32
392	12/27/2005	565.74	497.03	634.45	49,068.23	160,838.31	60,931.77
393	01/10/2006	565.74	0.00	0.00	49,068.23	160,838.31	60,931.77
394	01/24/2006	565.74	490.68	640.80	48,427.43	161,328.99	61,572.57

Table 11-8   Continued

Names: MR. ALAN SPALDING

PMT #	PAYMENT DATE	PAYMENT AMOUNT	INTEREST PAID	PRINCIPAL PAID	BALANCE OWED	ACCUMULATED INTEREST	ACCUMULATED PRINCIPAL
395	02/07/2006	565.74	0.00	0.00	48,427.43	161,328.99	61,572.57
396	02/21/2006	565.74	484.27	647.21	47,780.22	161,813.26	62,219.78
397	03/07/2006	565.74	0.00	0.00	47,780.22	161,813.26	62,219.78
398	03/21/2006	565.74	477.80	653.68	47,126.54	162,291.06	62,873.46
399	04/04/2006	565.74	0.00	0.00	47,126.54	162,291.06	62,873.46
400	04/18/2006	565.74	471.27	660.21	46,466.33	162,762.33	63,533.67
401	05/02/2006	565.74	0.00	0.00	46,466.33	162,762.33	63,533.67
402	05/16/2006	565.74	464.66	666.82	45,799.51	163,226.99	64,200.49
403	05/30/2006	565.74	0.00	0.00	45,799.51	163,226.99	64,200.49
404	06/13/2006	565.74	458.00	673.48	45,126.03	163,684.99	64,873.97
405	06/27/2006	565.74	0.00	0.00	45,126.03	163,684.99	64,873.97
406	07/11/2006	565.74	451.26	680.22	44,445.81	164,136.25	65,554.19
407	07/25/2006	565.74	0.00	0.00	44,445.81	164,136.25	65,554.19
408	08/08/2006	565.74	444.46	687.02	43,758.79	164,580.71	66,241.21
409	08/22/2006	565.74	0.00	0.00	43,758.79	164,580.71	66,241.21
410	09/05/2006	565.74	437.59	693.89	43,064.90	165,018.30	66,935.10
411	09/19/2006	565.74	0.00	0.00	43,064.90	165,018.30	66,935.10
412	10/03/2006	565.74	430.65	700.83	42,364.07	165,448.95	67,635.93
413	10/17/2006	565.74	0.00	0.00	42,364.07	165,448.95	67,635.93
414	10/31/2006	565.74	423.64	707.84	41,656.23	165,872.59	68,343.77
415	11/14/2006	565.74	0.00	0.00	41,656.23	165,872.59	68,343.77
416	11/28/2006	565.74	0.00	1,131.48	40,524.75	165,872.59	69,475.25
417	12/12/2006	565.74	0.00	0.00	40,524.75	165,872.59	69,475.25
418	12/26/2006	565.74	405.25	726.23	39,798.52	166,277.84	70,201.48
419	01/09/2007	565.74	0.00	0.00	39,798.52	166,277.84	70,201.48
420	01/23/2007	565.74	397.99	733.49	39,065.03	166,675.83	70,934.97
421	02/06/2007	565.74	0.00	0.00	39,065.03	166,675.83	70,934.97
422	02/20/2007	565.74	390.65	740.83	38,324.20	167,066.48	71,675.80
423	03/06/2007	565.74	0.00	0.00	38,324.20	167,066.48	71,675.80
424	03/20/2007	565.74	383.24	748.24	37,575.96	167,449.72	72,424.04
425	04/03/2007	565.74	0.00	0.00	37,575.96	167,449.72	72,424.04
426	04/17/2007	565.74	375.76	755.72	36,820.24	167,825.48	73,179.76
427	05/01/2007	565.74	0.00	0.00	36,820.24	167,825.48	73,179.76
428	05/15/2007	565.74	368.20	763.28	36,056.96	168,193.68	73,943.04
429	05/29/2007	565.74	0.00	0.00	36,056.96	168,193.68	73,943.04
430	06/12/2007	565.74	360.57	770.91	35,286.05	168,554.25	74,713.95
431	06/26/2007	565.74	0.00	0.00	35,286.05	168,554.25	74,713.95
432	07/10/2007	565.74	352.86	778.62	34,507.43	168,907.11	75,492.57
433	07/24/2007	565.74	0.00	0.00	34,507.43	168,907.11	75,492.57
434	08/07/2007	565.74	345.07	786.41	33,721.02	169,252.18	76,278.98
435	08/21/2007	565.74	0.00	0.00	33,721.02	169,252.18	76,278.98
436	09/04/2007	565.74	337.21	794.27	32,926.75	169,589.39	77,073.25
437	09/18/2007	565.74	0.00	0.00	32,926.75	169,589.39	77,073.25
438	10/02/2007	565.74	329.27	802.21	32,124.54	169,918.66	77,875.46
439	10/16/2007	565.74	0.00	0.00	32,124.54	169,918.66	77,875.46

Table 11–8   Continued

Names: MR. ALAN SPALDING

PMT #	PAYMENT DATE	PAYMENT AMOUNT	INTEREST PAID	PRINCIPAL PAID	BALANCE OWED	ACCUMULATED INTEREST	ACCUMULATED PRINCIPAL
440	10/30/2007	565.74	321.25	810.23	31,314.31	170,239.91	78,685.69
441	11/13/2007	565.74	0.00	0.00	31,314.31	170,239.91	78,685.69
442	11/27/2007	565.74	0.00	1,131.48	30,182.83	170,239.91	79,817.17
443	12/11/2007	565.74	0.00	0.00	30,182.83	170,239.91	79,817.17
444	12/25/2007	565.74	301.83	829.65	29,353.18	170,541.74	80,646.82
445	01/08/2008	565.74	0.00	0.00	29,353.18	170,541.74	80,646.82
446	01/22/2008	565.74	293.53	837.95	28,515.23	170,835.27	81,484.77
447	02/05/2008	565.74	0.00	0.00	28,515.23	170,835.27	81,484.77
448	02/19/2008	565.74	285.15	846.33	27,668.90	171,120.42	82,331.10
449	03/04/2008	565.74	0.00	0.00	27,668.90	171,120.42	82,331.10
450	03/18/2008	565.74	276.69	854.79	26,814.11	171,397.11	83,185.89
451	04/01/2008	565.74	0.00	0.00	26,814.11	171,397.11	83,185.89
452	04/15/2008	565.74	268.14	863.34	25,950.77	171,665.25	84,049.23
453	04/29/2008	565.74	0.00	0.00	25,950.77	171,665.25	84,049.23
454	05/13/2008	565.74	259.51	871.97	25,078.80	171,924.76	84,921.20
455	05/27/2008	565.74	0.00	0.00	25,078.80	171,924.76	84,921.20
456	06/10/2008	565.74	250.79	880.69	24,198.11	172,175.55	85,801.89
457	06/24/2008	565.74	0.00	0.00	24,198.11	172,175.55	85,801.89
458	07/08/2008	565.74	241.98	889.50	23,308.61	172,417.53	86,691.39
459	07/22/2008	565.74	0.00	0.00	23,308.61	172,417.53	86,691.39
460	08/05/2008	565.74	233.09	898.39	22,410.22	172,650.62	87,589.78
461	08/19/2008	565.74	0.00	0.00	22,410.22	172,650.62	87,589.78
462	09/02/2008	565.74	224.10	907.38	21,502.84	172,874.72	88,497.16
463	09/16/2008	565.74	0.00	0.00	21,502.84	172,874.72	88,497.16
464	09/30/2008	565.74	215.03	916.45	20,586.39	173,089.75	89,413.61
465	10/14/2008	565.74	0.00	0.00	20,586.39	173,089.75	89,413.61
466	10/28/2008	565.74	205.86	925.62	19,660.77	173,295.61	90,339.23
467	11/11/2008	565.74	0.00	0.00	19,660.77	173,295.61	90,339.23
468	11/25/2008	565.74	0.00	1,131.48	18,529.29	173,295.61	91,470.71
469	12/09/2008	565.74	0.00	0.00	18,529.29	173,295.61	91,470.71
470	12/23/2008	565.74	185.29	946.19	17,583.10	173,480.90	92,416.90
471	01/06/2009	565.74	0.00	0.00	17,583.10	173,480.90	92,416.90
472	01/20/2009	565.74	175.83	955.65	16,627.45	173,656.73	93,372.55
473	02/03/2009	565.74	0.00	0.00	16,627.45	173,656.73	93,372.55
474	02/17/2009	565.74	166.27	965.21	15,662.24	173,823.00	94,337.76
475	03/03/2009	565.74	0.00	0.00	15,662.24	173,823.00	94,337.76
476	03/17/2009	565.74	156.62	974.86	14,687.38	173,979.62	95,312.62
477	03/31/2009	565.74	0.00	0.00	14,687.38	173,979.62	95,312.62
478	04/14/2009	565.74	146.87	984.61	13,702.77	174,126.49	96,297.23
479	04/28/2009	565.74	0.00	0.00	13,702.77	174,126.49	96,297.23
480	05/12/2009	565.74	137.03	994.45	12,708.32	174,263.52	97,291.68
481	05/26/2009	565.74	0.00	0.00	12,708.32	174,263.52	97,291.68
482	06/09/2009	565.74	127.08	1,004.40	11,703.92	174,390.60	98,296.08
483	06/23/2009	565.74	0.00	0.00	11,703.92	174,390.60	98,296.08
484	07/07/2009	565.74	117.04	1,014.44	10,689.48	174,507.64	99,310.52

Table 11–8   Continued

Names: MR. ALAN SPALDING

PMT #	PAYMENT DATE	PAYMENT AMOUNT	INTEREST PAID	PRINCIPAL PAID	BALANCE OWED	ACCUMULATED INTEREST	ACCUMULATED PRINCIPAL
485	07/21/2009	565.74	0.00	0.00	10,689.48	174,507.64	99,310.52
486	08/04/2009	565.74	106.89	1,024.59	9,664.89	174,614.53	100,335.11
487	08/18/2009	565.74	0.00	0.00	9,664.89	174,614.53	100,335.11
488	09/01/2009	565.74	96.65	1,034.83	8,630.06	174,711.18	101,369.94
489	09/15/2009	565.74	0.00	0.00	8,630.06	174,711.18	101,369.94
490	09/29/2009	565.74	86.30	1,045.18	7,584.88	174,797.48	102,415.12
491	10/13/2009	565.74	0.00	0.00	7,584.88	174,797.48	102,415.12
492	10/27/2009	565.74	75.85	1,055.63	6,529.25	174,873.33	103,470.75
493	11/10/2009	565.74	0.00	0.00	6,529.25	174,873.33	103,470.75
494	11/24/2009	565.74	0.00	1,131.48	5,397.77	174,873.33	104,602.23
495	12/08/2009	565.74	0.00	0.00	5,397.77	174,873.33	104,602.23
496	12/22/2009	565.74	53.98	1,077.50	4,320.27	174,927.31	105,679.73
497	01/05/2010	565.74	0.00	0.00	4,320.27	174,927.31	105,679.73
498	01/19/2010	565.74	43.20	1,088.28	3,231.99	174,970.51	106,768.01
499	02/02/2010	565.74	0.00	0.00	3,231.99	174,970.51	106,768.01
500	02/16/2010	565.74	32.32	1,099.16	2,132.83	175,002.83	107,867.17
501	03/02/2010	565.74	0.00	0.00	2,132.83	175,002.83	107,867.17
502	03/16/2010	565.74	21.33	1,110.15	1,022.68	175,024.16	108,977.32
503	03/30/2010	565.74	0.00	0.00	1,022.68	175,024.16	108,977.32
504	04/13/2010	467.17	10.23	1,022.68	0.00	175,034.39	110,000.00

Table 11–9   Comparison of Costs and Savings for Mr. & Mrs. Robert Hughes—Homeowners Conventional vs. Biweekly Programs Summary

ORIGINAL LOAN AMOUNT:	150,000.00		ANNUAL INTEREST RATE:	11.000 %
ORIGINAL LOAN TERM:	15 (YEARS)		CURRENT MONTHLY PAYMENT:	1,704.90
NUMBER OF PREVIOUS PAYMENTS:	0		'NEW' BIWEEKLY PAYMENT:	852.45
CURRENT LOAN BALANCE:	150,000.00			

	CURRENT MONTHLY			'NEW' BIWEEKLY			DIFFERENCE	
END OF YEAR	REMAINING BALANCE	INTEREST PAID TO-DATE	(EQUITY) PRINCIPAL PAID TO-DATE	REMAINING BALANCE	INTEREST PAID TO-DATE	(EQUITY) PRINCIPAL PAID TO-DATE	EQUTIY GROWTH TO-DATE	INTEREST SAVED TO-DATE
1	145,835.38	16,294.18	4,164.62	144,130.48	16,294.18	5,869.52	1,704.90	0.00
2	141,188.84	32,106.44	8,811.16	137,581.75	31,909.15	12,418.25	3,607.09	197.29
3	136,004.59	47,380.99	13,995.41	130,275.20	46,766.30	19,724.80	5,729.39	614.69
4	130,220.44	62,055.64	19,779.56	122,123.16	60,777.96	27,876.84	8,097.28	1,277.68
5	123,766.95	76,060.95	26,233.05	113,027.77	73,846.27	36,972.23	10,739.18	2,214.68
6	116,566.68	89,319.48	33,433.32	102,879.88	85,862.08	47,120.12	13,686.80	3,457.40
7	108,533.21	101,744.81	41,466.79	91,557.68	96,703.58	58,442.32	16,975.53	5,041.23
8	99,570.10	113,240.50	50,429.90	78,925.30	106,234.90	71,074.70	20,644.80	7,005.60
9	89,569.80	123,699.00	60,430.20	64,831.11	114,304.41	85,168.89	24,738.69	9,394.59
10	78,412.28	133,000.28	71,587.72	49,105.94	120,742.94	100,894.06	29,306.34	12,257.34
11	65,963.62	141,010.42	84,036.38	31,561.07	125,361.77	118,438.93	34,402.55	15,648.65
12	52,074.43	147,580.03	97,925.57	11,985.95	127,950.35	138,014.05	40,088.48	19,629.68
13	36,578.00	152,542.40	113,422.00	DEBT FREE	128,412.33	150,000.00		24,130.07
14	19,288.30	155,711.50	130,711.70					27,299.17
15	1,687.31	156,879.88	150,000.00					28,467.55

TOTAL INTEREST SAVED: 28,467.55
TOTAL TERM SAVED: 29.28 (PAYMENTS)   2.44 (YEARS)

Table 11–10 Amortization Schedule Re: Table 11–9

Names:	MR. & MRS. ROBERT HUGHES
Property:	61487 ELLSWORTH DR., MOUNTAIN LAKE, CO 18467
Telephone:	(782)555-8888
Tax I.D.:	123-45-6789

```
========================================================================================
| ORIGINAL LOAN AMOUNT:       150,000.00   BIWEEKLY PAYMENT:                   852.45 |
| ORIGINAL INTEREST RATE:         11.000   TOTAL BIWEEKLY INTEREST PAID:    128,412.33 |
| ORIGINAL TERM OF LOAN:       15 (YRS)    LAST BIWEEKLY PAYMENT DATE:       07/01/2003 |
| NUMBER OF PREVIOUS PAYMENTS:         0   NEW TERM OF LOAN:                 12.56 (YRS) |
| CURRENT LOAN BALANCE:       150,000.00                                               |
========================================================================================
```

PMT #	PAYMENT DATE	PAYMENT AMOUNT	INTEREST PAID	PRINCIPAL PAID	BALANCE OWED	ACCUMULATED INTEREST	ACCUMULATED PRINCIPAL
1	01/01/1991	852.45	0.00	0.00	150,000.00	0.00	0.00
2	01/15/1991	852.45	1,375.00	329.90	149,670.10	1,375.00	329.90
3	01/29/1991	852.45	0.00	0.00	149,670.10	1,375.00	329.90
4	02/12/1991	852.45	1,371.98	332.92	149,337.18	2,746.98	662.82
5	02/26/1991	852.45	0.00	0.00	149,337.18	2,746.98	662.82
6	03/12/1991	852.45	1,368.92	335.98	149,001.20	4,115.90	998.80
7	03/26/1991	852.45	0.00	0.00	149,001.20	4,115.90	998.80
8	04/09/1991	852.45	1,365.84	339.06	148,662.14	5,481.74	1,337.86
9	04/23/1991	852.45	0.00	0.00	148,662.14	5,481.74	1,337.86
10	05/07/1991	852.45	1,362.74	342.16	148,319.98	6,844.48	1,680.02
11	05/21/1991	852.45	0.00	0.00	148,319.98	6,844.48	1,680.02
12	06/04/1991	852.45	1,359.60	345.30	147,974.68	8,204.08	2,025.32
13	06/18/1991	852.45	0.00	0.00	147,974.68	8,204.08	2,025.32
14	07/02/1991	852.45	1,356.43	348.47	147,626.21	9,560.51	2,373.79
15	07/16/1991	852.45	0.00	0.00	147,626.21	9,560.51	2,373.79
16	07/30/1991	852.45	1,353.24	351.66	147,274.55	10,913.75	2,725.45
17	08/13/1991	852.45	0.00	0.00	147,274.55	10,913.75	2,725.45
18	08/27/1991	852.45	1,350.02	354.88	146,919.67	12,263.77	3,080.33
19	09/10/1991	852.45	0.00	0.00	146,919.67	12,263.77	3,080.33
20	09/24/1991	852.45	1,346.76	358.14	146,561.53	13,610.53	3,438.47
21	10/08/1991	852.45	0.00	0.00	146,561.53	13,610.53	3,438.47
22	10/22/1991	852.45	1,343.48	361.42	146,200.11	14,954.01	3,799.89
23	11/05/1991	852.45	0.00	0.00	146,200.11	14,954.01	3,799.89
24	11/19/1991	852.45	1,340.17	364.73	145,835.38	16,294.18	4,164.62
25	12/03/1991	852.45	0.00	0.00	145,835.38	16,294.18	4,164.62
26	12/17/1991	852.45	0.00	1,704.90	144,130.48	16,294.18	5,869.52
27	12/31/1991	852.45	0.00	0.00	144,130.48	16,294.18	5,869.52
28	01/14/1992	852.45	1,321.20	383.70	143,746.78	17,615.38	6,253.22
29	01/28/1992	852.45	0.00	0.00	143,746.78	17,615.38	6,253.22
30	02/11/1992	852.45	1,317.68	387.22	143,359.56	18,933.06	6,640.44
31	02/25/1992	852.45	0.00	0.00	143,359.56	18,933.06	6,640.44
32	03/10/1992	852.45	1,314.13	390.77	142,968.79	20,247.19	7,031.21
33	03/24/1992	852.45	0.00	0.00	142,968.79	20,247.19	7,031.21
34	04/07/1992	852.45	1,310.55	394.35	142,574.44	21,557.74	7,425.56

Table 11-10 Continued

Names: MR. & MRS. ROBERT HUGHES

PMT #	PAYMENT DATE	PAYMENT AMOUNT	INTEREST PAID	PRINCIPAL PAID	BALANCE OWED	ACCUMULATED INTEREST	ACCUMULATED PRINCIPAL
35	04/21/1992	852.45	0.00	0.00	142,574.44	21,557.74	7,425.56
36	05/05/1992	852.45	1,306.93	397.97	142,176.47	22,864.67	7,823.53
37	05/19/1992	852.45	0.00	0.00	142,176.47	22,864.67	7,823.53
38	06/02/1992	852.45	1,303.28	401.62	141,774.85	24,167.95	8,225.15
39	06/16/1992	852.45	0.00	0.00	141,774.85	24,167.95	8,225.15
40	06/30/1992	852.45	1,299.60	405.30	141,369.55	25,467.55	8,630.45
41	07/14/1992	852.45	0.00	0.00	141,369.55	25,467.55	8,630.45
42	07/28/1992	852.45	1,295.89	409.01	140,960.54	26,763.44	9,039.46
43	08/11/1992	852.45	0.00	0.00	140,960.54	26,763.44	9,039.46
44	08/25/1992	852.45	1,292.14	412.76	140,547.78	28,055.58	9,452.22
45	09/08/1992	852.45	0.00	0.00	140,547.78	28,055.58	9,452.22
46	09/22/1992	852.45	1,288.35	416.55	140,131.23	29,343.93	9,868.77
47	10/06/1992	852.45	0.00	0.00	140,131.23	29,343.93	9,868.77
48	10/20/1992	852.45	1,284.54	420.36	139,710.87	30,628.47	10,289.13
49	11/03/1992	852.45	0.00	0.00	139,710.87	30,628.47	10,289.13
50	11/17/1992	852.45	1,280.68	424.22	139,286.65	31,909.15	10,713.35
51	12/01/1992	852.45	0.00	0.00	139,286.65	31,909.15	10,713.35
52	12/15/1992	852.45	0.00	1,704.90	137,581.75	31,909.15	12,418.25
53	12/29/1992	852.45	0.00	0.00	137,581.75	31,909.15	12,418.25
54	01/12/1993	852.45	1,261.17	443.73	137,138.02	33,170.32	12,861.98
55	01/26/1993	852.45	0.00	0.00	137,138.02	33,170.32	12,861.98
56	02/09/1993	852.45	1,257.10	447.80	136,690.22	34,427.42	13,309.78
57	02/23/1993	852.45	0.00	0.00	136,690.22	34,427.42	13,309.78
58	03/09/1993	852.45	1,252.99	451.91	136,238.31	35,680.41	13,761.69
59	03/23/1993	852.45	0.00	0.00	136,238.31	35,680.41	13,761.69
60	04/06/1993	852.45	1,248.85	456.05	135,782.26	36,929.26	14,217.74
61	04/20/1993	852.45	0.00	0.00	135,782.26	36,929.26	14,217.74
62	05/04/1993	852.45	1,244.67	460.23	135,322.03	38,173.93	14,677.97
63	05/18/1993	852.45	0.00	0.00	135,322.03	38,173.93	14,677.97
64	06/01/1993	852.45	1,240.45	464.45	134,857.58	39,414.38	15,142.42
65	06/15/1993	852.45	0.00	0.00	134,857.58	39,414.38	15,142.42
66	06/29/1993	852.45	1,236.19	468.71	134,388.87	40,650.57	15,611.13
67	07/13/1993	852.45	0.00	0.00	134,388.87	40,650.57	15,611.13
68	07/27/1993	852.45	1,231.90	473.00	133,915.87	41,882.47	16,084.13
69	08/10/1993	852.45	0.00	0.00	133,915.87	41,882.47	16,084.13
70	08/24/1993	852.45	1,227.56	477.34	133,438.53	43,110.03	16,561.47
71	09/07/1993	852.45	0.00	0.00	133,438.53	43,110.03	16,561.47
72	09/21/1993	852.45	1,223.19	481.71	132,956.82	44,333.22	17,043.18
73	10/05/1993	852.45	0.00	0.00	132,956.82	44,333.22	17,043.18
74	10/19/1993	852.45	1,218.77	486.13	132,470.69	45,551.99	17,529.31
75	11/02/1993	852.45	0.00	0.00	132,470.69	45,551.99	17,529.31
76	11/16/1993	852.45	1,214.31	490.59	131,980.10	46,766.30	18,019.90
77	11/30/1993	852.45	0.00	0.00	131,980.10	46,766.30	18,019.90
78	12/14/1993	852.45	0.00	1,704.90	130,275.20	46,766.30	19,724.80
79	12/28/1993	852.45	0.00	0.00	130,275.20	46,766.30	19,724.80

Table 11–10 Continued

Names:　　　MR. & MRS. ROBERT HUGHES

PMT #	PAYMENT DATE	PAYMENT AMOUNT	INTEREST PAID	PRINCIPAL PAID	BALANCE OWED	ACCUMULATED INTEREST	ACCUMULATED PRINCIPAL
80	01/11/1994	852.45	1,194.19	510.71	129,764.49	47,960.49	20,235.51
81	01/25/1994	852.45	0.00	0.00	129,764.49	47,960.49	20,235.51
82	02/08/1994	852.45	1,189.51	515.39	129,249.10	49,150.00	20,750.90
83	02/22/1994	852.45	0.00	0.00	129,249.10	49,150.00	20,750.90
84	03/08/1994	852.45	1,184.78	520.12	128,728.98	50,334.78	21,271.02
85	03/22/1994	852.45	0.00	0.00	128,728.98	50,334.78	21,271.02
86	04/05/1994	852.45	1,180.02	524.88	128,204.10	51,514.80	21,795.90
87	04/19/1994	852.45	0.00	0.00	128,204.10	51,514.80	21,795.90
88	05/03/1994	852.45	1,175.20	529.70	127,674.40	52,690.00	22,325.60
89	05/17/1994	852.45	0.00	0.00	127,674.40	52,690.00	22,325.60
90	05/31/1994	852.45	1,170.35	534.55	127,139.85	53,860.35	22,860.15
91	06/14/1994	852.45	0.00	0.00	127,139.85	53,860.35	22,860.15
92	06/28/1994	852.45	1,165.45	539.45	126,600.40	55,025.80	23,399.60
93	07/12/1994	852.45	0.00	0.00	126,600.40	55,025.80	23,399.60
94	07/26/1994	852.45	1,160.50	544.40	126,056.00	56,186.30	23,944.00
95	08/09/1994	852.45	0.00	0.00	126,056.00	56,186.30	23,944.00
96	08/23/1994	852.45	1,155.51	549.39	125,506.61	57,341.81	24,493.39
97	09/06/1994	852.45	0.00	0.00	125,506.61	57,341.81	24,493.39
98	09/20/1994	852.45	1,150.48	554.42	124,952.19	58,492.29	25,047.81
99	10/04/1994	852.45	0.00	0.00	124,952.19	58,492.29	25,047.81
100	10/18/1994	852.45	1,145.40	559.50	124,392.69	59,637.69	25,607.31
101	11/01/1994	852.45	0.00	0.00	124,392.69	59,637.69	25,607.31
102	11/15/1994	852.45	1,140.27	564.63	123,828.06	60,777.96	26,171.94
103	11/29/1994	852.45	0.00	0.00	123,828.06	60,777.96	26,171.94
104	12/13/1994	852.45	0.00	1,704.90	122,123.16	60,777.96	27,876.84
105	12/27/1994	852.45	0.00	0.00	122,123.16	60,777.96	27,876.84
106	01/10/1995	852.45	1,119.46	585.44	121,537.72	61,897.42	28,462.28
107	01/24/1995	852.45	0.00	0.00	121,537.72	61,897.42	28,462.28
108	02/07/1995	852.45	1,114.10	590.80	120,946.92	63,011.52	29,053.08
109	02/21/1995	852.45	0.00	0.00	120,946.92	63,011.52	29,053.08
110	03/07/1995	852.45	1,108.68	596.22	120,350.70	64,120.20	29,649.30
111	03/21/1995	852.45	0.00	0.00	120,350.70	64,120.20	29,649.30
112	04/04/1995	852.45	1,103.21	601.69	119,749.01	65,223.41	30,250.99
113	04/18/1995	852.45	0.00	0.00	119,749.01	65,223.41	30,250.99
114	05/02/1995	852.45	1,097.70	607.20	119,141.81	66,321.11	30,858.19
115	05/16/1995	852.45	0.00	0.00	119,141.81	66,321.11	30,858.19
116	05/30/1995	852.45	1,092.13	612.77	118,529.04	67,413.24	31,470.96
117	06/13/1995	852.45	0.00	0.00	118,529.04	67,413.24	31,470.96
118	06/27/1995	852.45	1,086.52	618.38	117,910.66	68,499.76	32,089.34
119	07/11/1995	852.45	0.00	0.00	117,910.66	68,499.76	32,089.34
120	07/25/1995	852.45	1,080.85	624.05	117,286.61	69,580.61	32,713.39
121	08/08/1995	852.45	0.00	0.00	117,286.61	69,580.61	32,713.39
122	08/22/1995	852.45	1,075.13	629.77	116,656.84	70,655.74	33,343.16
123	09/05/1995	852.45	0.00	0.00	116,656.84	70,655.74	33,343.16
124	09/19/1995	852.45	1,069.35	635.55	116,021.29	71,725.09	33,978.71

Table 11–10 Continued

Names: MR. & MRS. ROBERT HUGHES

PMT #	PAYMENT DATE	PAYMENT AMOUNT	INTEREST PAID	PRINCIPAL PAID	BALANCE OWED	ACCUMULATED INTEREST	ACCUMULATED PRINCIPAL
125	10/03/1995	852.45	0.00	0.00	116,021.29	71,725.09	33,978.71
126	10/17/1995	852.45	1,063.53	641.37	115,379.92	72,788.62	34,620.08
127	10/31/1995	852.45	0.00	0.00	115,379.92	72,788.62	34,620.08
128	11/14/1995	852.45	1,057.65	647.25	114,732.67	73,846.27	35,267.33
129	11/28/1995	852.45	0.00	0.00	114,732.67	73,846.27	35,267.33
130	12/12/1995	852.45	0.00	1,704.90	113,027.77	73,846.27	36,972.23
131	12/26/1995	852.45	0.00	0.00	113,027.77	73,846.27	36,972.23
132	01/09/1996	852.45	1,036.09	668.81	112,358.96	74,882.36	37,641.04
133	01/23/1996	852.45	0.00	0.00	112,358.96	74,882.36	37,641.04
134	02/06/1996	852.45	1,029.96	674.94	111,684.02	75,912.32	38,315.98
135	02/20/1996	852.45	0.00	0.00	111,684.02	75,912.32	38,315.98
136	03/05/1996	852.45	1,023.77	681.13	111,002.89	76,936.09	38,997.11
137	03/19/1996	852.45	0.00	0.00	111,002.89	76,936.09	38,997.11
138	04/02/1996	852.45	1,017.53	687.37	110,315.52	77,953.62	39,684.48
139	04/16/1996	852.45	0.00	0.00	110,315.52	77,953.62	39,684.48
140	04/30/1996	852.45	1,011.23	693.67	109,621.85	78,964.85	40,378.15
141	05/14/1996	852.45	0.00	0.00	109,621.85	78,964.85	40,378.15
142	05/28/1996	852.45	1,004.87	700.03	108,921.82	79,969.72	41,078.18
143	06/11/1996	852.45	0.00	0.00	108,921.82	79,969.72	41,078.18
144	06/25/1996	852.45	998.45	706.45	108,215.37	80,968.17	41,784.63
145	07/09/1996	852.45	0.00	0.00	108,215.37	80,968.17	41,784.63
146	07/23/1996	852.45	991.97	712.93	107,502.44	81,960.14	42,497.56
147	08/06/1996	852.45	0.00	0.00	107,502.44	81,960.14	42,497.56
148	08/20/1996	852.45	985.44	719.46	106,782.98	82,945.58	43,217.02
149	09/03/1996	852.45	0.00	0.00	106,782.98	82,945.58	43,217.02
150	09/17/1996	852.45	978.84	726.06	106,056.92	83,924.42	43,943.08
151	10/01/1996	852.45	0.00	0.00	106,056.92	83,924.42	43,943.08
152	10/15/1996	852.45	972.19	732.71	105,324.21	84,896.61	44,675.79
153	10/29/1996	852.45	0.00	0.00	105,324.21	84,896.61	44,675.79
154	11/12/1996	852.45	965.47	739.43	104,584.78	85,862.08	45,415.22
155	11/26/1996	852.45	0.00	0.00	104,584.78	85,862.08	45,415.22
156	12/10/1996	852.45	0.00	1,704.90	102,879.88	85,862.08	47,120.12
157	12/24/1996	852.45	0.00	0.00	102,879.88	85,862.08	47,120.12
158	01/07/1997	852.45	943.07	761.83	102,118.05	86,805.15	47,881.95
159	01/21/1997	852.45	0.00	0.00	102,118.05	86,805.15	47,881.95
160	02/04/1997	852.45	936.08	768.82	101,349.23	87,741.23	48,650.77
161	02/18/1997	852.45	0.00	0.00	101,349.23	87,741.23	48,650.77
162	03/04/1997	852.45	929.03	775.87	100,573.36	88,670.26	49,426.64
163	03/18/1997	852.45	0.00	0.00	100,573.36	88,670.26	49,426.64
164	04/01/1997	852.45	921.92	782.98	99,790.38	89,592.18	50,209.62
165	04/15/1997	852.45	0.00	0.00	99,790.38	89,592.18	50,209.62
166	04/29/1997	852.45	914.75	790.15	99,000.23	90,506.93	50,999.77
167	05/13/1997	852.45	0.00	0.00	99,000.23	90,506.93	50,999.77
168	05/27/1997	852.45	907.50	797.40	98,202.83	91,414.43	51,797.17
169	06/10/1997	852.45	0.00	0.00	98,202.83	91,414.43	51,797.17

Table 11-10 Continued

Names: MR. & MRS. ROBERT HUGHES

PMT #	PAYMENT DATE	PAYMENT AMOUNT	INTEREST PAID	PRINCIPAL PAID	BALANCE OWED	ACCUMULATED INTEREST	ACCUMULATED PRINCIPAL
170	06/24/1997	852.45	900.19	804.71	97,398.12	92,314.62	52,601.88
171	07/08/1997	852.45	0.00	0.00	97,398.12	92,314.62	52,601.88
172	07/22/1997	852.45	892.82	812.08	96,586.04	93,207.44	53,413.96
173	08/05/1997	852.45	0.00	0.00	96,586.04	93,207.44	53,413.96
174	08/19/1997	852.45	885.37	819.53	95,766.51	94,092.81	54,233.49
175	09/02/1997	852.45	0.00	0.00	95,766.51	94,092.81	54,233.49
176	09/16/1997	852.45	877.86	827.04	94,939.47	94,970.67	55,060.53
177	09/30/1997	852.45	0.00	0.00	94,939.47	94,970.67	55,060.53
178	10/14/1997	852.45	870.28	834.62	94,104.85	95,840.95	55,895.15
179	10/28/1997	852.45	0.00	0.00	94,104.85	95,840.95	55,895.15
180	11/11/1997	852.45	862.63	842.27	93,262.58	96,703.58	56,737.42
181	11/25/1997	852.45	0.00	0.00	93,262.58	96,703.58	56,737.42
182	12/09/1997	852.45	0.00	1,704.90	91,557.68	96,703.58	58,442.32
183	12/23/1997	852.45	0.00	0.00	91,557.68	96,703.58	58,442.32
184	01/06/1998	852.45	839.28	865.62	90,692.06	97,542.86	59,307.94
185	01/20/1998	852.45	0.00	0.00	90,692.06	97,542.86	59,307.94
186	02/03/1998	852.45	831.34	873.56	89,818.50	98,374.20	60,181.50
187	02/17/1998	852.45	0.00	0.00	89,818.50	98,374.20	60,181.50
188	03/03/1998	852.45	823.34	881.56	88,936.94	99,197.54	61,063.06
189	03/17/1998	852.45	0.00	0.00	88,936.94	99,197.54	61,063.06
190	03/31/1998	852.45	815.26	889.64	88,047.30	100,012.80	61,952.70
191	04/14/1998	852.45	0.00	0.00	88,047.30	100,012.80	61,952.70
192	04/28/1998	852.45	807.10	897.80	87,149.50	100,819.90	62,850.50
193	05/12/1998	852.45	0.00	0.00	87,149.50	100,819.90	62,850.50
194	05/26/1998	852.45	798.87	906.03	86,243.47	101,618.77	63,756.53
195	06/09/1998	852.45	0.00	0.00	86,243.47	101,618.77	63,756.53
196	06/23/1998	852.45	790.57	914.33	85,329.14	102,409.34	64,670.86
197	07/07/1998	852.45	0.00	0.00	85,329.14	102,409.34	64,670.86
198	07/21/1998	852.45	782.18	922.72	84,406.42	103,191.52	65,593.58
199	08/04/1998	852.45	0.00	0.00	84,406.42	103,191.52	65,593.58
200	08/18/1998	852.45	773.73	931.17	83,475.25	103,965.25	66,524.75
201	09/01/1998	852.45	0.00	0.00	83,475.25	103,965.25	66,524.75
202	09/15/1998	852.45	765.19	939.71	82,535.54	104,730.44	67,464.46
203	09/29/1998	852.45	0.00	0.00	82,535.54	104,730.44	67,464.46
204	10/13/1998	852.45	756.58	948.32	81,587.22	105,487.02	68,412.78
205	10/27/1998	852.45	0.00	0.00	81,587.22	105,487.02	68,412.78
206	11/10/1998	852.45	747.88	957.02	80,630.20	106,234.90	69,369.80
207	11/24/1998	852.45	0.00	0.00	80,630.20	106,234.90	69,369.80
208	12/08/1998	852.45	0.00	1,704.90	78,925.30	106,234.90	71,074.70
209	12/22/1998	852.45	0.00	0.00	78,925.30	106,234.90	71,074.70
210	01/05/1999	852.45	723.48	981.42	77,943.88	106,958.38	72,056.12
211	01/19/1999	852.45	0.00	0.00	77,943.88	106,958.38	72,056.12
212	02/02/1999	852.45	714.49	990.41	76,953.47	107,672.87	73,046.53
213	02/16/1999	852.45	0.00	0.00	76,953.47	107,672.87	73,046.53
214	03/02/1999	852.45	705.41	999.49	75,953.98	108,378.28	74,046.02

Table 11–10 Continued

Names: MR. & MRS. ROBERT HUGHES

PMT #	PAYMENT DATE	PAYMENT AMOUNT	INTEREST PAID	PRINCIPAL PAID	BALANCE OWED	ACCUMULATED INTEREST	ACCUMULATED PRINCIPAL
215	03/16/1999	852.45	0.00	0.00	75,953.98	108,378.28	74,046.02
216	03/30/1999	852.45	696.24	1,008.66	74,945.32	109,074.52	75,054.68
217	04/13/1999	852.45	0.00	0.00	74,945.32	109,074.52	75,054.68
218	04/27/1999	852.45	687.00	1,017.90	73,927.42	109,761.52	76,072.58
219	05/11/1999	852.45	0.00	0.00	73,927.42	109,761.52	76,072.58
220	05/25/1999	852.45	677.67	1,027.23	72,900.19	110,439.19	77,099.81
221	06/08/1999	852.45	0.00	0.00	72,900.19	110,439.19	77,099.81
222	06/22/1999	852.45	668.25	1,036.65	71,863.54	111,107.44	78,136.46
223	07/06/1999	852.45	0.00	0.00	71,863.54	111,107.44	78,136.46
224	07/20/1999	852.45	658.75	1,046.15	70,817.39	111,766.19	79,182.61
225	08/03/1999	852.45	0.00	0.00	70,817.39	111,766.19	79,182.61
226	08/17/1999	852.45	649.16	1,055.74	69,761.65	112,415.35	80,238.35
227	08/31/1999	852.45	0.00	0.00	69,761.65	112,415.35	80,238.35
228	09/14/1999	852.45	639.48	1,065.42	68,696.23	113,054.83	81,303.77
229	09/28/1999	852.45	0.00	0.00	68,696.23	113,054.83	81,303.77
230	10/12/1999	852.45	629.72	1,075.18	67,621.05	113,684.55	82,378.95
231	10/26/1999	852.45	0.00	0.00	67,621.05	113,684.55	82,378.95
232	11/09/1999	852.45	619.86	1,085.04	66,536.01	114,304.41	83,463.99
233	11/23/1999	852.45	0.00	0.00	66,536.01	114,304.41	83,463.99
234	12/07/1999	852.45	0.00	1,704.90	64,831.11	114,304.41	85,168.89
235	12/21/1999	852.45	0.00	0.00	64,831.11	114,304.41	85,168.89
236	01/04/2000	852.45	594.29	1,110.61	63,720.50	114,898.70	86,279.50
237	01/18/2000	852.45	0.00	0.00	63,720.50	114,898.70	86,279.50
238	02/01/2000	852.45	584.10	1,120.80	62,599.70	115,482.80	87,400.30
239	02/15/2000	852.45	0.00	0.00	62,599.70	115,482.80	87,400.30
240	02/29/2000	852.45	573.83	1,131.07	61,468.63	116,056.63	88,531.37
241	03/14/2000	852.45	0.00	0.00	61,468.63	116,056.63	88,531.37
242	03/28/2000	852.45	563.46	1,141.44	60,327.19	116,620.09	89,672.81
243	04/11/2000	852.45	0.00	0.00	60,327.19	116,620.09	89,672.81
244	04/25/2000	852.45	553.00	1,151.90	59,175.29	117,173.09	90,824.71
245	05/09/2000	852.45	0.00	0.00	59,175.29	117,173.09	90,824.71
246	05/23/2000	852.45	542.44	1,162.46	58,012.83	117,715.53	91,987.17
247	06/06/2000	852.45	0.00	0.00	58,012.83	117,715.53	91,987.17
248	06/20/2000	852.45	531.78	1,173.12	56,839.71	118,247.31	93,160.29
249	07/04/2000	852.45	0.00	0.00	56,839.71	118,247.31	93,160.29
250	07/18/2000	852.45	521.03	1,183.87	55,655.84	118,768.34	94,344.16
251	08/01/2000	852.45	0.00	0.00	55,655.84	118,768.34	94,344.16
252	08/15/2000	852.45	510.18	1,194.72	54,461.12	119,278.52	95,538.88
253	08/29/2000	852.45	0.00	0.00	54,461.12	119,278.52	95,538.88
254	09/12/2000	852.45	499.23	1,205.67	53,255.45	119,777.75	96,744.55
255	09/26/2000	852.45	0.00	0.00	53,255.45	119,777.75	96,744.55
256	10/10/2000	852.45	488.17	1,216.73	52,038.72	120,265.92	97,961.28
257	10/24/2000	852.45	0.00	0.00	52,038.72	120,265.92	97,961.28
258	11/07/2000	852.45	477.02	1,227.88	50,810.84	120,742.94	99,189.16
259	11/21/2000	852.45	0.00	0.00	50,810.84	120,742.94	99,189.16

Table 11–10 Continued

Names: MR. & MRS. ROBERT HUGHES

PMT #	PAYMENT DATE	PAYMENT AMOUNT	INTEREST PAID	PRINCIPAL PAID	BALANCE OWED	ACCUMULATED INTEREST	ACCUMULATED PRINCIPAL
260	12/05/2000	852.45	0.00	1,704.90	49,105.94	120,742.94	100,894.06
261	12/19/2000	852.45	0.00	0.00	49,105.94	120,742.94	100,894.06
262	01/02/2001	852.45	450.14	1,254.76	47,851.18	121,193.08	102,148.82
263	01/16/2001	852.45	0.00	0.00	47,851.18	121,193.08	102,148.82
264	01/30/2001	852.45	438.64	1,266.26	46,584.92	121,631.72	103,415.08
265	02/13/2001	852.45	0.00	0.00	46,584.92	121,631.72	103,415.08
266	02/27/2001	852.45	427.03	1,277.87	45,307.05	122,058.75	104,692.95
267	03/13/2001	852.45	0.00	0.00	45,307.05	122,058.75	104,692.95
268	03/27/2001	852.45	415.31	1,289.59	44,017.46	122,474.06	105,982.54
269	04/10/2001	852.45	0.00	0.00	44,017.46	122,474.06	105,982.54
270	04/24/2001	852.45	403.49	1,301.41	42,716.05	122,877.55	107,283.95
271	05/08/2001	852.45	0.00	0.00	42,716.05	122,877.55	107,283.95
272	05/22/2001	852.45	391.56	1,313.34	41,402.71	123,269.11	108,597.29
273	06/05/2001	852.45	0.00	0.00	41,402.71	123,269.11	108,597.29
274	06/19/2001	852.45	379.52	1,325.38	40,077.33	123,648.63	109,922.67
275	07/03/2001	852.45	0.00	0.00	40,077.33	123,648.63	109,922.67
276	07/17/2001	852.45	367.38	1,337.52	38,739.81	124,016.01	111,260.19
277	07/31/2001	852.45	0.00	0.00	38,739.81	124,016.01	111,260.19
278	08/14/2001	852.45	355.11	1,349.79	37,390.02	124,371.12	112,609.98
279	08/28/2001	852.45	0.00	0.00	37,390.02	124,371.12	112,609.98
280	09/11/2001	852.45	342.74	1,362.16	36,027.86	124,713.86	113,972.14
281	09/25/2001	852.45	0.00	0.00	36,027.86	124,713.86	113,972.14
282	10/09/2001	852.45	330.26	1,374.64	34,653.22	125,044.12	115,346.78
283	10/23/2001	852.45	0.00	0.00	34,653.22	125,044.12	115,346.78
284	11/06/2001	852.45	317.65	1,387.25	33,265.97	125,361.77	116,734.03
285	11/20/2001	852.45	0.00	0.00	33,265.97	125,361.77	116,734.03
286	12/04/2001	852.45	0.00	1,704.90	31,561.07	125,361.77	118,438.93
287	12/18/2001	852.45	0.00	0.00	31,561.07	125,361.77	118,438.93
288	01/01/2002	852.45	289.31	1,415.59	30,145.48	125,651.08	119,854.52
289	01/15/2002	852.45	0.00	0.00	30,145.48	125,651.08	119,854.52
290	01/29/2002	852.45	276.33	1,428.57	28,716.91	125,927.41	121,283.09
291	02/12/2002	852.45	0.00	0.00	28,716.91	125,927.41	121,283.09
292	02/26/2002	852.45	263.24	1,441.66	27,275.25	126,190.65	122,724.75
293	03/12/2002	852.45	0.00	0.00	27,275.25	126,190.65	122,724.75
294	03/26/2002	852.45	250.02	1,454.88	25,820.37	126,440.67	124,179.63
295	04/09/2002	852.45	0.00	0.00	25,820.37	126,440.67	124,179.63
296	04/23/2002	852.45	236.69	1,468.21	24,352.16	126,677.36	125,647.84
297	05/07/2002	852.45	0.00	0.00	24,352.16	126,677.36	125,647.84
298	05/21/2002	852.45	223.23	1,481.67	22,870.49	126,900.59	127,129.51
299	06/04/2002	852.45	0.00	0.00	22,870.49	126,900.59	127,129.51
300	06/18/2002	852.45	209.65	1,495.25	21,375.24	127,110.24	128,624.76
301	07/02/2002	852.45	0.00	0.00	21,375.24	127,110.24	128,624.76
302	07/16/2002	852.45	195.94	1,508.96	19,866.28	127,306.18	130,133.72
303	07/30/2002	852.45	0.00	0.00	19,866.28	127,306.18	130,133.72
304	08/13/2002	852.45	182.11	1,522.79	18,343.49	127,488.29	131,656.51

Table 11–10 Continued

Names: MR. & MRS. ROBERT HUGHES

PMT #	PAYMENT DATE	PAYMENT AMOUNT	INTEREST PAID	PRINCIPAL PAID	BALANCE OWED	ACCUMULATED INTEREST	ACCUMULATED PRINCIPAL
305	08/27/2002	852.45	0.00	0.00	18,343.49	127,488.29	131,656.51
306	09/10/2002	852.45	168.15	1,536.75	16,806.74	127,656.44	133,193.26
307	09/24/2002	852.45	0.00	0.00	16,806.74	127,656.44	133,193.26
308	10/08/2002	852.45	154.06	1,550.84	15,255.90	127,810.50	134,744.10
309	10/22/2002	852.45	0.00	0.00	15,255.90	127,810.50	134,744.10
310	11/05/2002	852.45	139.85	1,565.05	13,690.85	127,950.35	136,309.15
311	11/19/2002	852.45	0.00	0.00	13,690.85	127,950.35	136,309.15
312	12/03/2002	852.45	0.00	1,704.90	11,985.95	127,950.35	138,014.05
313	12/17/2002	852.45	0.00	0.00	11,985.95	127,950.35	138,014.05
314	12/31/2002	852.45	109.87	1,595.03	10,390.92	128,060.22	139,609.08
315	01/14/2003	852.45	0.00	0.00	10,390.92	128,060.22	139,609.08
316	01/28/2003	852.45	95.25	1,609.65	8,781.27	128,155.47	141,218.73
317	02/11/2003	852.45	0.00	0.00	8,781.27	128,155.47	141,218.73
318	02/25/2003	852.45	80.49	1,624.41	7,156.86	128,235.96	142,843.14
319	03/11/2003	852.45	0.00	0.00	7,156.86	128,235.96	142,843.14
320	03/25/2003	852.45	65.60	1,639.30	5,517.56	128,301.56	144,482.44
321	04/08/2003	852.45	0.00	0.00	5,517.56	128,301.56	144,482.44
322	04/22/2003	852.45	50.58	1,654.32	3,863.24	128,352.14	146,136.76
323	05/06/2003	852.45	0.00	0.00	3,863.24	128,352.14	146,136.76
324	05/20/2003	852.45	35.41	1,669.49	2,193.75	128,387.55	147,806.25
325	06/03/2003	852.45	0.00	0.00	2,193.75	128,387.55	147,806.25
326	06/17/2003	852.45	20.11	1,684.79	508.96	128,407.66	149,491.04
327	07/01/2003	513.63	4.67	508.96	0.00	128,412.33	150,000.00

Table 11–11 Comparison of Costs and Savings for Mr. John Dixon—Homeowner Conventional vs. Biweekly Programs Summary

```
=================================================================================================
| ORIGINAL LOAN AMOUNT:          150,000.00        ANNUAL INTEREST RATE:            11.000 % |
| ORIGINAL LOAN TERM:            30 (YEARS)         CURRENT MONTHLY PAYMENT:        1,428.49 |
| NUMBER OF PREVIOUS PAYMENTS:    0                 'NEW' BIWEEKLY PAYMENT:           714.25 |
| CURRENT LOAN BALANCE:          150,000.00                                                  |
=================================================================================================
```

END OF YEAR	CURRENT MONTHLY REMAINING BALANCE	INTEREST PAID TO-DATE	(EQUITY) PRINCIPAL PAID TO-DATE	'NEW' BIWEEKLY REMAINING BALANCE	INTEREST PAID TO-DATE	(EQUITY) PRINCIPAL PAID TO-DATE	DIFFERENCE EQUITY GROWTH TO-DATE	INTEREST SAVED TO-DATE
1	149,324.74	16,466.62	675.26	147,896.12	16,466.62	2,103.88	1,428.62	0.00
2	148,571.33	32,855.09	1,428.67	145,548.77	32,689.77	4,451.23	3,022.56	165.32
3	147,730.75	49,156.39	2,269.25	142,929.81	48,641.31	7,070.19	4,800.94	515.08
4	146,792.91	65,360.43	3,207.09	140,007.79	64,289.79	9,992.21	6,785.12	1,070.64
5	145,746.53	81,455.93	4,253.47	136,747.61	79,600.11	13,252.39	8,998.92	1,855.82
6	144,579.07	97,430.35	5,420.93	133,110.18	94,533.18	16,889.82	11,468.89	2,897.17
7	143,276.50	113,269.66	6,723.50	129,051.84	109,045.34	20,948.16	14,224.66	4,224.32
8	141,823.20	128,958.24	8,176.80	124,523.86	123,087.86	25,476.14	17,299.34	5,870.38
9	140,201.73	144,478.65	9,798.27	119,471.92	136,606.42	30,528.08	20,729.81	7,872.23
10	138,392.64	159,811.44	11,607.36	113,835.37	149,540.37	36,164.63	24,557.27	10,271.07
11	136,374.19	174,934.87	13,625.81	107,546.57	161,822.07	42,453.43	28,827.62	13,112.80
12	134,122.19	189,824.75	15,877.81	100,530.04	173,376.04	49,469.96	33,592.15	16,448.71
13	131,609.58	204,454.02	18,390.42	92,701.58	184,118.08	57,298.42	38,908.00	20,335.94
14	128,806.19	218,792.51	21,193.81	83,967.20	193,954.20	66,032.80	44,838.99	24,838.31
15	125,678.41	232,806.61	24,321.59	74,222.10	202,779.60	75,777.90	51,456.31	30,027.01
16	122,188.70	246,458.78	27,811.30	63,349.30	210,477.30	86,650.70	58,839.40	35,981.48
17	118,295.17	259,707.13	31,704.83	51,218.31	216,916.81	98,781.69	67,076.86	42,790.32
18	113,951.06	272,504.90	36,048.94	37,683.54	221,952.54	112,316.46	76,267.52	50,552.36
19	109,104.27	284,799.99	40,895.73	22,582.51	225,422.01	127,417.49	86,521.76	59,377.98
20	103,696.62	296,534.22	46,303.38	5,734.05	227,144.05	144,265.95	97,962.57	69,390.17
21	97,663.21	307,642.69	52,336.79	DEBT FREE	227,279.57	150,000.00		80,363.12
22	90,931.61	318,052.97	59,068.39					90,773.40
23	83,421.04	327,684.28	66,578.96					100,404.71
24	75,041.36	336,446.48	74,958.64					109,166.91
25	65,691.99	344,238.99	84,308.01					116,959.42
26	55,260.70	350,949.58	94,739.30					123,670.01
27	43,622.33	356,453.09	106,377.67					129,173.52
28	30,637.17	360,609.81	119,362.83					133,330.24
29	16,149.39	363,263.91	133,850.61					135,984.34
30	1,400.76	364,241.51	150,000.00					136,961.94

```
TOTAL INTEREST SAVED:   136,961.94
TOTAL TERM SAVED:       116.16 (PAYMENTS)   9.68  (YEARS)
```

Table 11–12 Amortization Schedule Re: Table 11-11

```
Names:        MR. JOHN DIXON
Property:     609 S.E. 16TH WAY, ATLANTA, GA 39206
Telephone:    (615)555-8888
Tax I.D.:     123-45-6789
```

ORIGINAL LOAN AMOUNT:	150,000.00	BIWEEKLY PAYMENT: 714.25
ORIGINAL INTEREST RATE:	11.000	TOTAL BIWEEKLY INTEREST PAID: 227,279.57
ORIGINAL TERM OF LOAN:	30 (YRS)	LAST BIWEEKLY PAYMENT DATE: 03/29/2011
NUMBER OF PREVIOUS PAYMENTS:	0	NEW TERM OF LOAN: 20.32 (YRS)
CURRENT LOAN BALANCE:	150,000.00	

PMT #	PAYMENT DATE	PAYMENT AMOUNT	INTEREST PAID	PRINCIPAL PAID	BALANCE OWED	ACCUMULATED INTEREST	ACCUMULATED PRINCIPAL
1	01/01/1991	714.25	0.00	0.00	150,000.00	0.00	0.00
2	01/15/1991	714.25	1,375.00	53.50	149,946.50	1,375.00	53.50
3	01/29/1991	714.25	0.00	0.00	149,946.50	1,375.00	53.50
4	02/12/1991	714.25	1,374.51	53.99	149,892.51	2,749.51	107.49
5	02/26/1991	714.25	0.00	0.00	149,892.51	2,749.51	107.49
6	03/12/1991	714.25	1,374.01	54.49	149,838.02	4,123.52	161.98
7	03/26/1991	714.25	0.00	0.00	149,838.02	4,123.52	161.98
8	04/09/1991	714.25	1,373.52	54.98	149,783.04	5,497.04	216.96
9	04/23/1991	714.25	0.00	0.00	149,783.04	5,497.04	216.96
10	05/07/1991	714.25	1,373.01	55.49	149,727.55	6,870.05	272.45
11	05/21/1991	714.25	0.00	0.00	149,727.55	6,870.05	272.45
12	06/04/1991	714.25	1,372.50	56.00	149,671.55	8,242.55	328.45
13	06/18/1991	714.25	0.00	0.00	149,671.55	8,242.55	328.45
14	07/02/1991	714.25	1,371.99	56.51	149,615.04	9,614.54	384.96
15	07/16/1991	714.25	0.00	0.00	149,615.04	9,614.54	384.96
16	07/30/1991	714.25	1,371.47	57.03	149,558.01	10,986.01	441.99
17	08/13/1991	714.25	0.00	0.00	149,558.01	10,986.01	441.99
18	08/27/1991	714.25	1,370.95	57.55	149,500.46	12,356.96	499.54
19	09/10/1991	714.25	0.00	0.00	149,500.46	12,356.96	499.54
20	09/24/1991	714.25	1,370.42	58.08	149,442.38	13,727.38	557.62
21	10/08/1991	714.25	0.00	0.00	149,442.38	13,727.38	557.62
22	10/22/1991	714.25	1,369.89	58.61	149,383.77	15,097.27	616.23
23	11/05/1991	714.25	0.00	0.00	149,383.77	15,097.27	616.23
24	11/19/1991	714.25	1,369.35	59.15	149,324.62	16,466.62	675.38
25	12/03/1991	714.25	0.00	0.00	149,324.62	16,466.62	675.38
26	12/17/1991	714.25	0.00	1,428.50	147,896.12	16,466.62	2,103.88
27	12/31/1991	714.25	0.00	0.00	147,896.12	16,466.62	2,103.88
28	01/14/1992	714.25	1,355.71	72.79	147,823.33	17,822.33	2,176.67
29	01/28/1992	714.25	0.00	0.00	147,823.33	17,822.33	2,176.67
30	02/11/1992	714.25	1,355.05	73.45	147,749.88	19,177.38	2,250.12
31	02/25/1992	714.25	0.00	0.00	147,749.88	19,177.38	2,250.12
32	03/10/1992	714.25	1,354.37	74.13	147,675.75	20,531.75	2,324.25
33	03/24/1992	714.25	0.00	0.00	147,675.75	20,531.75	2,324.25
34	04/07/1992	714.25	1,353.69	74.81	147,600.94	21,885.44	2,399.06

Table 11–12 Continued

Names: MR. JOHN DIXON

PMT #	PAYMENT DATE	PAYMENT AMOUNT	INTEREST PAID	PRINCIPAL PAID	BALANCE OWED	ACCUMULATED INTEREST	ACCUMULATED PRINCIPAL
35	04/21/1992	714.25	0.00	0.00	147,600.94	21,885.44	2,399.06
36	05/05/1992	714.25	1,353.01	75.49	147,525.45	23,238.45	2,474.55
37	05/19/1992	714.25	0.00	0.00	147,525.45	23,238.45	2,474.55
38	06/02/1992	714.25	1,352.32	76.18	147,449.27	24,590.77	2,550.73
39	06/16/1992	714.25	0.00	0.00	147,449.27	24,590.77	2,550.73
40	06/30/1992	714.25	1,351.62	76.88	147,372.39	25,942.39	2,627.61
41	07/14/1992	714.25	0.00	0.00	147,372.39	25,942.39	2,627.61
42	07/28/1992	714.25	1,350.91	77.59	147,294.80	27,293.30	2,705.20
43	08/11/1992	714.25	0.00	0.00	147,294.80	27,293.30	2,705.20
44	08/25/1992	714.25	1,350.20	78.30	147,216.50	28,643.50	2,783.50
45	09/08/1992	714.25	0.00	0.00	147,216.50	28,643.50	2,783.50
46	09/22/1992	714.25	1,349.48	79.02	147,137.48	29,992.98	2,862.52
47	10/06/1992	714.25	0.00	0.00	147,137.48	29,992.98	2,862.52
48	10/20/1992	714.25	1,348.76	79.74	147,057.74	31,341.74	2,942.26
49	11/03/1992	714.25	0.00	0.00	147,057.74	31,341.74	2,942.26
50	11/17/1992	714.25	1,348.03	80.47	146,977.27	32,689.77	3,022.73
51	12/01/1992	714.25	0.00	0.00	146,977.27	32,689.77	3,022.73
52	12/15/1992	714.25	0.00	1,428.50	145,548.77	32,689.77	4,451.23
53	12/29/1992	714.25	0.00	0.00	145,548.77	32,689.77	4,451.23
54	01/12/1993	714.25	1,334.20	94.30	145,454.47	34,023.97	4,545.53
55	01/26/1993	714.25	0.00	0.00	145,454.47	34,023.97	4,545.53
56	02/09/1993	714.25	1,333.33	95.17	145,359.30	35,357.30	4,640.70
57	02/23/1993	714.25	0.00	0.00	145,359.30	35,357.30	4,640.70
58	03/09/1993	714.25	1,332.46	96.04	145,263.26	36,689.76	4,736.74
59	03/23/1993	714.25	0.00	0.00	145,263.26	36,689.76	4,736.74
60	04/06/1993	714.25	1,331.58	96.92	145,166.34	38,021.34	4,833.66
61	04/20/1993	714.25	0.00	0.00	145,166.34	38,021.34	4,833.66
62	05/04/1993	714.25	1,330.69	97.81	145,068.53	39,352.03	4,931.47
63	05/18/1993	714.25	0.00	0.00	145,068.53	39,352.03	4,931.47
64	06/01/1993	714.25	1,329.79	98.71	144,969.82	40,681.82	5,030.18
65	06/15/1993	714.25	0.00	0.00	144,969.82	40,681.82	5,030.18
66	06/29/1993	714.25	1,328.89	99.61	144,870.21	42,010.71	5,129.79
67	07/13/1993	714.25	0.00	0.00	144,870.21	42,010.71	5,129.79
68	07/27/1993	714.25	1,327.98	100.52	144,769.69	43,338.69	5,230.31
69	08/10/1993	714.25	0.00	0.00	144,769.69	43,338.69	5,230.31
70	08/24/1993	714.25	1,327.06	101.44	144,668.25	44,665.75	5,331.75
71	09/07/1993	714.25	0.00	0.00	144,668.25	44,665.75	5,331.75
72	09/21/1993	714.25	1,326.13	102.37	144,565.88	45,991.88	5,434.12
73	10/05/1993	714.25	0.00	0.00	144,565.88	45,991.88	5,434.12
74	10/19/1993	714.25	1,325.19	103.31	144,462.57	47,317.07	5,537.43
75	11/02/1993	714.25	0.00	0.00	144,462.57	47,317.07	5,537.43
76	11/16/1993	714.25	1,324.24	104.26	144,358.31	48,641.31	5,641.69
77	11/30/1993	714.25	0.00	0.00	144,358.31	48,641.31	5,641.69
78	12/14/1993	714.25	0.00	1,428.50	142,929.81	48,641.31	7,070.19
79	12/28/1993	714.25	0.00	0.00	142,929.81	48,641.31	7,070.19

Table 11–12 Continued

Names: MR. JOHN DIXON

PMT #	PAYMENT DATE	PAYMENT AMOUNT	INTEREST PAID	PRINCIPAL PAID	BALANCE OWED	ACCUMULATED INTEREST	ACCUMULATED PRINCIPAL
80	01/11/1994	714.25	1,310.19	118.31	142,811.50	49,951.50	7,188.50
81	01/25/1994	714.25	0.00	0.00	142,811.50	49,951.50	7,188.50
82	02/08/1994	714.25	1,309.11	119.39	142,692.11	51,260.61	7,307.89
83	02/22/1994	714.25	0.00	0.00	142,692.11	51,260.61	7,307.89
84	03/08/1994	714.25	1,308.01	120.49	142,571.62	52,568.62	7,428.38
85	03/22/1994	714.25	0.00	0.00	142,571.62	52,568.62	7,428.38
86	04/05/1994	714.25	1,306.91	121.59	142,450.03	53,875.53	7,549.97
87	04/19/1994	714.25	0.00	0.00	142,450.03	53,875.53	7,549.97
88	05/03/1994	714.25	1,305.79	122.71	142,327.32	55,181.32	7,672.68
89	05/17/1994	714.25	0.00	0.00	142,327.32	55,181.32	7,672.68
90	05/31/1994	714.25	1,304.67	123.83	142,203.49	56,485.99	7,796.51
91	06/14/1994	714.25	0.00	0.00	142,203.49	56,485.99	7,796.51
92	06/28/1994	714.25	1,303.53	124.97	142,078.52	57,789.52	7,921.48
93	07/12/1994	714.25	0.00	0.00	142,078.52	57,789.52	7,921.48
94	07/26/1994	714.25	1,302.39	126.11	141,952.41	59,091.91	8,047.59
95	08/09/1994	714.25	0.00	0.00	141,952.41	59,091.91	8,047.59
96	08/23/1994	714.25	1,301.23	127.27	141,825.14	60,393.14	8,174.86
97	09/06/1994	714.25	0.00	0.00	141,825.14	60,393.14	8,174.86
98	09/20/1994	714.25	1,300.06	128.44	141,696.70	61,693.20	8,303.30
99	10/04/1994	714.25	0.00	0.00	141,696.70	61,693.20	8,303.30
100	10/18/1994	714.25	1,298.89	129.61	141,567.09	62,992.09	8,432.91
101	11/01/1994	714.25	0.00	0.00	141,567.09	62,992.09	8,432.91
102	11/15/1994	714.25	1,297.70	130.80	141,436.29	64,289.79	8,563.71
103	11/29/1994	714.25	0.00	0.00	141,436.29	64,289.79	8,563.71
104	12/13/1994	714.25	0.00	1,428.50	140,007.79	64,289.79	9,992.21
105	12/27/1994	714.25	0.00	0.00	140,007.79	64,289.79	9,992.21
106	01/10/1995	714.25	1,283.40	145.10	139,862.69	65,573.19	10,137.31
107	01/24/1995	714.25	0.00	0.00	139,862.69	65,573.19	10,137.31
108	02/07/1995	714.25	1,282.07	146.43	139,716.26	66,855.26	10,283.74
109	02/21/1995	714.25	0.00	0.00	139,716.26	66,855.26	10,283.74
110	03/07/1995	714.25	1,280.73	147.77	139,568.49	68,135.99	10,431.51
111	03/21/1995	714.25	0.00	0.00	139,568.49	68,135.99	10,431.51
112	04/04/1995	714.25	1,279.38	149.12	139,419.37	69,415.37	10,580.63
113	04/18/1995	714.25	0.00	0.00	139,419.37	69,415.37	10,580.63
114	05/02/1995	714.25	1,278.01	150.49	139,268.88	70,693.38	10,731.12
115	05/16/1995	714.25	0.00	0.00	139,268.88	70,693.38	10,731.12
116	05/30/1995	714.25	1,276.63	151.87	139,117.01	71,970.01	10,882.99
117	06/13/1995	714.25	0.00	0.00	139,117.01	71,970.01	10,882.99
118	06/27/1995	714.25	1,275.24	153.26	138,963.75	73,245.25	11,036.25
119	07/11/1995	714.25	0.00	0.00	138,963.75	73,245.25	11,036.25
120	07/25/1995	714.25	1,273.83	154.67	138,809.08	74,519.08	11,190.92
121	08/08/1995	714.25	0.00	0.00	138,809.08	74,519.08	11,190.92
122	08/22/1995	714.25	1,272.42	156.08	138,653.00	75,791.50	11,347.00
123	09/05/1995	714.25	0.00	0.00	138,653.00	75,791.50	11,347.00
124	09/19/1995	714.25	1,270.99	157.51	138,495.49	77,062.49	11,504.51

Table 11–12 Continued

Names: MR. JOHN DIXON

PMT #	PAYMENT DATE	PAYMENT AMOUNT	INTEREST PAID	PRINCIPAL PAID	BALANCE OWED	ACCUMULATED INTEREST	ACCUMULATED PRINCIPAL
125	10/03/1995	714.25	0.00	0.00	138,495.49	77,062.49	11,504.51
126	10/17/1995	714.25	1,269.54	158.96	138,336.53	78,332.03	11,663.47
127	10/31/1995	714.25	0.00	0.00	138,336.53	78,332.03	11,663.47
128	11/14/1995	714.25	1,268.08	160.42	138,176.11	79,600.11	11,823.89
129	11/28/1995	714.25	0.00	0.00	138,176.11	79,600.11	11,823.89
130	12/12/1995	714.25	0.00	1,428.50	136,747.61	79,600.11	13,252.39
131	12/26/1995	714.25	0.00	0.00	136,747.61	79,600.11	13,252.39
132	01/09/1996	714.25	1,253.52	174.98	136,572.63	80,853.63	13,427.37
133	01/23/1996	714.25	0.00	0.00	136,572.63	80,853.63	13,427.37
134	02/06/1996	714.25	1,251.92	176.58	136,396.05	82,105.55	13,603.95
135	02/20/1996	714.25	0.00	0.00	136,396.05	82,105.55	13,603.95
136	03/05/1996	714.25	1,250.30	178.20	136,217.85	83,355.85	13,782.15
137	03/19/1996	714.25	0.00	0.00	136,217.85	83,355.85	13,782.15
138	04/02/1996	714.25	1,248.66	179.84	136,038.01	84,604.51	13,961.99
139	04/16/1996	714.25	0.00	0.00	136,038.01	84,604.51	13,961.99
140	04/30/1996	714.25	1,247.02	181.48	135,856.53	85,851.53	14,143.47
141	05/14/1996	714.25	0.00	0.00	135,856.53	85,851.53	14,143.47
142	05/28/1996	714.25	1,245.35	183.15	135,673.38	87,096.88	14,326.62
143	06/11/1996	714.25	0.00	0.00	135,673.38	87,096.88	14,326.62
144	06/25/1996	714.25	1,243.67	184.83	135,488.55	88,340.55	14,511.45
145	07/09/1996	714.25	0.00	0.00	135,488.55	88,340.55	14,511.45
146	07/23/1996	714.25	1,241.98	186.52	135,302.03	89,582.53	14,697.97
147	08/06/1996	714.25	0.00	0.00	135,302.03	89,582.53	14,697.97
148	08/20/1996	714.25	1,240.27	188.23	135,113.80	90,822.80	14,886.20
149	09/03/1996	714.25	0.00	0.00	135,113.80	90,822.80	14,886.20
150	09/17/1996	714.25	1,238.54	189.96	134,923.84	92,061.34	15,076.16
151	10/01/1996	714.25	0.00	0.00	134,923.84	92,061.34	15,076.16
152	10/15/1996	714.25	1,236.80	191.70	134,732.14	93,298.14	15,267.86
153	10/29/1996	714.25	0.00	0.00	134,732.14	93,298.14	15,267.86
154	11/12/1996	714.25	1,235.04	193.46	134,538.68	94,533.18	15,461.32
155	11/26/1996	714.25	0.00	0.00	134,538.68	94,533.18	15,461.32
156	12/10/1996	714.25	0.00	1,428.50	133,110.18	94,533.18	16,889.82
157	12/24/1996	714.25	0.00	0.00	133,110.18	94,533.18	16,889.82
158	01/07/1997	714.25	1,220.18	208.32	132,901.86	95,753.36	17,098.14
159	01/21/1997	714.25	0.00	0.00	132,901.86	95,753.36	17,098.14
160	02/04/1997	714.25	1,218.27	210.23	132,691.63	96,971.63	17,308.37
161	02/18/1997	714.25	0.00	0.00	132,691.63	96,971.63	17,308.37
162	03/04/1997	714.25	1,216.34	212.16	132,479.47	98,187.97	17,520.53
163	03/18/1997	714.25	0.00	0.00	132,479.47	98,187.97	17,520.53
164	04/01/1997	714.25	1,214.40	214.10	132,265.37	99,402.37	17,734.63
165	04/15/1997	714.25	0.00	0.00	132,265.37	99,402.37	17,734.63
166	04/29/1997	714.25	1,212.43	216.07	132,049.30	100,614.80	17,950.70
167	05/13/1997	714.25	0.00	0.00	132,049.30	100,614.80	17,950.70
168	05/27/1997	714.25	1,210.45	218.05	131,831.25	101,825.25	18,168.75
169	06/10/1997	714.25	0.00	0.00	131,831.25	101,825.25	18,168.75

Table 11–12 Continued

Names: MR. JOHN DIXON

PMT #	PAYMENT DATE	PAYMENT AMOUNT	INTEREST PAID	PRINCIPAL PAID	BALANCE OWED	ACCUMULATED INTEREST	ACCUMULATED PRINCIPAL
170	06/24/1997	714.25	1,208.45	220.05	131,611.20	103,033.70	18,388.80
171	07/08/1997	714.25	0.00	0.00	131,611.20	103,033.70	18,388.80
172	07/22/1997	714.25	1,206.44	222.06	131,389.14	104,240.14	18,610.86
173	08/05/1997	714.25	0.00	0.00	131,389.14	104,240.14	18,610.86
174	08/19/1997	714.25	1,204.40	224.10	131,165.04	105,444.54	18,834.96
175	09/02/1997	714.25	0.00	0.00	131,165.04	105,444.54	18,834.96
176	09/16/1997	714.25	1,202.35	226.15	130,938.89	106,646.89	19,061.11
177	09/30/1997	714.25	0.00	0.00	130,938.89	106,646.89	19,061.11
178	10/14/1997	714.25	1,200.27	228.23	130,710.66	107,847.16	19,289.34
179	10/28/1997	714.25	0.00	0.00	130,710.66	107,847.16	19,289.34
180	11/11/1997	714.25	1,198.18	230.32	130,480.34	109,045.34	19,519.66
181	11/25/1997	714.25	0.00	0.00	130,480.34	109,045.34	19,519.66
182	12/09/1997	714.25	0.00	1,428.50	129,051.84	109,045.34	20,948.16
183	12/23/1997	714.25	0.00	0.00	129,051.84	109,045.34	20,948.16
184	01/06/1998	714.25	1,182.98	245.52	128,806.32	110,228.32	21,193.68
185	01/20/1998	714.25	0.00	0.00	128,806.32	110,228.32	21,193.68
186	02/03/1998	714.25	1,180.72	247.78	128,558.54	111,409.04	21,441.46
187	02/17/1998	714.25	0.00	0.00	128,558.54	111,409.04	21,441.46
188	03/03/1998	714.25	1,178.45	250.05	128,308.49	112,587.49	21,691.51
189	03/17/1998	714.25	0.00	0.00	128,308.49	112,587.49	21,691.51
190	03/31/1998	714.25	1,176.16	252.34	128,056.15	113,763.65	21,943.85
191	04/14/1998	714.25	0.00	0.00	128,056.15	113,763.65	21,943.85
192	04/28/1998	714.25	1,173.85	254.65	127,801.50	114,937.50	22,198.50
193	05/12/1998	714.25	0.00	0.00	127,801.50	114,937.50	22,198.50
194	05/26/1998	714.25	1,171.51	256.99	127,544.51	116,109.01	22,455.49
195	06/09/1998	714.25	0.00	0.00	127,544.51	116,109.01	22,455.49
196	06/23/1998	714.25	1,169.16	259.34	127,285.17	117,278.17	22,714.83
197	07/07/1998	714.25	0.00	0.00	127,285.17	117,278.17	22,714.83
198	07/21/1998	714.25	1,166.78	261.72	127,023.45	118,444.95	22,976.55
199	08/04/1998	714.25	0.00	0.00	127,023.45	118,444.95	22,976.55
200	08/18/1998	714.25	1,164.38	264.12	126,759.33	119,609.33	23,240.67
201	09/01/1998	714.25	0.00	0.00	126,759.33	119,609.33	23,240.67
202	09/15/1998	714.25	1,161.96	266.54	126,492.79	120,771.29	23,507.21
203	09/29/1998	714.25	0.00	0.00	126,492.79	120,771.29	23,507.21
204	10/13/1998	714.25	1,159.52	268.98	126,223.81	121,930.81	23,776.19
205	10/27/1998	714.25	0.00	0.00	126,223.81	121,930.81	23,776.19
206	11/10/1998	714.25	1,157.05	271.45	125,952.36	123,087.86	24,047.64
207	11/24/1998	714.25	0.00	0.00	125,952.36	123,087.86	24,047.64
208	12/08/1998	714.25	0.00	1,428.50	124,523.86	123,087.86	25,476.14
209	12/22/1998	714.25	0.00	0.00	124,523.86	123,087.86	25,476.14
210	01/05/1999	714.25	1,141.47	287.03	124,236.83	124,229.33	25,763.17
211	01/19/1999	714.25	0.00	0.00	124,236.83	124,229.33	25,763.17
212	02/02/1999	714.25	1,138.84	289.66	123,947.17	125,368.17	26,052.83
213	02/16/1999	714.25	0.00	0.00	123,947.17	125,368.17	26,052.83
214	03/02/1999	714.25	1,136.18	292.32	123,654.85	126,504.35	26,345.15

Table 11–12 Continued

Names: MR. JOHN DIXON

PMT #	PAYMENT DATE	PAYMENT AMOUNT	INTEREST PAID	PRINCIPAL PAID	BALANCE OWED	ACCUMULATED INTEREST	ACCUMULATED PRINCIPAL
215	03/16/1999	714.25	0.00	0.00	123,654.85	126,504.35	26,345.15
216	03/30/1999	714.25	1,133.50	295.00	123,359.85	127,637.85	26,640.15
217	04/13/1999	714.25	0.00	0.00	123,359.85	127,637.85	26,640.15
218	04/27/1999	714.25	1,130.80	297.70	123,062.15	128,768.65	26,937.85
219	05/11/1999	714.25	0.00	0.00	123,062.15	128,768.65	26,937.85
220	05/25/1999	714.25	1,128.07	300.43	122,761.72	129,896.72	27,238.28
221	06/08/1999	714.25	0.00	0.00	122,761.72	129,896.72	27,238.28
222	06/22/1999	714.25	1,125.32	303.18	122,458.54	131,022.04	27,541.46
223	07/06/1999	714.25	0.00	0.00	122,458.54	131,022.04	27,541.46
224	07/20/1999	714.25	1,122.54	305.96	122,152.58	132,144.58	27,847.42
225	08/03/1999	714.25	0.00	0.00	122,152.58	132,144.58	27,847.42
226	08/17/1999	714.25	1,119.73	308.77	121,843.81	133,264.31	28,156.19
227	08/31/1999	714.25	0.00	0.00	121,843.81	133,264.31	28,156.19
228	09/14/1999	714.25	1,116.90	311.60	121,532.21	134,381.21	28,467.79
229	09/28/1999	714.25	0.00	0.00	121,532.21	134,381.21	28,467.79
230	10/12/1999	714.25	1,114.05	314.45	121,217.76	135,495.26	28,782.24
231	10/26/1999	714.25	0.00	0.00	121,217.76	135,495.26	28,782.24
232	11/09/1999	714.25	1,111.16	317.34	120,900.42	136,606.42	29,099.58
233	11/23/1999	714.25	0.00	0.00	120,900.42	136,606.42	29,099.58
234	12/07/1999	714.25	0.00	1,428.50	119,471.92	136,606.42	30,528.08
235	12/21/1999	714.25	0.00	0.00	119,471.92	136,606.42	30,528.08
236	01/04/2000	714.25	1,095.16	333.34	119,138.58	137,701.58	30,861.42
237	01/18/2000	714.25	0.00	0.00	119,138.58	137,701.58	30,861.42
238	02/01/2000	714.25	1,092.10	336.40	118,802.18	138,793.68	31,197.82
239	02/15/2000	714.25	0.00	0.00	118,802.18	138,793.68	31,197.82
240	02/29/2000	714.25	1,089.02	339.48	118,462.70	139,882.70	31,537.30
241	03/14/2000	714.25	0.00	0.00	118,462.70	139,882.70	31,537.30
242	03/28/2000	714.25	1,085.91	342.59	118,120.11	140,968.61	31,879.89
243	04/11/2000	714.25	0.00	0.00	118,120.11	140,968.61	31,879.89
244	04/25/2000	714.25	1,082.77	345.73	117,774.38	142,051.38	32,225.62
245	05/09/2000	714.25	0.00	0.00	117,774.38	142,051.38	32,225.62
246	05/23/2000	714.25	1,079.60	348.90	117,425.48	143,130.98	32,574.52
247	06/06/2000	714.25	0.00	0.00	117,425.48	143,130.98	32,574.52
248	06/20/2000	714.25	1,076.40	352.10	117,073.38	144,207.38	32,926.62
249	07/04/2000	714.25	0.00	0.00	117,073.38	144,207.38	32,926.62
250	07/18/2000	714.25	1,073.17	355.33	116,718.05	145,280.55	33,281.95
251	08/01/2000	714.25	0.00	0.00	116,718.05	145,280.55	33,281.95
252	08/15/2000	714.25	1,069.92	358.58	116,359.47	146,350.47	33,640.53
253	08/29/2000	714.25	0.00	0.00	116,359.47	146,350.47	33,640.53
254	09/12/2000	714.25	1,066.63	361.87	115,997.60	147,417.10	34,002.40
255	09/26/2000	714.25	0.00	0.00	115,997.60	147,417.10	34,002.40
256	10/10/2000	714.25	1,063.31	365.19	115,632.41	148,480.41	34,367.59
257	10/24/2000	714.25	0.00	0.00	115,632.41	148,480.41	34,367.59
258	11/07/2000	714.25	1,059.96	368.54	115,263.87	149,540.37	34,736.13
259	11/21/2000	714.25	0.00	0.00	115,263.87	149,540.37	34,736.13

Table 11–12 Continued

Names: MR. JOHN DIXON

PMT #	PAYMENT DATE	PAYMENT AMOUNT	INTEREST PAID	PRINCIPAL PAID	BALANCE OWED	ACCUMULATED INTEREST	ACCUMULATED PRINCIPAL
260	12/05/2000	714.25	0.00	1,428.50	113,835.37	149,540.37	36,164.63
261	12/19/2000	714.25	0.00	0.00	113,835.37	149,540.37	36,164.63
262	01/02/2001	714.25	1,043.49	385.01	113,450.36	150,583.86	36,549.64
263	01/16/2001	714.25	0.00	0.00	113,450.36	150,583.86	36,549.64
264	01/30/2001	714.25	1,039.96	388.54	113,061.82	151,623.82	36,938.18
265	02/13/2001	714.25	0.00	0.00	113,061.82	151,623.82	36,938.18
266	02/27/2001	714.25	1,036.40	392.10	112,669.72	152,660.22	37,330.28
267	03/13/2001	714.25	0.00	0.00	112,669.72	152,660.22	37,330.28
268	03/27/2001	714.25	1,032.81	395.69	112,274.03	153,693.03	37,725.97
269	04/10/2001	714.25	0.00	0.00	112,274.03	153,693.03	37,725.97
270	04/24/2001	714.25	1,029.18	399.32	111,874.71	154,722.21	38,125.29
271	05/08/2001	714.25	0.00	0.00	111,874.71	154,722.21	38,125.29
272	05/22/2001	714.25	1,025.52	402.98	111,471.73	155,747.73	38,528.27
273	06/05/2001	714.25	0.00	0.00	111,471.73	155,747.73	38,528.27
274	06/19/2001	714.25	1,021.82	406.68	111,065.05	156,769.55	38,934.95
275	07/03/2001	714.25	0.00	0.00	111,065.05	156,769.55	38,934.95
276	07/17/2001	714.25	1,018.10	410.40	110,654.65	157,787.65	39,345.35
277	07/31/2001	714.25	0.00	0.00	110,654.65	157,787.65	39,345.35
278	08/14/2001	714.25	1,014.33	414.17	110,240.48	158,801.98	39,759.52
279	08/28/2001	714.25	0.00	0.00	110,240.48	158,801.98	39,759.52
280	09/11/2001	714.25	1,010.54	417.96	109,822.52	159,812.52	40,177.48
281	09/25/2001	714.25	0.00	0.00	109,822.52	159,812.52	40,177.48
282	10/09/2001	714.25	1,006.71	421.79	109,400.73	160,819.23	40,599.27
283	10/23/2001	714.25	0.00	0.00	109,400.73	160,819.23	40,599.27
284	11/06/2001	714.25	1,002.84	425.66	108,975.07	161,822.07	41,024.93
285	11/20/2001	714.25	0.00	0.00	108,975.07	161,822.07	41,024.93
286	12/04/2001	714.25	0.00	1,428.50	107,546.57	161,822.07	42,453.43
287	12/18/2001	714.25	0.00	0.00	107,546.57	161,822.07	42,453.43
288	01/01/2002	714.25	985.84	442.66	107,103.91	162,807.91	42,896.09
289	01/15/2002	714.25	0.00	0.00	107,103.91	162,807.91	42,896.09
290	01/29/2002	714.25	981.79	446.71	106,657.20	163,789.70	43,342.80
291	02/12/2002	714.25	0.00	0.00	106,657.20	163,789.70	43,342.80
292	02/26/2002	714.25	977.69	450.81	106,206.39	164,767.39	43,793.61
293	03/12/2002	714.25	0.00	0.00	106,206.39	164,767.39	43,793.61
294	03/26/2002	714.25	973.56	454.94	105,751.45	165,740.95	44,248.55
295	04/09/2002	714.25	0.00	0.00	105,751.45	165,740.95	44,248.55
296	04/23/2002	714.25	969.39	459.11	105,292.34	166,710.34	44,707.66
297	05/07/2002	714.25	0.00	0.00	105,292.34	166,710.34	44,707.66
298	05/21/2002	714.25	965.18	463.32	104,829.02	167,675.52	45,170.98
299	06/04/2002	714.25	0.00	0.00	104,829.02	167,675.52	45,170.98
300	06/18/2002	714.25	960.93	467.57	104,361.45	168,636.45	45,638.55
301	07/02/2002	714.25	0.00	0.00	104,361.45	168,636.45	45,638.55
302	07/16/2002	714.25	956.65	471.85	103,889.60	169,593.10	46,110.40
303	07/30/2002	714.25	0.00	0.00	103,889.60	169,593.10	46,110.40
304	08/13/2002	714.25	952.32	476.18	103,413.42	170,545.42	46,586.58

Table 11–12 Continued

Names: MR. JOHN DIXON

PMT #	PAYMENT DATE	PAYMENT AMOUNT	INTEREST PAID	PRINCIPAL PAID	BALANCE OWED	ACCUMULATED INTEREST	ACCUMULATED PRINCIPAL
305	08/27/2002	714.25	0.00	0.00	103,413.42	170,545.42	46,586.58
306	09/10/2002	714.25	947.96	480.54	102,932.88	171,493.38	47,067.12
307	09/24/2002	714.25	0.00	0.00	102,932.88	171,493.38	47,067.12
308	10/08/2002	714.25	943.55	484.95	102,447.93	172,436.93	47,552.07
309	10/22/2002	714.25	0.00	0.00	102,447.93	172,436.93	47,552.07
310	11/05/2002	714.25	939.11	489.39	101,958.54	173,376.04	48,041.46
311	11/19/2002	714.25	0.00	0.00	101,958.54	173,376.04	48,041.46
312	12/03/2002	714.25	0.00	1,428.50	100,530.04	173,376.04	49,469.96
313	12/17/2002	714.25	0.00	0.00	100,530.04	173,376.04	49,469.96
314	12/31/2002	714.25	921.53	506.97	100,023.07	174,297.57	49,976.93
315	01/14/2003	714.25	0.00	0.00	100,023.07	174,297.57	49,976.93
316	01/28/2003	714.25	916.88	511.62	99,511.45	175,214.45	50,488.55
317	02/11/2003	714.25	0.00	0.00	99,511.45	175,214.45	50,488.55
318	02/25/2003	714.25	912.19	516.31	98,995.14	176,126.64	51,004.86
319	03/11/2003	714.25	0.00	0.00	98,995.14	176,126.64	51,004.86
320	03/25/2003	714.25	907.46	521.04	98,474.10	177,034.10	51,525.90
321	04/08/2003	714.25	0.00	0.00	98,474.10	177,034.10	51,525.90
322	04/22/2003	714.25	902.68	525.82	97,948.28	177,936.78	52,051.72
323	05/06/2003	714.25	0.00	0.00	97,948.28	177,936.78	52,051.72
324	05/20/2003	714.25	897.86	530.64	97,417.64	178,834.64	52,582.36
325	06/03/2003	714.25	0.00	0.00	97,417.64	178,834.64	52,582.36
326	06/17/2003	714.25	893.00	535.50	96,882.14	179,727.64	53,117.86
327	07/01/2003	714.25	0.00	0.00	96,882.14	179,727.64	53,117.86
328	07/15/2003	714.25	888.09	540.41	96,341.73	180,615.73	53,658.27
329	07/29/2003	714.25	0.00	0.00	96,341.73	180,615.73	53,658.27
330	08/12/2003	714.25	883.13	545.37	95,796.36	181,498.86	54,203.64
331	08/26/2003	714.25	0.00	0.00	95,796.36	181,498.86	54,203.64
332	09/09/2003	714.25	878.13	550.37	95,245.99	182,376.99	54,754.01
333	09/23/2003	714.25	0.00	0.00	95,245.99	182,376.99	54,754.01
334	10/07/2003	714.25	873.09	555.41	94,690.58	183,250.08	55,309.42
335	10/21/2003	714.25	0.00	0.00	94,690.58	183,250.08	55,309.42
336	11/04/2003	714.25	868.00	560.50	94,130.08	184,118.08	55,869.92
337	11/18/2003	714.25	0.00	0.00	94,130.08	184,118.08	55,869.92
338	12/02/2003	714.25	0.00	1,428.50	92,701.58	184,118.08	57,298.42
339	12/16/2003	714.25	0.00	0.00	92,701.58	184,118.08	57,298.42
340	12/30/2003	714.25	849.76	578.74	92,122.84	184,967.84	57,877.16
341	01/13/2004	714.25	0.00	0.00	92,122.84	184,967.84	57,877.16
342	01/27/2004	714.25	844.46	584.04	91,538.80	185,812.30	58,461.20
343	02/10/2004	714.25	0.00	0.00	91,538.80	185,812.30	58,461.20
344	02/24/2004	714.25	839.11	589.39	90,949.41	186,651.41	59,050.59
345	03/09/2004	714.25	0.00	0.00	90,949.41	186,651.41	59,050.59
346	03/23/2004	714.25	833.70	594.80	90,354.61	187,485.11	59,645.39
347	04/06/2004	714.25	0.00	0.00	90,354.61	187,485.11	59,645.39
348	04/20/2004	714.25	828.25	600.25	89,754.36	188,313.36	60,245.64
349	05/04/2004	714.25	0.00	0.00	89,754.36	188,313.36	60,245.64

Table 11–12 Continued

Names: MR. JOHN DIXON

PMT #	PAYMENT DATE	PAYMENT AMOUNT	INTEREST PAID	PRINCIPAL PAID	BALANCE OWED	ACCUMULATED INTEREST	ACCUMULATED PRINCIPAL
350	05/18/2004	714.25	822.75	605.75	89,148.61	189,136.11	60,851.39
351	06/01/2004	714.25	0.00	0.00	89,148.61	189,136.11	60,851.39
352	06/15/2004	714.25	817.20	611.30	88,537.31	189,953.31	61,462.69
353	06/29/2004	714.25	0.00	0.00	88,537.31	189,953.31	61,462.69
354	07/13/2004	714.25	811.59	616.91	87,920.40	190,764.90	62,079.60
355	07/27/2004	714.25	0.00	0.00	87,920.40	190,764.90	62,079.60
356	08/10/2004	714.25	805.94	622.56	87,297.84	191,570.84	62,702.16
357	08/24/2004	714.25	0.00	0.00	87,297.84	191,570.84	62,702.16
358	09/07/2004	714.25	800.23	628.27	86,669.57	192,371.07	63,330.43
359	09/21/2004	714.25	0.00	0.00	86,669.57	192,371.07	63,330.43
360	10/05/2004	714.25	794.47	634.03	86,035.54	193,165.54	63,964.46
361	10/19/2004	714.25	0.00	0.00	86,035.54	193,165.54	63,964.46
362	11/02/2004	714.25	788.66	639.84	85,395.70	193,954.20	64,604.30
363	11/16/2004	714.25	0.00	0.00	85,395.70	193,954.20	64,604.30
364	11/30/2004	714.25	0.00	1,428.50	83,967.20	193,954.20	66,032.80
365	12/14/2004	714.25	0.00	0.00	83,967.20	193,954.20	66,032.80
366	12/28/2004	714.25	769.70	658.80	83,308.40	194,723.90	66,691.60
367	01/11/2005	714.25	0.00	0.00	83,308.40	194,723.90	66,691.60
368	01/25/2005	714.25	763.66	664.84	82,643.56	195,487.56	67,356.44
369	02/08/2005	714.25	0.00	0.00	82,643.56	195,487.56	67,356.44
370	02/22/2005	714.25	757.57	670.93	81,972.63	196,245.13	68,027.37
371	03/08/2005	714.25	0.00	0.00	81,972.63	196,245.13	68,027.37
372	03/22/2005	714.25	751.42	677.08	81,295.55	196,996.55	68,704.45
373	04/05/2005	714.25	0.00	0.00	81,295.55	196,996.55	68,704.45
374	04/19/2005	714.25	745.21	683.29	80,612.26	197,741.76	69,387.74
375	05/03/2005	714.25	0.00	0.00	80,612.26	197,741.76	69,387.74
376	05/17/2005	714.25	738.95	689.55	79,922.71	198,480.71	70,077.29
377	05/31/2005	714.25	0.00	0.00	79,922.71	198,480.71	70,077.29
378	06/14/2005	714.25	732.62	695.88	79,226.83	199,213.33	70,773.17
379	06/28/2005	714.25	0.00	0.00	79,226.83	199,213.33	70,773.17
380	07/12/2005	714.25	726.25	702.25	78,524.58	199,939.58	71,475.42
381	07/26/2005	714.25	0.00	0.00	78,524.58	199,939.58	71,475.42
382	08/09/2005	714.25	719.81	708.69	77,815.89	200,659.39	72,184.11
383	08/23/2005	714.25	0.00	0.00	77,815.89	200,659.39	72,184.11
384	09/06/2005	714.25	713.31	715.19	77,100.70	201,372.70	72,899.30
385	09/20/2005	714.25	0.00	0.00	77,100.70	201,372.70	72,899.30
386	10/04/2005	714.25	706.76	721.74	76,378.96	202,079.46	73,621.04
387	10/18/2005	714.25	0.00	0.00	76,378.96	202,079.46	73,621.04
388	11/01/2005	714.25	700.14	728.36	75,650.60	202,779.60	74,349.40
389	11/15/2005	714.25	0.00	0.00	75,650.60	202,779.60	74,349.40
390	11/29/2005	714.25	0.00	1,428.50	74,222.10	202,779.60	75,777.90
391	12/13/2005	714.25	0.00	0.00	74,222.10	202,779.60	75,777.90
392	12/27/2005	714.25	680.37	748.13	73,473.97	203,459.97	76,526.03
393	01/10/2006	714.25	0.00	0.00	73,473.97	203,459.97	76,526.03
394	01/24/2006	714.25	673.51	754.99	72,718.98	204,133.48	77,281.02

Table 11–12 Continued

Names: MR. JOHN DIXON

PMT #	PAYMENT DATE	PAYMENT AMOUNT	INTEREST PAID	PRINCIPAL PAID	BALANCE OWED	ACCUMULATED INTEREST	ACCUMULATED PRINCIPAL
395	02/07/2006	714.25	0.00	0.00	72,718.98	204,133.48	77,281.02
396	02/21/2006	714.25	666.59	761.91	71,957.07	204,800.07	78,042.93
397	03/07/2006	714.25	0.00	0.00	71,957.07	204,800.07	78,042.93
398	03/21/2006	714.25	659.61	768.89	71,188.18	205,459.68	78,811.82
399	04/04/2006	714.25	0.00	0.00	71,188.18	205,459.68	78,811.82
400	04/18/2006	714.25	652.56	775.94	70,412.24	206,112.24	79,587.76
401	05/02/2006	714.25	0.00	0.00	70,412.24	206,112.24	79,587.76
402	05/16/2006	714.25	645.45	783.05	69,629.19	206,757.69	80,370.81
403	05/30/2006	714.25	0.00	0.00	69,629.19	206,757.69	80,370.81
404	06/13/2006	714.25	638.27	790.23	68,838.96	207,395.96	81,161.04
405	06/27/2006	714.25	0.00	0.00	68,838.96	207,395.96	81,161.04
406	07/11/2006	714.25	631.02	797.48	68,041.48	208,026.98	81,958.52
407	07/25/2006	714.25	0.00	0.00	68,041.48	208,026.98	81,958.52
408	08/08/2006	714.25	623.71	804.79	67,236.69	208,650.69	82,763.31
409	08/22/2006	714.25	0.00	0.00	67,236.69	208,650.69	82,763.31
410	09/05/2006	714.25	616.34	812.16	66,424.53	209,267.03	83,575.47
411	09/19/2006	714.25	0.00	0.00	66,424.53	209,267.03	83,575.47
412	10/03/2006	714.25	608.89	819.61	65,604.92	209,875.92	84,395.08
413	10/17/2006	714.25	0.00	0.00	65,604.92	209,875.92	84,395.08
414	10/31/2006	714.25	601.38	827.12	64,777.80	210,477.30	85,222.20
415	11/14/2006	714.25	0.00	0.00	64,777.80	210,477.30	85,222.20
416	11/28/2006	714.25	0.00	1,428.50	63,349.30	210,477.30	86,650.70
417	12/12/2006	714.25	0.00	0.00	63,349.30	210,477.30	86,650.70
418	12/26/2006	714.25	580.70	847.80	62,501.50	211,058.00	87,498.50
419	01/09/2007	714.25	0.00	0.00	62,501.50	211,058.00	87,498.50
420	01/23/2007	714.25	572.93	855.57	61,645.93	211,630.93	88,354.07
421	02/06/2007	714.25	0.00	0.00	61,645.93	211,630.93	88,354.07
422	02/20/2007	714.25	565.09	863.41	60,782.52	212,196.02	89,217.48
423	03/06/2007	714.25	0.00	0.00	60,782.52	212,196.02	89,217.48
424	03/20/2007	714.25	557.17	871.33	59,911.19	212,753.19	90,088.81
425	04/03/2007	714.25	0.00	0.00	59,911.19	212,753.19	90,088.81
426	04/17/2007	714.25	549.19	879.31	59,031.88	213,302.38	90,968.12
427	05/01/2007	714.25	0.00	0.00	59,031.88	213,302.38	90,968.12
428	05/15/2007	714.25	541.13	887.37	58,144.51	213,843.51	91,855.49
429	05/29/2007	714.25	0.00	0.00	58,144.51	213,843.51	91,855.49
430	06/12/2007	714.25	532.99	895.51	57,249.00	214,376.50	92,751.00
431	06/26/2007	714.25	0.00	0.00	57,249.00	214,376.50	92,751.00
432	07/10/2007	714.25	524.78	903.72	56,345.28	214,901.28	93,654.72
433	07/24/2007	714.25	0.00	0.00	56,345.28	214,901.28	93,654.72
434	08/07/2007	714.25	516.50	912.00	55,433.28	215,417.78	94,566.72
435	08/21/2007	714.25	0.00	0.00	55,433.28	215,417.78	94,566.72
436	09/04/2007	714.25	508.14	920.36	54,512.92	215,925.92	95,487.08
437	09/18/2007	714.25	0.00	0.00	54,512.92	215,925.92	95,487.08
438	10/02/2007	714.25	499.70	928.80	53,584.12	216,425.62	96,415.88
439	10/16/2007	714.25	0.00	0.00	53,584.12	216,425.62	96,415.88

Table 11–12 Continued

Names: MR. JOHN DIXON

PMT #	PAYMENT DATE	PAYMENT AMOUNT	INTEREST PAID	PRINCIPAL PAID	BALANCE OWED	ACCUMULATED INTEREST	ACCUMULATED PRINCIPAL
440	10/30/2007	714.25	491.19	937.31	52,646.81	216,916.81	97,353.19
441	11/13/2007	714.25	0.00	0.00	52,646.81	216,916.81	97,353.19
442	11/27/2007	714.25	0.00	1,428.50	51,218.31	216,916.81	98,781.69
443	12/11/2007	714.25	0.00	0.00	51,218.31	216,916.81	98,781.69
444	12/25/2007	714.25	469.50	959.00	50,259.31	217,386.31	99,740.69
445	01/08/2008	714.25	0.00	0.00	50,259.31	217,386.31	99,740.69
446	01/22/2008	714.25	460.71	967.79	49,291.52	217,847.02	100,708.48
447	02/05/2008	714.25	0.00	0.00	49,291.52	217,847.02	100,708.48
448	02/19/2008	714.25	451.84	976.66	48,314.86	218,298.86	101,685.14
449	03/04/2008	714.25	0.00	0.00	48,314.86	218,298.86	101,685.14
450	03/18/2008	714.25	442.89	985.61	47,329.25	218,741.75	102,670.75
451	04/01/2008	714.25	0.00	0.00	47,329.25	218,741.75	102,670.75
452	04/15/2008	714.25	433.85	994.65	46,334.60	219,175.60	103,665.40
453	04/29/2008	714.25	0.00	0.00	46,334.60	219,175.60	103,665.40
454	05/13/2008	714.25	424.73	1,003.77	45,330.83	219,600.33	104,669.17
455	05/27/2008	714.25	0.00	0.00	45,330.83	219,600.33	104,669.17
456	06/10/2008	714.25	415.53	1,012.97	44,317.86	220,015.86	105,682.14
457	06/24/2008	714.25	0.00	0.00	44,317.86	220,015.86	105,682.14
458	07/08/2008	714.25	406.25	1,022.25	43,295.61	220,422.11	106,704.39
459	07/22/2008	714.25	0.00	0.00	43,295.61	220,422.11	106,704.39
460	08/05/2008	714.25	396.88	1,031.62	42,263.99	220,818.99	107,736.01
461	08/19/2008	714.25	0.00	0.00	42,263.99	220,818.99	107,736.01
462	09/02/2008	714.25	387.42	1,041.08	41,222.91	221,206.41	108,777.09
463	09/16/2008	714.25	0.00	0.00	41,222.91	221,206.41	108,777.09
464	09/30/2008	714.25	377.88	1,050.62	40,172.29	221,584.29	109,827.71
465	10/14/2008	714.25	0.00	0.00	40,172.29	221,584.29	109,827.71
466	10/28/2008	714.25	368.25	1,060.25	39,112.04	221,952.54	110,887.96
467	11/11/2008	714.25	0.00	0.00	39,112 04	221,952.54	110,887.96
468	11/25/2008	714.25	0.00	1,428.50	37,683.54	221,952.54	112,316.46
469	12/09/2008	714.25	0.00	0.00	37,683.54	221,952.54	112,316.46
470	12/23/2008	714.25	345.43	1,083.07	36,600.47	222,297.97	113,399.53
471	01/06/2009	714.25	0.00	0.00	36,600.47	222,297.97	113,399.53
472	01/20/2009	714.25	335.50	1,093.00	35,507.47	222,633.47	114,492.53
473	02/03/2009	714.25	0.00	0.00	35,507.47	222,633.47	114,492.53
474	02/17/2009	714.25	325.49	1,103.01	34,404.46	222,958.96	115,595.54
475	03/03/2009	714.25	0.00	0.00	34,404.46	222,958.96	115,595.54
476	03/17/2009	714.25	315.37	1,113.13	33,291.33	223,274.33	116,708.67
477	03/31/2009	714.25	0.00	0.00	33,291.33	223,274.33	116,708.67
478	04/14/2009	714.25	305.17	1,123.33	32,168.00	223,579.50	117,832.00
479	04/28/2009	714.25	0.00	0.00	32,168.00	223,579.50	117,832.00
480	05/12/2009	714.25	294.87	1,133.63	31,034.37	223,874.37	118,965.63
481	05/26/2009	714.25	0.00	0.00	31,034.37	223,874.37	118,965.63
482	06/09/2009	714.25	284.48	1,144.02	29,890.35	224,158.85	120,109.65
483	06/23/2009	714.25	0.00	0.00	29,890.35	224,158.85	120,109.65
484	07/07/2009	714.25	273.99	1,154.51	28,735.84	224,432.84	121,264.16

Table 11–12 Continued

Names: MR. JOHN DIXON

PMT #	PAYMENT DATE	PAYMENT AMOUNT	INTEREST PAID	PRINCIPAL PAID	BALANCE OWED	ACCUMULATED INTEREST	ACCUMULATED PRINCIPAL
485	07/21/2009	714.25	0.00	0.00	28,735.84	224,432.84	121,264.16
486	08/04/2009	714.25	263.41	1,165.09	27,570.75	224,696.25	122,429.25
487	08/18/2009	714.25	0.00	0.00	27,570.75	224,696.25	122,429.25
488	09/01/2009	714.25	252.73	1,175.77	26,394.98	224,948.98	123,605.02
489	09/15/2009	714.25	0.00	0.00	26,394.98	224,948.98	123,605.02
490	09/29/2009	714.25	241.95	1,186.55	25,208.43	225,190.93	124,791.57
491	10/13/2009	714.25	0.00	0.00	25,208.43	225,190.93	124,791.57
492	10/27/2009	714.25	231.08	1,197.42	24,011.01	225,422.01	125,988.99
493	11/10/2009	714.25	0.00	0.00	24,011.01	225,422.01	125,988.99
494	11/24/2009	714.25	0.00	1,428.50	22,582.51	225,422.01	127,417.49
495	12/08/2009	714.25	0.00	0.00	22,582.51	225,422.01	127,417.49
496	12/22/2009	714.25	207.01	1,221.49	21,361.02	225,629.02	128,638.98
497	01/05/2010	714.25	0.00	0.00	21,361.02	225,629.02	128,638.98
498	01/19/2010	714.25	195.81	1,232.69	20,128.33	225,824.83	129,871.67
499	02/02/2010	714.25	0.00	0.00	20,128.33	225,824.83	129,871.67
500	02/16/2010	714.25	184.51	1,243.99	18,884.34	226,009.34	131,115.66
501	03/02/2010	714.25	0.00	0.00	18,884.34	226,009.34	131,115.66
502	03/16/2010	714.25	173.11	1,255.39	17,628.95	226,182.45	132,371.05
503	03/30/2010	714.25	0.00	0.00	17,628.95	226,182.45	132,371.05
504	04/13/2010	714.25	161.60	1,266.90	16,362.05	226,344.05	133,637.95
505	04/27/2010	714.25	0.00	0.00	16,362.05	226,344.05	133,637.95
506	05/11/2010	714.25	149.99	1,278.51	15,083.54	226,494.04	134,916.46
507	05/25/2010	714.25	0.00	0.00	15,083.54	226,494.04	134,916.46
508	06/08/2010	714.25	138.27	1,290.23	13,793.31	226,632.31	136,206.69
509	06/22/2010	714.25	0.00	0.00	13,793.31	226,632.31	136,206.69
510	07/06/2010	714.25	126.44	1,302.06	12,491.25	226,758.75	137,508.75
511	07/20/2010	714.25	0.00	0.00	12,491.25	226,758.75	137,508.75
512	08/03/2010	714.25	114.50	1,314.00	11,177.25	226,873.25	138,822.75
513	08/17/2010	714.25	0.00	0.00	11,177.25	226,873.25	138,822.75
514	08/31/2010	714.25	102.46	1,326.04	9,851.21	226,975.71	140,148.79
515	09/14/2010	714.25	0.00	0.00	9,851.21	226,975.71	140,148.79
516	09/28/2010	714.25	90.30	1,338.20	8,513.01	227,066.01	141,486.99
517	10/12/2010	714.25	0.00	0.00	8,513.01	227,066.01	141,486.99
518	10/26/2010	714.25	78.04	1,350.46	7,162.55	227,144.05	142,837.45
519	11/09/2010	714.25	0.00	0.00	7,162.55	227,144.05	142,837.45
520	11/23/2010	714.25	0.00	1,428.50	5,734.05	227,144.05	144,265.95
521	12/07/2010	714.25	0.00	0.00	5,734.05	227,144.05	144,265.95
522	12/21/2010	714.25	52.56	1,375.94	4,358.11	227,196.61	145,641.89
523	01/04/2011	714.25	0.00	0.00	4,358.11	227,196.61	145,641.89
524	01/18/2011	714.25	39.95	1,388.55	2,969.56	227,236.56	147,030.44
525	02/01/2011	714.25	0.00	0.00	2,969.56	227,236.56	147,030.44
526	02/15/2011	714.25	27.22	1,401.28	1,568.28	227,263.78	148,431.72
527	03/01/2011	714.25	0.00	0.00	1,568.28	227,263.78	148,431.72
528	03/15/2011	714.25	14.38	1,414.12	154.16	227,278.16	149,845.84
529	03/29/2011	155.57	1.41	154.16	0.00	227,279.57	150,000.00

Chapter 12

Your Key to Savings

Throughout this book, we have used our own examples to illustrate our points. If, however, you are interested in the results using your mortgage situation, you can order your own personal evaluation on your current mortgage or mortgages. We offer you a personal computerized amortization projection and summary analysis of biweekly payments and interest savings of your present mortgage or mortgages.

Upon receipt of the enclosed application form, together with your check or money order in the amount of $32.45 ($29.95 plus $2.50 for delivery and handling charges), we will send you a complete amortization schedule of payments of the "Biweekly" System of your individual mortgage. In addition, you will receive a summary analysis as to the yearly savings you can achieve on your specific mortgage, and when the earlier payoff date will occur.

We offer you a money back guarantee if we cannot show you a savings of at least $10,000 over the remaining term of your mortgage. The service fee of $29.95 plus $2.50 for delivery and handling charges will be promptly refunded in that unlikely eventuality. Order Now!

APPLICATION AND ORDER FORM

I (we) understand that unless you can show interest savings in excess of $10,000 over the remaining term of my (our) mortgage loan (or Deed of Trust), the information of which is given by me (us) below, the entire $29.95 + $2.50 (for delivery and handling charges) service fee will be refunded.

OWNER _____

     Last Name   First Name   Initial

CO-OWNER_____

     Last Name   First Name   Initial

MAILING ADDRESS (No P.O. Box, Please)

_____

Street   City   State   Zip

PROPERTY ADDRESS

_____

Street   City   State   Zip

Loan Number   Original Term

Original Amount   Original Interest Rate

Current Interest Rate (If adjustable)

Original Monthly Payment (principal & interest only)

Current Monthly Payment (principal & interest only)

Current Escrow Payment Taxes & Insurance

Current Loan Balance

Date First Payment Ever Made   Date Last Payment Made

No. of Payments Made to Date

Interest Rate Program (Fixed, Adjustable, Graduated, Other)

I (we) have enclosed a copy of my (our) latest mortgage loan (or deed of trust) statement from my (our) financial institution.

My (our) check or money order (sorry, no CODs) for $29.95 plus $2.50 for delivery and handling (Total—$32.45) is enclosed for the personalized Computerized Amortization Schedule and Summary Analysis of projected interest savings using the biweekly method of payment.

Make check or money order payable to Financial Enterprises and mail to:

Financial Enterprises
P.O. Box 2741
Boca Raton, FL 33427

Please allow 3-4 weeks for delivery.

Signature

Signature

NOTE: If you want additional amortization schedules for other properties you own, residential or commercial, use separate sheet of paper for each property and enclose $32.45 for each additional Amortization and Summary Analysis ordered.

TRUTH-IN-LENDING FORM

FEDERAL TRUTH - IN - LENDING DISCLOSURE STATEMENT
For use with Fixed-Rate, GPM, or Balloon Mortgage Loans

Date _____ 19_____ Loan No.: _____

Borrowers_____

Property
Location: _____

_____

ANNUAL PERCENTAGE RATE	FINANCE CHARGE	Amount Financed	Total Payments
The cost of your credit as a yearly rate	The dollar amount the credit will cost you	The amount of credit provided to you or on your behalf	The amount you will have paid after you have made all payments as scheduled
%	$	$	$

You have the right to receive at this time an itemization of the Amount Financed.
☐ I want an itemization   ☐ I do not want an itemization.

Your payment schedule will be:

Number of Payments	Amount of Payments	When Payments are Due
	$	
	$	
	$	
	$	
	$	
	$	
	$	

☐ Required Deposit: The annual percentage rate does not take into account your required deposit.
☐ This obligation has a demand Feature.

Insurance: Credit life insurance and credit disability insurance are not required to obtain credit, and will not be provided unless you sign and agree to pay the additional cost. No such insurance will be in force until you have completed an application, the insurance company has issued the policy, the effective date of that policy has arrived and the required premium has been paid.

Type	Premium	Term	Signature
Credit Life	$		I want to apply for credit life insurance _____ Signature
Credit Disability	$		I want to apply for credit disability insurance. _____ Signature
Credit Life and Credit Disability	$		I want to apply for credit life and disability insurance. _____ Signature

You may obtain property insurance from anyone you want that is acceptable to this institution. If you get the insurance from
_____ you will pay $ _____ for a term of _____

Security: You are giving a security interest in:

☐ the property being purchased.

☐ _____

Late Charge: If payment is _____ late, you will be charged $ _____ / _____ % of the payment.

Prepayment: If you pay off early, you

☐ may   ☐ will not   have to pay a penalty

☐ may   ☐ will not   be entitled to a refund of part of the finance charge.

Assumption: Someone buying your home

☐ cannot assume the remainder of the mortgage on the original terms.

☐ may, subject to conditions, be allowed to assume the remainder of the mortgage on the original terms.

See your contract documents for any additional information about nonpayment, default, any required repayment in full before the scheduled date, and prepayment refunds and penalties.

_____
e means an estimate

I/We hereby acknowledge receipt of this disclosure.

_____
DATE

110

TRUTH -IN-LENDING FORM

DOC. 200

■ Originating Office:

Date:
Loan:
Property:

, is the Creditor in this loan transaction. We are furnishing you this disclosure to comply with Federal Truth in Lending Regulations.

This is not an approval of, or commitment to make, the loan applied for. If an approval and commitment are made at a rate other than that disclosed on this form, a new disclosure will be furnished to you.

For us to consider approving the loan you have applied for, we need you to acknowledge that you have received this disclosure. Please sign and date the Acknowledgement on the yellow copy. Return it to us today in the enclosed envelope. Keep the white copy for your records.

Sincerely,

ANNUAL PERCENTAGE RATE The cost of your credit as a yearly rate.	FINANCE CHARGE The dollar amount the credit will cost you.	Amount Financed The amount of credit provided to you or on your behalf	Total of Payments The amount you will have paid after you have made all payments as scheduled.	Total Sale Price The total cost of your purchase on credit, including your downpayment of $
%	$	$	$	$

Attached is: ☐ Itemization of the Amount Financed. ☐ GOOD FAITH ESTIMATES OF CLOSING COSTS.

Your Payment Schedule will be:

Number of Payments	Amount of Payments	Payments Are Due Monthly Beginning	Number of Payments	Amount of Payments	Payments Are Due Monthly Beginning

VARIABLE RATE: The ANNUAL PERCENTAGE RATE of the obligation
☐ is subject to increases or decreases. For details, see the disclosure furnished to you when you made your initial inquiry about a loan.
☐ is not subject to increases or decreases.

DEMAND FEATURE: This obligation ☐ has a demand feature. ☐ has no demand feature.

LATE CHARGE: If a payment is late, you will be charged _____ % of the payment.

PREPAYMENT: If you pay off early, you
☐ may have to pay a charge ☐ will not have to pay a charge.

SECURITY: You are giving a security interest in the property being purchased or refinanced.

INSURANCE: You may obtain property insurance from anyone that is acceptable to the Association.

ASSUMPTION: Someone buying your house ☐ may, subject to conditions, be allowed to assume the remainder of the mortgage on the original terms.
☐ cannot assume the remainder of the mortgage on the original terms.

See your contract documents for any additional information about nonpayment, default, any required repayment in full before the schedule date, and prepayment charges.

ACKNOWLEDGEMENT: I acknowledge receipt of this disclosure.

_____
date

Example 1

DISCLOSURE STATEMENT—FIXED RATE MORTGAGE LOAN

_____

_____

Note: The above checked lender is hereafter referred to as "Lender." The information contained in this disclosure relates specifically to:

Property Address:_____

Purchase Price: _____ Loan Amount:_____

Application Date: _____

This disclosure contains information on Lender's fixed rate mortgage loan.

The purpose of the disclosure is to insure full understanding of the terms of the loan for which you are or may be applying. Please read the information below. It describes the differences between this type of financing and other mortgages or residential loans with which you may be familiar. This disclosure does not constitute a commitment on the part of Lender to make a loan to you.

Questions: Should you have any questions regarding this disclosure or any of the information it contains, please contact:

_____ at (____) _____

_____

General Description of Lender's Fixed Rate Mortgage

This program provides a loan in which the interest rate is fixed for the entire term of the loan. This means that your monthly payments of principal and interest will neither increase or decrease over the loan term. The security or collateral for the loan will consist of an interest in favor of Lender in the property noted above. Your failure to comply with the loan terms and fulfil your obligations under the loan may result in the entire unpaid loan amount, interest and other charges becoming immediately due and payable and possibly in the forced sale of the property. The terms and operation of this loan are explained in detail below.

1. **Loan Term**
   The maximum term of this loan is the lesser of _____ years or the remaining economic life of the property as determined by the appraisal.

2. **Interest Rate**
   Your interest rate is determined by market conditions expected to prevail at the time you close your loan. This determination may be further based upon such factors as the amount of your loan, the amount of the origination or discount fee you wish to pay and whether you intend to occupy the mortgaged property. For example, if your loan were for $100,000, you intended to occupy the property and were closing today, your initial rate would be _____ if you paid _____ percent of the loan as an origination or discount fee. Your interest rate will be disclosed to you at the time you are given a loan commitment by Lender.

3. **Monthly Payment Amount and Repayment Explanation**
   Your monthly payment will be set at an amount which will fully repay the loan over its term. Your payments will consist of interest, principal and escrow charges (escrow charges are described in paragraph 8 below). All payments are applied first to any late charges, then to escrow charges, if any, then to interest and, lastly, to principal. The following example demonstrates how Lender would establish a payment schedule for your loan, how your monthly payment is determined and what portion of the payment is credited to interest and to principal:

   In this example, the loan amount is $100,000 with a term of 25 years and an interest rate of ten percent per year. Monthly payments of principal and interest would be $908.70, which is the amount required to reduce the original loan amount to zero at the end of 25 years. The interest portion of the payment would be calculated by multiplying the loan amount ($100,000) by the interest rate (10%) and dividing the result by 12 to get an interest figure in the first month of $833.33. Subtracting the interest ($833.33) from the payment ($908.70) leaves $75.37, or the amount the outstanding loan amount is reduced in the first month of the loan. Using the new loan balance ($99,924.63) and repeating the steps above will produce an interest figure of $832.71, a principal figure of $75.99 and a new balance of $99,848.64 after the second month of the loan. Continued repetition of these steps will result in the full repayment of the loan by the end of the term.

Please note that your interest rate, term, loan amount and monthly payment may be different from those in this example and will be disclosed to you in your commitment letter and in the loan documents.

4. **Late Charges**

If Lender does not receive your full monthly payment within 15 days after the date it is due, you will be charged a late charge equal to ___ percent (___%) of your overdue payment of principal and interest. This charge will be imposed only once on any late payment.

5. **Prepayments**

You may prepay this loan in whole or in part without penalty at any time during the loan term. All partial prepayments will be used to reduce the unpaid loan balance and will not allow you to delay or skip any monthly payments.

6. **Loan Obligations and Lender's Rights**

The loan documents contain provisions which may result in the loan becoming immediately due and payable. If you fail or are unable to immediately repay the loan amount and all loan charges, the forced sale of the property may result.

Lender may require immediate payment in full if a change in a law makes any provision of the loan documents unenforceable. In addition, your failure to comply with all of your obligations and responsibilities under the loan may result in Lender's requiring immediate payment. Some of the most important obligations which may be included in the loan documents are as follows: 1) making payments for all loan charges including not only monthly payments, but escrow charges and payments resulting from

Lender's need to protect its security in the property; 2) paying all taxes, assessments, fines and liens imposed on the property not paid by escrow charges; 3) obtaining Lender's prior written permission to sell or transfer any interest in the property; 4) obtaining adequate hazard insurance; and, 5) keeping the property in good repair and complying with all laws, ordinances and governmental regulations. Details regarding these and other obligations are set forth in the loan documents.

7. **Assumption and Transfer of Property**

The documents for this loan contain a "Due on Sale" clause which provides that if all or part of the property securing the loan is sold or transferred without Lender's prior written consent, Lender may, at its option, require immediate payment in full of the loan balance and all other monies due under the loan. If Lender chooses to allow an assumption or transfer it may condition its consent upon the party assuming the loan agreeing to changes in the loan terms, including the interest rate.

Please note that even where Lender consents to an assumption, the original borrower may remain obligated under the loan documents unless expressly released in writing by Lender.

8. **Escrow Charges**

Except where prohibited by applicable law, the loan documents will require you to make payments into an escrow account to be applied toward the payment of taxes, assessments, insurance premiums and ground rents, if any. The purpose of this account is to assure the existence of funds to pay such items, the non-payment of which might endanger your interest in the property and Lender's security interest. The use of the escrow account spreads the collection of funds for these items evenly throughout the year rather than requiring a number of large annual payments.

The monthly escrow payments will equal 1/12th of the total yearly taxes and assessments on the property, 1/12th of ground rents on the property, if any, 1/12th of the total yearly premium for hazard insurance and 1/12th of the total yearly premiums for flood and mortgage insurance, if any.

If you do not make your escrow payments as scheduled or if the monies in the escrow account are insufficient, Lender will advance such funds on your behalf and will separately bill you for these advances. Your continued failure to pay such funds may result in Lender demanding immediate payment of the outstanding loan amount, any interest and all other unpaid charges. Your failure to pay all amounts due under your loan when required could result in the forced sale of the property.

9. **Loan Documents**

The exact terms of the loan and the rights of the borrower and of Lender are contained in a note and a security instrument (which may be called a mortgage, deed of trust or security deed). The borrower and Lender become bound to the terms of the loan upon signing these documents. Although either party may subsequently request modification of the loan terms, neither party is required to agree to such a request. As a borrower, you should understand and become familiar with the provisions of the note and security instrument. Copies of these documents are available to you upon request.

Acknowledgments

I have read the contents of this disclosure and I acknowledge receipt of a fully completed copy of this disclosure.

_____ DATE _____
Borrower

_____ DATE _____
Co-Borrower

_____ DATE _____
Signature of Lender Employee

Example 2

DISCLOSURE STATEMENT

ONE-YEAR ADJUSTABLE RATE MORTGAGE LOAN

_____

_____

Lender is: _____

The information contained in this disclosure relates specifically to:

Property Address: _____

Purchase Price:_____ Loan Amount:_____

Application Date:_____

This disclosure contains information on one of Lender's adjustable rate mortgage ("ARM") loans.

The purpose of the disclosure is to insure full understanding of the terms of the loan for which you are or may be applying. Please read the information below. It describes the differences between this type of financing and other mortgages or residential loans with which you may be familiar. This disclosure does not constitute a commitment on the part of Lender to make a loan to you.

Questions: Should you have any questions regarding this disclosure or any of the information it contains, please contact:

_____ at (____)_____

General Description of Lender's One-Year ARM Loan

This program provides an ARM loan with an interest rate which may change every year, but which limits the yearly and cumulative changes in the interest rate. Interest changes are computed using an index. The monthly payment due under the loan will increase and decrease as the interest rate increases and decreases. The index reflects market and economic conditions and thus its changes and the corresponding changes in your interest rate and your monthly payments may not be predicted in advance. The terms and operation of this loan are explained in greater detail below.

1. **Loan Term**
   The maximum term of an ARM loan under this program is the lesser of 30 years or the remaining economic life of the property. The minimum term is ten years. Within these guidelines you may select the term.

2. **Initial Interest Rate and Monthly Payment Amount**
   Your initial interest rate is determined by market conditions expected to prevail at the time you close your loan. This determination may be further based upon such factors as the amount of your loan, the amount of the origination or discount fee you wish to pay and whether you intend to occupy the mortgaged property. For example, if your loan were for $100,000, and you intended to occupy the property and were closing today, your initial rate would be _____ percent if you paid _____ percent of the loan amount as an origination and/or discount fee. Your initial interest rate will be disclosed to you at the time you are given a loan commitment by the Lender.

   Your initial monthly payment will be set at an amount which will fully repay the loan at the initial interest rate over the term of the loan. Your payments will consist of interest, principal and escrow charges (escrow charges are described in Paragraph 13 below). All payments are applied first to late charges, (if any) then to escrow charges, if any, then to interest and, lastly, to principal. The interest rate and monthly payment amount will change according to the rules set forth below.

3. **Index for Determining Interest Rate Changes**
   Interest rate changes in ARM loan are based upon calculations which use an "index." The index used for this ARM loan is the

weekly average yield of United States Treasury securities adjusted to a constant maturity of one year. Information on this index is published weekly in the Federal Reserve Board's Statistical Release H.15 (519) is published monthly in the Federal Reserve Bulletin. If this index is no longer available, Lender will use an alternative index which is based on information Lender believes to be comparable.

4. **Frequency of Interest Rate Changes (Caps)**
   The interest rate for this ARM loan can be adjusted up or down every twelve months. The first potential interest rate changes will occur on the first day of every twelfth month thereafter. These dates are known as Interest Rate Change Dates. The exact date of the first change date for your loan will be determined when you fix or "lock in" your loan terms and will be disclosed in your loan documents.

5. **Calculation of Interest Rate Changes**
   Approximately 45 days before each Interest Rate Change Date, your interest rate will be reviewed. The interest rate for the next twelve months will be determined by adding a fixed percent, known as the margin, to the then current index and rounding the sum to the nearest one-eighth of one percent (0.125%). The current margin for this type of ARM loan is _____ percent. The margin for your loan will be determined when you fix or "lock in" your loan terms and will be disclosed in your loan documents.

6. **Limits on Interest Rate Changes (Caps)**
   The interest rate set on the first and on following Interest Rate Change Dates shall never be increased or decreased by more than one percentage point (1.0%) from the interest rate in effect for the month preceding the Change Date. In addition, the interest rate may never increase more than the maximum interest rate. The current maximum interest rate for this type of ARM loan is _____ percent. The maximum interest rate for your loan will be determined when you fix or "lock in" your loan terms and will be disclosed in your loan documents.

7. **Frequency and Calculation of Payment Changes**
   Changes in your interest rate will be reflected in your monthly payment. Changes will become effective for the payment due on the first of the month following the Interest Rate Change Date.

The date is called the Payment Change Date. For example, if the Interest Rate Change Date was the first day of July, the Payment Change Date would be the first day of August. Subsequent payment changes would occur on the first day of every twelfth month thereafter.

The new monthly payment will be calculated by computing the payment necessary to pay off the remaining loan balance at the new interest rate. Monthly escrow charges (if any), will be added to this amount to arrive at the new full monthly payment.

Please note that your monthly payment could change more frequently if there is an increase in taxes, insurance premiums or other assessments paid from the escrow account, as discussed in paragraph 13 below.

8. **Notice of Interest Rate and Payment Changes**
    Lender will send you written notice of interest rate and payment changes at least 30 days before the changes become effective. This notice will be mailed to the most current mailing address supplied by you and will contain the following information and any other information required by law:

    a) The scheduled date of interest rate and payment changes

    b) The amount of your new payment

    c) The new interest rate

    d) The index on which the new interest rate is based

    e) The outstanding balance of your loan on the Interest Rate Change Date (assuming timely receipt of the payments due by that date)

    f) The date of the next Interest Rate and Payment Change Dates

    g) The name and telephone number of a representative of Lender who can answer questions about the notice.

    The notice will also be sent prior to Change Dates even when no changes will occur in the monthly payment.

9. **Late Charges**
    If Lender does not receive your full monthly payment within 15 days after the date it is due, you will be charged a late charge equal to _____ percent of your overdue payment of principal and

interest. This charge will be imposed only once on any late payment.

10. **Prepayments**

You may prepay this ARM loan in whole or in part without penalty at any time during the loan term. All partial prepayments will be used to reduce the unpaid loan balance and will not allow you to delay or skip any monthly payments.

11. **Loan Obligations and Lender's Rights**

The loan documents contain provisions which may result in the loan becoming immediately due and payable. If you fail or are unable to immediately repay the loan amount and all loan charges, the forced sale of the property may result. Lender may require immediate payment in full if a change in a law makes any provision of the loan documents unenforceable. In addition, your failure to comply with all of your obligations and responsibilities under the loan may result in Lender's requiring immediate payment. Some of the most important obligations which may be included in the loan documents are as follows: 1) making payments for all loan charges including not only monthly payments but escrow charges and payments resulting from Lender's need to protect its security in the property; 2) paying all taxes, assessments, fines and liens imposed on the property not paid by escrow charges; 3) obtaining Lender's prior written permission to sell or transfer any interest in the property; 4) obtaining adequate hazard insurance; and, 5) keeping the property in good repair and complying with all laws, ordinances and governmental regulations. Details regarding these and other obligations are set forth in the loan documents.

12. **Assumption and Transfer of Property**

The documents for this loan contain a "Due on Sale" clause which provides that if all or part of the property securing the loan is sold or transferred without Lender's prior written consent, Lender may require immediate payment in full of the principal balance and all other monies due under the loan.

To obtain Lender's consent to a transfer of the property and the assumption of the loan, you must submit to Lender information regarding the person(s) who will assume the loan. If Lender determines that such person(s) are qualified to assume the loan's obligation and that Lender's security interest will not be impaired by the transfer and assumption, Lender must allow the assumption without changes in the loan terms. Lender may further condition its consent upon the payment of an assumption fee and the signing of an assumption agreement.

Please note that even where Lender consents to an assumption, the original borrower may remain obligated under the loan documents unless expressly released in writing by Lender.

13. Escrow Charges

Except where prohibited by applicable law, the loan documents will require you to make payments into an escrow account to be applied toward the payment of taxes, assessments, insurance premiums and ground rents, if any. The purpose of this account is to assure the existence of funds to pay such items, the non-payment of which might endanger your interest in the property and Lender's security interest. The use of the escrow account spreads the collection of funds for these items evenly throughout the year rather than requiring a number of large annual payments. The monthly escrow payments will equal 1/12th of the total yearly taxes and assessments on the property, 1/12th of ground rents on the property, if any, 1/12th of the total yearly premium for hazard insurance and 1/12th of the total yearly premiums for flood and mortgage insurance, if any.

If you do not make your escrow payments as scheduled or if the monies in the escrow account are insufficient, Lender will advance such funds on your behalf and will separately bill you for these advances. Your continued failure to pay such funds may result in Lender demanding immediate payment of the unpaid loan amount, interest and all other unpaid charges. Your failure to pay all amounts due under your loan when required could result in the forced sale of the property.

14. Hypothetical Transaction

Assume the following transaction:

Loan Amount: $100,000	Margin: 2.625%
Initial Interest Rate: 7.375%	1st Interest Rate Change Date: May 1, 1991
Initial Payment: $690.67	Index in Effect on First Change Date: 7.00%
Closing Date: March 15, 1990	

The initial monthly payment noted above and other monthly payment figures used below are for principal and interest only. Escrow charges could be added to such payment to arrive at the full monthly payment obligation.

On the first Interest Rate Change Date (May 1, 1991, the margin (2.625%) would be added to the then current index (7.00%). The sum would be 9.625 percent. This would not be the new interest rate as it would create an interest increase of more than one percent from the interest rate in effect prior to the Interest Rate Change Date (7.375%). The limits on interest rate changes set forth in paragraph 6 above would result in the new interest rate being 8.375 percent. The new monthly payment would be $758.66. This payment would be due June 1, 1991, and would be in effect until the next Payment Change Date.

The interest rate and monthly payment would continue to be computed each year using the then current indexes and the margin of 2.625 percent. The interest rate would never change more than one percent on any one change date and could ever be greater than the maximum interest rate described in paragraph 6 above. There is no minimum interest rate. Monthly payments would adjust each year taking into consideration the new interest rates and the then outstanding loan balance. The payments would always be set at a level which would provide for the full repayment of the loan within the loan term. Please note, your initial interest rate, first Interest Change Date, margin and maximum interest rate may be different than those noted above and, thus, the changes in the interest rate on your loan may be different.

Please also note that the value of the Index as of _____ _____ is _____ percent. The round sum of this Index and the current margin noted above is _____ percent. If this sum is greater than your initial interest rate and if the Index is higher or unchanged at the time of your first Interest Rate Change Date, then your interest rate (and your monthly payments) will increase on and after the first Interest Rate Change Date.

15. Loan Documents

The exact terms of the loan and the rights of the borrower and of Lender are contained in a note and a security instrument (which may be called a mortgage, deed of trust or security deed). The borrower and Lender become bound to the terms of the loan upon the signing of these documents. Although either party may subsequently request modification of the loan terms, neither party is required to agree to such a request. As a borrower, you should understand and become familiar with the provisions of the note and security instrument. Copies of these documents are available to you upon request.

Acknowledgments

I have read the contents of this disclosure and I acknowledge receipt of a fully completed copy of this disclosure. I also acknowledge that I have received a copy of the Federal Home Loan Bank Board's "Consumer Handbook on Adjustable Rate Mortgages."

_____ DATE _____
Borrower

_____ DATE _____
Co-Borrower

_____ DATE _____
Signature of Lender Employee

Example 3

DISCLOSURE STATEMENT

**THREE-YEAR ADJUSTABLE RATE
MORTGAGE LOAN WITH FIXED RATE CONVERSION OPTION**

_____

_____

Lender is: _____

The information contained in this disclosure relates specifically to:

Property Address: _____

Purchase Price: _____   Loan Amount:_____

Application Date: _____

This disclosure contains information on one of Lender's adjustable rate mortgage ("ARM") loans.

The purpose of the disclosure is to insure full understanding of the terms of the loan for which you are or may be applying. Please read the information below. It describes the differences between this type of financing and other mortgages or residential loans with which you may be familiar. This disclosure does not constitute a commitment on the part of Lender to make a loan to you.

Questions: Should you have any questions regarding this disclosure or any of the information it contains, please contact:

_____ at (____)_____

_____

General Description of Lender's Three-Year ARM Loan

This program provides an ARM loan with an interest rate which may change every three years but which limits the changes in the interest rate. Interest changes are computed using an index. The monthly payment due under the loan will increase and decrease as the interest rate increases and decreases. The index reflects market and economic conditions and thus, its changes and the corresponding changes in your interest rate and your monthly payments may not be predicted in advance. This program also includes an option to convert the loan to a fixed rate loan. The terms and operation of this loan are explained in greater detail below.

1. **Loan Term**
    The minimum term of an ARM loan under this program is 15 years. The maximum term is the lesser of 30 years or the maximum economic life of the property as determined by the appraisal. Within these guidelines you may select the term.

2. **Initial Interest Rate and Monthly Payment Amount**
    Your initial interest rate is determined by market conditions expected to prevail at the time you close your loan. This determination may be further based upon such factors as the amount of your loan and the amount of the origination or discount fee you wish to pay. For example, if your loan were for $100,000 and you were closing today, your initial rate would be ____ percent if you paid ____ percent of the loan amount as an origination and/or discount fee. Your initial interest rate will be disclosed to you at the time you are given a loan commitment by Lender.

    Your initial monthly payment will be set at an amount which will fully repay the loan at the initial interest rate over the term of the loan. Your payments will consist of interest, principal and escrow charges (escrow charges are described in paragraph 14 below). All payments are applied first to late charges (if any), then to escrow charges, then to interest and, lastly, to principal.

    The interest rate and monthly payment amount will change according to the rules set forth below.

3. **Index for Determining Interest Rate Changes**
    Interest rate changes in ARM loans are based upon calculations which use an "index." The index used for this ARM loan is the weekly average yield of United States Treasury securities adjusted to a constant maturity of three years. Information on this

index is published weekly in the Federal Reserve Board's Statistical Release H.15 (519) and is published monthly in the Federal Reserve Bulletin. If this index is no longer available, Lender will use an alternative index which is based on information Lender believes to be comparable.

4. **Frequency of Interest Rate Changes**
   The interest rate for this ARM loan can be adjusted up or down every three years or 36 months. The first potential interest rate change for your loan will occur on the first day of the thirty-sixth or thirty-seventh month of your loan term. For example, if your loan closed in December and your first payment was on February 1st, the first change would occur on January 1st of the third following year. Subsequent interest rate changes will occur on the same date every 36 months thereafter. These dates are known as the Interest Rate Change Dates. The exact date of the first change date will be disclosed in your loan documents.

5. **Calculation of Interest Rate Changes**
   Approximately 45 days before each Interest Rate Change Date, your interest rate will be reviewed. The interest rate for the next three years or 36 months will be determined by adding a fixed percent, known as the margin, to the then current index and rounding the sum to the nearest one eighth of one percent (0.125%). The margin for this type of ARM loan is two and three-quarters percent (2.75%).

6. **Limits on Interest Rate Changes (Caps)**
   The interest rate set on the first and on following Interest Rate Change Dates shall never be increased or decreased by more than two percentage points (2.0%) from the interest rate in effect for the month preceding the Change Date. In addition, the interest rate may never decrease lower than the initial interest rate and may never increase more than six percentage points (6.0%) over the initial interest rate.

7. **Frequency and Calculation of Payment Changes**
   Changes in your interest rate will be reflected in your monthly payment. Changes will become effective for the payment due on the first of the month following the Interest Rate Change Date. The date is called the Payment Change Date. For example, if the Interest Rate Change Date was the first day of February, the Payment Change Date would change on the first day of March. Sub-

sequent payment changes would occur on the first day of every thirty-sixth month thereafter.

The new monthly payment will be calculated by computing the payment necessary to pay off the remaining loan balance at the new interest rate. Monthly escrow charges will be added to this amount to arrive at the new full monthly payment.

Please note that your monthly payment could change more frequently if there is an increase in taxes, insurance premiums or other assessments paid from the escrow account, as discussed in paragraph 14 below.

8. **Option to Convert Loan to Fixed Interest Rate Loan**
On the first and second Interest Rate Change Dates you may exercise an option to convert your adjustable rate loan to a loan with a fixed interest rate. These Change Dates are also known as the Conversion Dates and are the only dates upon which this option can be exercised.

If you choose to exercise the option, you must give Lender notice of your intention to exercise the option at least 15 days before the Conversion Date. Your loan must not be in default and you must sign any documents which Lender requires. You must also pay Lender a conversion fee equal to $100 plus one percent (1%) of the unpaid loan amount.

If you convert your loan to a fixed interest rate as set forth in this paragraph, the new fixed interest rate will be equal to the Federal National Mortgage Association's required net yield for: (a) 15-year fixed rate mortgages covered by 30-day mandatory delivery commitments in effect 45 days before the Conversion Date plus five-eighths of one percent (0.625%), if the original term is 15 years; or (b) 30-year fixed rate mortgages covered by 30-day mandatory delivery comitments; in effect, 45 days before the conversion date plus five-eighths of one percent (0.625%), if the original term is greater than 15 years. If FNMA's net yield figures are not available, Lender may determine your interest rate by using a comparable figure.

Your new monthly payment will be calculated by determining the monthly payment sufficient at your new fixed interest rate to pay back the unpaid loan amount in substantially equal monthly payments over the remainder of the loan term. The new monthly payment will be effective with the first monthly payment due after the Conversion Date and will continue until the loan is paid in full.

9. **Notice of Interest Rate and Payment Changes**

Lender will send you written notice of interest rate and payment changes at least 30 days before the changes become effective. This notice will be mailed to the most current mailing address supplied by you and will contain the following information and any other information required by law:

a) The scheduled date of rate and payment changes.

b) The amount of your new payment.

c) The new interest rate.

d) The index on which the new interest rate is based.

e) The outstanding balance of your loan on the Interest Rate Change Date (assuming timely receipt of the payments due by that date).

f) The date of the next Interest Rate and Payment Change Dates.

g) The name and telephone number of a Lender representative who can answer questions about the notice.

The notice will also be sent prior to Change Dates even when no changes will occur in the monthly payment.

Lender will also send you a notice containing the following information at least 30 days prior to the Conversion Dates described in paragraph 8 above:

a) The interest rate which you would pay if you convert to a fixed interest rate loan.

b) The amount of the new monthly payment if you choose to convert to a fixed interest rate loan.

c) The date by which you must execute and deliver to the Lender all required documents relating to the modification of the loan to a fixed interest rate.

d) The current interest rate under the loan document should you decide to retain your adjustable rate loan and not exercise your option to convert.

10. **Late Charges**

If Lender does not receive your full monthly payment within 15 days after the date it is due, you will be charged a late charge equal to _____ percent of your overdue payment of principal and interest. This charge will be imposed only once on any late payment.

11. Prepayments

You may prepay this ARM loan in whole or in part without penalty at any time during the loan term. All partial prepayments will be used to reduce the unpaid loan balance and will not allow you to delay or skip any monthly payments.

12. Loan Obligations and Lender's Rights

The loan documents contain provisions which may result in the loan becoming immediately due and payable. If you fail or are unable to immediately repay the loan amount and all loan charges, the forced sale of the property may result.

Lender may require immediate payment in full if a change in a law makes any provision of the loan documents unenforceable. In addition, your failure to comply with all of your obligations and responsibilities under the loan may result in Lender's requiring immediate payment. Some of the most important obligations which may be included in the loan documents are as follows: 1) making payments for all loan charges including not only monthly payments, but escrow charges and payments resulting from Lender's need to protect its security in the property; 2) paying all taxes, assessments, fines and liens imposed on the property not paid by escrow charges; 3) obtaining Lender's prior written permission to sell or transfer any interest in the property; 4) obtaining adequate hazard insurance; and, 5) keeping the property in good repair and complying with all laws, ordinances and governmental regulations. Details regarding these and other obligations are set forth in the loan documents.

13. Assumption and Transfer of Property

The documents for this loan contain a "Due on Sale" clause which provides that if all or part of the property securing the loan is sold or transferred without Lender's prior written consent, Lender may require immediate payment in full of the principal balance and all other monies due under the loan. To obtain Lender's consent to a transfer of the property and the assumption of the loan, you must submit to Lender information regarding the person(s) who will assume the loan. If Lender determines that such person(s) are qualified to assume the loan's obligation and that Lender's security interest will not be impaired by the transfer and assumption, Lender must allow the assumption without changes in the loan terms. Lender may further condition its consent upon the payment of an assumption fee and the signing of an assumption agreement.

If you exercise your option to convert your ARM loan to a fixed interest rate loan (as set forth in paragraph 8 above), the "Due on Sale" provisions of the loan documents will be modified so that Lender need not allow any assumptions but may at its option, require payment in full upon the sale or transfer of the property.

Please note that even where Lender consents to an assumption, the original borrower may remain obligated under the loan documents unless expressly released in writing by Lender.

14. Escrow Charges

Except where prohibited by applicable law, the loan documents will require you to make payments into an escrow account to be applied toward the payment of taxes, assessments, insurance premiums and ground rents, if any. The purpose of this account is to assure the existence of funds to pay such items, the non-payment of which might endanger your interest in the property and Lender's security interest. The use of the escrow account spreads the collection of funds for these items evenly throughout the year rather than requiring a number of large annual payments. The monthly escrow payments will equal 1/12th of the total yearly taxes and assessments on the property, 1/12th of ground rents on the property, if any, 1/12th of the total yearly premium for hazard insurance and 1/12th of the total yearly premiums for flood and mortgage insurance, if any.

If you do not make your escrow payments as scheduled or if the monies in the escrow account are insufficient, Lender will advance such funds on your behalf and will separately bill you for these advances. Your continued failure to pay such funds may result in Lender demanding immediate payment of the unpaid loan amount, interest and all other unpaid charges. Your failure to pay all amounts due under your loan when required could result in the forced sale of the property.

15. Hypothetical Transaction

Assume the following transaction:

Loan Amount:	$100,000	Margin:	2.75%
Initial Interest Rate:	8.50%	First Interest Rate Change Date:	1/1/94

Initial Payment:	$76,91	Index in Effect on 1st Change Date:	8.125%
Closing Date:	12/15/90	Term:	30 Years

The initial monthly payment noted above and other monthly payment figures used below are for principal and interest only. Escrow charges would be added to such payment to arrive at the full monthly payment obligation.

On the first Interest Rate Change Date (January 1, 1994) the margin (2.75 percent) would be added to the then current index (8.125 percent). The sum would be 10.875 percent. This would not be the new interest rate as it would create an interest increase of more than 2.0 percent from the interest rate in effect prior to the Interest Rate Change Date (8.50 percent). The limits on interest rate changes set forth in paragraph 6 above would result in the new interest rate being 10.50 percent. The new monthly payment would be $907.29. This payment would be due February 1, 1994, and would be in effect until the next Payment Change Date.

The interest rate and monthly payment would continue to be computed at each Change Date (every three years) using the then current indexes and the margin of 2.75 percent. The interest rate would never change more than 2.0 percent on any one change date and could never be less than the initial interest rate or more than six percentage points over the initial interest rate. In this example, the minimum interest rate would, therefore, be 8.50 percent, and the maximum interest rate 14.50 percent. Monthly payments would adjust each third year taking into consideration the new interest rates and the then outstanding loan balance. The payments would always be set at a level which would provide for the full repayment of the loan within the loan term.

In this example, the Conversion Dates would be January 1, 1994 and January 1, 1997. You would be given an opportunity (as set forth in paragraph 8 above) to convert your ARM loan to a fixed rate loan on each of such dates and only on such dates. If FNMA's required Net Yield on the first conversion date was 10.50 percent, the offered fixed interest rate would be 1.125 perceent (10.50% + 0.625%). In this example, you would be required to pay a fee of $1,075.26 (one percent of the unpaid loan amount plus $100). Given an unpaid loan amount of $97,525.89 and a remaining term of 324 months, your new monthly payment would be $952.03. This payment would not change, but would continue to be your payment until the loan was fully paid.

Please note, your initial interest, margin and closing date may be different than those noted above and thus, the changes in your interest rate, the maximum and minimum interest rate, the Change Dates and Conversion Dates and fixed interest rate upon conversion for your loan may be different.

Please also note that the value of the Index as of _____ _____ is _____ percent. The round sum of this Index and the margin noted above is _____ percent. If this sum is greater than your initial interest rate and if the Index is higher or unchanged at the time of your first Interest Rate Change Date, then your interest rate (and your monthly payments) will increase on and after the first Interest Rate Change Date.

16. Loan Documents

The exact terms of the loan and the rights of the borrower and of Lender are contained in a note and a security instrument (which may be called a mortgage, deed of trust or security deed). The borrower and Lender become bound to the terms of the loan upon signing these documents. Although either party may subsequently request modification of the loan terms, neither party is required to agree to such a request. As a borrower, you should understand and become familiar with the provisions of the note and security instrument. Copies of these documents are available to you upon request.

Acknowledgments

I have read the contents of this disclosure and I acknowledge receipt of a fully complete copy of this disclosure. I also acknowledge that I have received a copy of the Federal Home Loan Bank Board's "Consumer Handbook on Adjustable Rate Mortgages."

_____ DATE _____
Borrower

_____ DATE _____
Co-Borrower

_____ DATE _____
Signature of Lender Employee

Example 4

DISCLOSURE STATEMENT—ONE-YEAR ADJUSTABLE RATE MORTGAGE LOAN (WITH INITIAL FIVE-YEAR FIXED RATE PERIOD AND FIXED RATE CONVERSION OPTION)

Lender is: _____

The information contained in this disclosure relates specifically to:

Property Address: _____

Purchase Price:_____ Loan Amount: _____

Disclosure Issue Date:_____

This disclosure contains information on one of Lender's adjustable rate mortgage ("ARM") loans.

The purpose of the disclosure is to insure full understanding of the terms of the loan for which you are or may be applying. Please read the information below. It describes the differences between this type of financing and other mortgages or residential loans with which you may be familiar. This disclosure does not constitute a commitment on the part of Lender to make a loan to you.

Questions: Should you have any questions regarding this disclosure or any of the information it contains, please contact:

_____ at (____) _____

General Description of Lender's One-Year ARM Loan

This program provides an ARM loan with an interest rate which may change every year after the first five (5) years but which limits the cumulative changes in the interest rate. Interest changes are computed using an index. The monthly payment due under the loan will increase and decrease as the interest rate increases and decreases. The index reflects market and economic conditions, and thus, its changes and the corresponding changes in your interest rate and your monthly payments may not be predicted in advance. The security for this loan will be a first lien or mortgage on your property, which property must be an owner occupied single family residential dwelling. Investment properties are not acceptable security. This program also includes an option to convert the loan to a fixed rate loan. The terms and operation of this loan are explained in greater detail below.

1. **Loan Term**

   The maximum term of an ARM loan under this program is the lesser of 30 years or the remaining economic life of the property as determined by the appraisal of the property. The minimum term is 10 years. Within these guidelines you may select the term.

2. **Initial Interest Rate**

   Your initial interest rate is determined by market conditions expected to prevail at the time you close your loan. This determination may be further based upon such factors as the amount of your loan and the amount of the origination or discount fee you wish to pay. For example, if your loan were for $100,000, and you were closing today, your initial interest rate would be _____ percent if you paid _____ percent of the loan amount as an origination and/or discount fee. Your initial interest rate will ordinarily be disclosed to you at the time you are given a loan commitment by Lender. You may have the option, however, to set or "lock" your interest rate (and origination or discount fees) for a set number of days at any time during the application process or pre-closing period. Your loan must be closed within the period set by the commitment or within the period set when you "lock" your interest rate. If your loan does not close within this period, your interest rate and origination or discount fees may change and your loan may be subject to re-underwriting. Upon closing, the initial interest rate will remain in effect until the first Interest Rate Change Date, as described more fully below.

3. **Initial Monthly Payment Amount**
Your initial monthly payment will be set at an amount which will fully repay the loan at the initial interest rate over the term of the loan. Your payments will consist of interest, principal and escrow charges (escrow charges are described in paragraph 15 below). All payments are applied first to escrow charges (if any), then to interest and, lastly, to principal. The principal and interest portion of your initial monthly payment will be disclosed to you in your commitment letter. Continuing the example above, if your loan was for $100,000 and the initial interest rate was 9.73 percent, your initial monthly payment of principal and interest would be $857.68. Of this amount, $810.83 would be applied to interest and the remainder, or $46.85 to principal. The proportion of the payment applied to interest and principal would change each month as the principal was repaid. The initial monthly payment would remain in effect until the first month after the first Interest Rate Change Date, as described more fully below.

4. **Index for Determining Interest Rate Changes**
Interest rate changes in ARM loans are based upon calculations which use an "index." The index used for this ARM loan is the weekly average yield of United States Treasury securities adjusted to a constant maturity of one year. Information on this index is published weekly in the Federal Reserve Board's Statistical Release H.15 (519) and is published monthly in the Federal Reserve Bulletin. If this index is no longer available, Lender will use an alternative index which is based on information Lender believes to be comparable.

5. **Frequency of Interest Rate Changes**
The first potential interest rate change for your loan will occur five (5) years from the first day of the month following your closing, or upon your sixtieth regular monthly payment, whichever occurs first. Subsequent interest rate changes will occur on the first day of every twelfth month thereafter. These dates are known as the Interest Rate Change Dates. For example, if your loan closed in September, 1991, and your first payment was No-

vember 1, 1991, your first Interest Rate Change Date would be October 1, 1996. Your second Interest Rate Change Date would be October 1, 1997. The exact date of the first change date will be disclosed in your loan documents.

6. **Calculation of Interest Rate Changes**
   Approximately 45 days before each Interest Rate Change Date, your interest rate will be reviewed. The interest rate for the next twelve months will be determined by adding a fixed percent, known as the margin, to the then current index and rounding the sum to the nearest one-eighth of one percent (0.125%). The margin for this type of ARM loan is two and three-quarters percent (2.75%).

7. **Limits on Interest Rate Changes (Caps)**
   The interest rate set on the first and on following Interest Rate Change Dates shall never be increased or decreased by more than two percentage points (2.0%) from the interest rate in effect for the month preceding the Interest Rate Change Date. In addition, the interest rate may never increase more than the maximum interest rate for your loan, which is five percentage points (5.0%) over your initial interest rate. There is no downward limit for interest rate decreases over the term of the loan. Please note that these limits do not apply to any changes in your interest rate which might occur as a result of the conversion of your loan to a fixed interest rate, as set forth in paragraph 9 below.

8. **Frequency and Calculation of Payment Changes**
   Changes in your interest rate may cause your monthly payment to increase or decrease. Changes will become effective for the payment due on the first of the month following the Interest Rate Change Date. This date is called the Payment Change Date. For example, if the Interest Rate Change Date was the first day of October, the Payment Change Date would be the first day of November. Subsequent payment changes would occur on the first day of every twelfth month thereafter.

   The new monthly payment will be calculated by computing the payment necessary to pay off the remaining loan balance at the new interest rate. Monthly escrow charges (if any), will be added to this amount to arrive at the new full monthly payment.

   Please note that your monthly payment could change more frequently if there is an increase or decrease in taxes, insurance premiums or other assessments paid from the escrow account, as discussed in paragraph 15 below.

9. **Option to Convert Loan to Fixed Interest Rate Loan**

On the first, second and third Interest Rate Change Dates you may exercise an option to convert your adjustable rate loan to a loan with a fixed interest rate. These dates are also known as the Conversion Dates and are the only dates upon which this option can be exercised.

If you choose to exercise the option, you must give Lender notice of your intention to exercise the option at least fifteen days before the Conversion Date. Your loan must not be in default and you must sign any documents which Lender requires. You must also pay Lender a conversion fee equal to $250 plus one percent (1%) of the unpaid loan amount.

If you convert your loan to a fixed interest rate as set forth in this paragraph, and if the original term of your loan was greater than 15 years, your new fixed interest rate will be equal to the sum of the Federal National Mortgage Association's required net yield for 30-year fixed rate mortgages covered by 60-day mandatory delivery commitments in effect 45 days before the Conversion Date plus five-eighths of one percent (0.625%), rounded to the nearest one-eighth of one percent (0.125%). If your original loan term is 15 years or less your new fixed interest rate will be equal to the sum of the Federal National Mortgage Association's required net yield for 15-year fixed rate mortgages covered by 60-day mandatory delivery commitments in effect 45 days before the Conversion Date plus five-eighths of one percent (0.625%) rounded to the nearest one-eighth of one percent (0.125%). If FNMA's net yield figures are not available, Lender may determine your interest rate by using a comparable figure.

Your new monthly payment will be calculated by determining the monthly payment sufficient at your new fixed interest rate to pay back the unpaid loan amount in substantially equal monthly payments over the remainder of the loan term. The new monthly payment will be effective with the first monthly payment due after the Conversion Date and will continue until the loan is paid in full.

10. **Notice of Interest Rate and Payment Changes**

Lender will send you written notice of interest rate and payment changes at least 30 days before the changes become effective. This notice will be mailed to the most current mailing address supplied by you and will contain the following information and any other information required by law:

a) The scheduled dates for rate and payment changes.

b) The amount of your new payment.

c) The new interest rate.

d) The index on which the new interest rate is based.

e) The outstanding balance of your loan on the Interest Rate Change Date (assuming timely receipt of the payments due by that date).

f) The date of the next Interest Rate and Payment Change Dates.

g) The name and telephone number of a representative of Lender who can answer questions about the notice.

The notice will also be sent prior to Interest Rate Change Dates even when no changes will occur in the monthly payment.

Lender will also send you a notice containing the following information at least 30 days prior to the Conversion Dates described in paragraph 9 above:

a) The interest rate which you would pay if you convert to a fixed interest rate loan.

b) The amount of the new monthly payment if you choose to convert to a fixed interest rate loan.

c) The date by which you must execute and deliver to Lender all required fees and documents relating to the modification of your loan to a fixed interest rate.

11. Late Charges

If Lender does not receive your full monthly payment within 15 days after the date it is due, you will be charged a late charge equal to _____ percent of your overdue payment of principal and interest. This charge will be imposed only once on any late payment.

12. Prepayments

You may prepay this ARM loan in whole or in part without penalty at any time during the loan term. All partial prepayments will be used to reduce the unpaid loan balance and will not allow you to delay or skip any monthly payments.

13. **Loan Obligations and Lender's Rights**

The loan documents contain provisions which may result in the loan becoming immediately due and payable. If you fail or are unable to immediately repay the loan amount and all loan charges, the forced sale of the property may result.

Lender may require immediate payment in full if a change in a law makes any provision of the loan documents unenforceable. In addition, your failure to comply with all of your obligations and responsibilities under the loan may result in Lender's requiring immediate payment. Some of the most important obligations which may be imposed upon you by the loan documents are as follows: 1) making payments for all loan charges including not only monthly principal and interest payments, but escrow charges and payments resulting from Lender's need to protect its security in the property; 2) paying all taxes, assessments, fines and liens imposed on the property not paid by escrow charges; 3) obtaining Lender's prior written permission to sell or transfer any interest in the property; 4) obtaining and maintaining adequate hazard insurance; and, 5) keeping the property in good repair and complying with all laws, ordinances and governmental regulations. Details regarding these and other obligations are set forth in the loan documents.

14. **Assumption and Transfer of Property**

The documents for this loan contain a "Due on Sale" clause which provides that if all or part of the property securing the loan is sold or transferred without Lender's prior written consent, Lender may require immediate payment in full of the principal balance and all other monies due under the loan. After the first Interest Rate Change Date, if you wish to obtain Lender's consent to a transfer of the property and the assumption of the loan, you must submit to Lender information regarding the person(s) who will assume the loan. If Lender determines that such person(s) are qualified to assume the loan's obligations and that Lender's security interest will not be impaired by the transfer and assumption, Lender must allow the assumption without changes in the loan terms. Lender may further condition its consent upon the payment of an assumption fee and the signing of an assumption agreement.

Please note that during the initial five years of your loan, and anytime after you exercise your option to convert your loan to a fixed interest rate loan (as set forth in paragraph 9 above), the "Due on Sale" provisions of your loan documents will be modified so that Lender need not allow any assumption, but may, at its option, require payment in full upon the sale or transfer of the property or may condition its consent upon the party assuming the loan agreeing to changes in the loan terms, including the interest rate.

Please note that even where Lender consents to an assumption, the original borrower may remain obligated under the loan documents unless expressly released in writing by Lender.

15. Escrow Charges

Except where prohibited by applicable law, the loan documents will require you to make payments into an escrow account to be applied toward the payment of taxes, assessments, insurance premiums and ground rents, if any. The purpose of this account is to assure the existence of funds to pay such items, the non-payment of which might endanger your interest in the property and Lender's security interest. The use of the escrow account spreads the collection of funds for these items evenly throughout the year rather than requiring a number of large annual payments. The monthly escrow payments will equal 1/12th of the total yearly taxes and assessments on the property, 1/12th of ground rents on the property, if any, 1/12th of the total yearly premium for hazard insurance and 1/12th of the total yearly premiums for flood and mortgage insurance, if any.

If you do not make your escrow payments as scheduled or if the monies in the escrow account are insufficient, Lender will advance such funds on your behalf and will bill you for these advances. Your continued failure to pay such funds may result in Lender demanding immediate payment of the unpaid loan amount, interest and all other unpaid charges. Your failure to pay all amounts due under your loan when required could result in the forced sale of the property.

16. Hypothetical Transaction

Assume the following transaction:

Loan Amount	$100,000	Margin	2.750%

Initial Interest Rate	9.73%	First Interest Rate Change Date	10/1/96
Initial Payment	$857.68	Index on Effect on First Change Date	9.00%

Closing Date 9/15/91

The initial monthly payment noted above and other monthly payment figures used below are for principal and interest only. Escrow charges (see paragraph 15 above) would be added to such payment to arrive at the full monthly payment obligation.

On the first Interest Rate Change Date (October 1, 1996), the margin (2.750%) would be added to the then current index (9.00%). The sum would be 11.75 percent. This would not be the new interest rate as it would create an interest increase of more than two percent from the interest rate in effect prior to the Interest Rate Change Date (9.73%). The limits on interest rate changes set forth in paragraph 7 above would result in a new interest rate of 11.73 percent. The new monthly payment would be $996.11. This payment would be due November 1, 1996, and would be in effect until the next Payment Change Date.

The interest rate and monthly payment would continue to be computed each year thereafter using the then current index and the margin of 2.750 percent. The interest rate would never change more than two percent on any one change date and could never be more than five percent over the initial interest rate (the maximum interest rate). There is no minimum interest rate. After the first five years, monthly payments would adjust each year taking into consideration the new interest rate and the then outstanding loan balance. The payments would always be set at a level which would provide for the full repayment of the loan within the remaining loan term. In this example, the Conversion Dates would be October 1, 1996, October 1, 1997 and October 1, 1998. You would be given an opportunity (as set forth in paragraph 9 above) to convert your ARM loan to a fixed rate loan on each of such dates and only on such dates. If FNMA's required Net Yield on the first Conversion Date was 12.00 percent, the offered fixed interest rate would be 12.625 percent (12.00% plus 0.625%). In this example you would be required to pay a fee of $1,213.98 (one percent of the unpaid loan amount plus $250.00). Given an unpaid loan amount of $96,398.10 and a remaining term of 300 months, your new monthly payment would be $1,060.08. This payment would not change but would

144

continue to be your payment until the loan was fully paid.

Please note, your initial interest rate, first Interest Rate Change Date, the Index in effect on such date and Conversion Dates may be different and thus the changes in the interest rate on your loan and fixed interest rate upon conversion may be different.

Please also note that the value of the Index as of _____ is ____ percent. The rounded sum of this Index and the margin noted above is ____ percent. If this sum is greater than your initial interest rate and if the Index is higher or unchanged at the time of your first Interest Rate Change Date, then your interest rate (and your monthly payments) will increase on and after the first Interest Rate Change Date.

17. **Loan Documents**

The exact terms of the loan and the rights of the borrower and of Lender are contained in a note and a security instrument (which may be called a mortgage, deed of trust or security deed). The borrower and Lender become bound to the terms of the loan upon signing these documents. Although either party may subsequently request modification of the loan terms, neither party is required to agree to such a request. As a borrower, you should understand and become familiar with the provisions of the note and security instrument. Copies of these documents are available to you upon request.

Acknowledgments

I have read the contents of this disclosure and I acknowledge receipt of a fully complete copy of this disclosure. I also acknowledge that I have received a copy of the Federal Home Loan Bank Board's "Consumer Handbook on Adjustable Rate Mortgages."

_____ DATE _____
Borrower

_____ DATE _____
Co-Borrower

_____ DATE _____
Signature of Lender Employee

Example 5

LOAN DISCLOSURE NOTICE
GRADUATED PAYMENT MORTGAGE (GPM)
IMPORTANT MORTGAGE LOAN INFORMATION

PLEASE READ CAREFULLY; If you wish to apply for a Graduated Payment Mortgage (GPM) loan with the lender, you should read the important information below concerning the differences between this mortgage and other mortgages with which you may be familiar.

GENERAL DESCRIPTION OF GRADUATED PAYMENT
MORTGAGE (GPM) LOAN

This disclosure statement contains a general description of the GPM Loan available from _____
(the Lender). *This disclosure is an example of how your GPM mortgage would work. It in no way constitutes a commitment on the part of the lender.* If your application is accepted you will be required to sign certain loan documents. When you have signed these loan documents, both you and the Lender will be bound by the terms of such documents, particularly the Note and Mortgage. You should become familiar with and understand the provisions of the loan documents. Samples of such documents are available to you or to your attorney during reasonable business hours.

1. Your GPM loan is a graduated payment, fixed rate mortgage loan which fully amortizes over a fifteen-year term. The interest rate (referenced in the NOTE as "NOTE RATE") is constant for the life of the loan, but the first year's payment rate is_____ below the NOTE RATE. The principal and interest payments increase five percent over the first five years. At the beginning of year six, your monthly payment will increase over the previous year's monthly payment by an amount which will allow your loan to fully amortize over its remaining term.

THERE IS NO NEGATIVE AMORTIZATION ON THIS LOAN

2. How your interest rate is established.
The interest rate on your loan will be set as agreed upon with the Lender. The rate will be based on FHLMC's 30-day mandatory delivery for GPM 15-year mortgages with a five percent annual increase plus 0.375 percent servicing fee.

Below you will find an example of how your GPM loan would work in practice. This example assumes no buydown funds.

LOAN: $50,000   **TERM:** 15 years   **NOTE RATE:** 10.000%

QUALIFYING RATE: 7.152%

Payment No.	Monthly Payment	Principal Balance
1–12	$453.68	$49,534.91
13–24	476.37	48,736.00
25–36	500.18	47.554.25
37–48	525.19	45,934.49
49–60	551.45	43,815.15
61–100	579.03	

Year six (6) is the year in which you reach a fully amortizing principal and interest payment for the remainder of the loan term. In order to permit the monthly payments to exactly repay the loan by the end of the 15th year, the adjustment of the monthly payment in year six will increase over the previous year's monthly payment to fully amortize the loan.

The Lender will require you to maintain an escrow account for the payment of taxes and insurance, unless state law prevents the requirement of establishing such an account.

THE UNDERSIGNED ACKNOWLEDGES RECEIPT OF THIS DISCLOSURE NOTICE PRIOR TO SIGNING THE RESIDENTIAL LOAN APPLICATION.

_____   _____
Date   Signature

_____   _____
Date   Signature

Example 6

LOAN DISCLOSURE NOTICE
GRADUATED EQUITY MORTGAGE (GEM)
IMPORTANT MORTGAGE LOAN INFORMATION

PLEASE READ CAREFULLY: If you wish to apply for a Graduated Equity Mortgage (GEM) loan with the lender, you should read the important information below concerning the differences between this mortgage and other mortgages with which you may be familiar.

GENERAL DESCRIPTION OF GRADUATED EQUITY
MORTGAGE (GEM) LOAN

This disclosure statement contains a general description of the GEM Loan available from _____ (the Lender). *This disclosure is an example of how your GEM mortgage would work. It in no way constitutes a commitment on the part of the lender.* If your application is accepted you will be required to sign certain loan documents. When you have signed these loan documents, both you and the Lender will be bound by the terms of such documents, particularly the Note and Mortgage. You should become familiar with and understand the provisions of the loan documents. Samples of such documents are available to you or to your attorney during reasonable business hours.

1. Your GEM loan will have an initial payment based upon a 15-year term with interest only payments of up to three years and may also include an interest rate buydown. The qualifying interest rate and corresponding payment may be bought down to an initial payment equivalent to that required to fully amortize a 30 years level payment loan bearing a 8 1/2 percent rate of interest. Payment increases may not exceed 7 1/2 percent of the prior year's payment (approximately 1% per year). The term of this loan may not exceed 15 years.

THERE IS NO NEGATIVE AMORTIZATION ON THIS LOAN

2. How your interest rate is established.
The interest rate on your loan will be set as agreed upon with the Lender. The rate will be based on FNMA's 30-day mandatory delivery for 15 year mortgages with SRS servicing plus ten basis points and 0.375 percent servicing.

Below you will find an example of how your GEM loan would work in practice. This example assumes no buydown funds.

LOAN: $55,000   **TERM:** 15 years   **NOTE RATE:** 9.625%

QUALIFYING RATE: 5.25%

Payment No.	Monthly Payment	Principal Balance
1–12	$453.68	$49,534.91
13–24	476.37	48,736.00
25–36	500.18	47.554.25
37–48	525.19	45,934.49
49–60	551.45	43,815.15
61–180	579.03	

Year six (6) is the year in which you reach a fully amortizing principal and interest payment for the remainder of the loan term. (In order to permit the monthly payments to exactly repay the loan by the end of the 15th year, the adjustment of the 1st monthly payment in year six (6) is less than 7 1/2 percent increase over the previous years monthly payments.)

The Lender will require you to maintain an escrow account for the payment of taxes and insurance, unless state law prevents the requirement of establishing such an account.

THE UNDERSIGNED ACKNOWLEDGES RECEIPT OF THIS DISCLOSURE NOTICE PRIOR TO SIGNING THE RESIDENTIAL LOAN APPLICATION.

_____   _____
Date   Signature

_____   _____
Date   Signature

Glossary

Terms and Fees Most Frequently Used in Mortgage Lending

Abstract of Title—A written history of the title transaction or conditions which affect the title to a designated parcel of land from the original source of title to the present, and consisting of a summary of all the instruments disclosed by the records setting forth their material parts.

Acceleration clause—A clause in a deed of trust or mortgage which accelerates or hastens the time when the debt becomes due. For example, most mortgages contain a provision that the note shall become due immediately upon the sale or transfer of title of the land or upon failure to pay an installment of principal or interest.

Ad valorem—Latin for "according to value." Used in connection with real estate taxation.

Affidavit—A statement or declaration reduced to writing and sworn or affirmed to before an officer who has authority to administer an oath or affirmation.

Agency—The business of one entrusted to another.

Alias—An assumed name, "also known as." From the Latin "alias dictus," "otherwise called."

Amortization—
A. Positive: The gradual reduction of a debt by means of periodic payments sufficient to pay principal and thereby liquidate the debt.
B. Negative: The graduated increase of a debt by means of periodic increases sufficient to satisfy an interest deficiency.

Appraisal—The act of placing an estimate of value on real property and the process of preparing such an estimate.

Assessed valuation—The valuation placed upon real or personal property for purposes of taxation.

151

Assessment—A charge made against property by the state, county, cities, and authorized districts.

Assignment—A transfer of any present or future interest in property, real or personal.

Attachment—A seizure of a defendant's property as security for any judgment plaintiff may recover in the pending action.

Attorney's fee—Fee charged by attorney for review of contract to purchase, document preparation, if necessary, and attendance at closing.

Bankrupt—Any person, firm or corporation unable to pay his or its debts and whose assets become liable to administration under bankruptcy law for the protection of creditors.

Beneficiary—The person designated to receive the income from a trust estate, or from a trust deed.

Biweekly—Occurring at intervals of two weeks.

Borrower—One who receives funds, with the expressed or implied intention of repaying the loan in full, or giving the equivalent.

Breach—Violation of a legal obligation.

Broker—One who for a commission or fee brings parties together and assists in negotiating contracts between them. In real estate transactions, the broker usually brings together the buyer and the seller and the mortgage lender.

Caveat emptor—Let the buyer beware.

Certificate of Claim—Certificate by the lender that a loan made under Section 501, 502, 503, 505 or 507 of the Servicemen's Readjustment Act of 1944 is in default and requesting that the VA make good the guaranty. This statement is made on Form VA 4-1874 A Certificate of Claim is also used where foreclosure has been completed and lender applies for FHA debentures. In the latter case, the Certificate of Claim comprises fees for advertising, notice of default charges, fees for recording, service charges covering delinquent payments, late charges covering delinquent payments, amounts expended for repairs, revenue stamps, travel expenses (if any), title insurance premium, trustee's fee, interest figures from date interest on the loan first became delinquent to the date notice of default was filed, and interest from date of filing notice of default to date of acceptance of title by the FHA. (This interest is computed at a rate on loan less rate carried in the debentures.)

Chattel mortgage—A mortgage on personal property.

Cloud on title—A proceeding or instrument such as a deed, or deed of trust, or mortgage, or a tax or assessment, judgment, or decrees which, if valid, would impair the title to land.

Coinsurance clause—A clause in an insurance policy ccontemplating that the policy holder will carry insurance to some named percentage of the value of the property covered. In return for this, the policy holder benefits through a reduction in rate.

Collateral—Stocks, bonds, evidence of deposit and other marketable properties which a borrower pledges as security for a loan. In mortgage lending, the collateral is the specific real property which the borrower pledges as security.

Commitment—A pledge or engagement, a contract involving financial responsibility or a contingent financial obligation to be performed in the future, a promise by a lender to make a specific loan to a prospective borrower.

Commitment points—A fee charged by the institution for a contingent financial obligation to a prospective borrower.

Conditional sale contract—A contract for the sale of property, the property to be delivered to the buyer, the seller to retain, however, the title thereof until the conditions of the contract have been fulfilled.

Construction loan—A loan which is made to finance the actual construction of improvements on land. It is the practice to divide the loan into four or five equal parts, or disbursements, which are paid as the construction progresses.

Contract—An agreement between two or more parties to do or not to do a particular thing.

Conveyance—The transfer of the title to land from one person or class of persons to another.

Courier fees—Fees charged by lender for special transmittal of borrower's documents or verifications of borrower's credit statements.

Covenant—An agreement between two or more persons, entered into by deed, whereby one of the parties promises the performance or nonperformance of certain acts, or that a given state of things does or shall, or does not or shall not exist.

Credit report fee—Charges for independent credit report of borrower.

Debentures—Form of payment made by the FHA to mortgage lenders upon completion of foreclosure and transfer of title to FHA.

Deed—An instrument in writing under seal, duly executed and delivered, containing a transfer, a bargain, or contract, used in conveying the title to real property from one party to another. There are two general types of deed—the quitclaim and the warranty. Under the quitclaim deed the seller conveys property to the purchaser, the title being only as good as the title held by the seller, who conveys all claim, interest, or right to the property as far as his own title is concerned. Under a warranty deed, the seller also conveys all claim, right, and title to the property, but, also warrants the title to be clear, subject only to such matters as may be shown in the deed. The warranty is recognized by law as the subject for future restitution of loss to the purchaser if any defects in the title are conveyed by the seller. A seal is not required in some states. The term "grant deed" is used in place of "warranty deed" in some states.

Deed of trust—A conveyance of the title to land to a trustee as collateral security for the payment of a debt with the condition that the trustee shall reconvey the title upon the payment of the debt, and with power of the trustee to sell the land and pay the debt in the event of a default on the part of the debtor.

Deed restrictions—Limitations placed in a deed limiting or restricting the use of the land.

Default—The nonperformance of a duty, whether arising under a contract or otherwise.

Deficiency judgment—A personal judgment against any person liable for the debt secured by a mortgage or deed of trust and being the amount remaining due to the mortgagee or beneficiary after foreclosure.

Demand mortgage—A mortgage which is payable on demand by the holder of the evidence of the debt.

Depreciation—Loss of value over a period of time or use.

Direct-reduction mortgage—A mortgage which directs that all payments have to be used for the reduction of the outstanding balance of principal.

Documentary or tax stamps—In some states a tax imposed upon the transfer of real property.

Documentation preparation—A lender's charges imposed for the preparation of the borrower's loan package.

Easement—A right or interest in the land of another which entitles the holder thereof to some use, privilege, or benefit, such as to place pole lines, pipeline, roads thereon or travel over.

Eminent domain—The inherent right of a sovereign power to appropriate all or any part of the private property within its borders for a necessary use by the public, with or without the consent of the owner, by making reasonable payment to such owner.

Encroachment—An unlawful extension of one's right upon the land of another.

Encumbrance—*See* "Incumbrance."

Escrow—Securities, instruments, or other property deposited by two or more persons with a third person, to be delivered on a certain contingency, or the happening of a certain event; when used in the expression "in escrow," the state of being so held. The subject matter of the transaction is the escrow; the terms with which it is deposited with the third person constitute the escrow agreement; and the third person is the escrow agent.

Estate—The degree, quantity, nature, and extent of interest which a person has in a real property.

Equity—Value in excess of a mortgage or deed of trust or value of an interest in a contract of sale.

Equity of redemption—A right which the mortgagor (borrower) of an estate has of redeeming it, after it has been forfeited by law by the nonpayment, at the time appointed, of the money secured by the mortgage to be paid by paying the amount of the debt, interest, and costs.

Escheat—The lapsing or reverting of land to the state.

Execution—A writ issued in the name of the people, under the seal of the court, and subscribed by the clerk, or issued by a justice of the peace directed to a sheriff, constable, marshal, or commissioner appointed by the court, to enforce a judgment against the property or person of a judgment debtor.

Extended coverage—Insurance agreed to, and paid for, by the insured which covers fire, lightning, windstorm, hail, aircraft damage, vehicle damage, riot, explosion, and smoke damage.

Federal Home Loan Banks—A system of eleven regional banks established by the Home Loan Bank Act of 1932 to provide certain facilities for savings and loan associations and like institutions, mutual savings banks, and life insurance companies in connection with their home mortgage lending activities, on condition that they become members of the system.

Federal National Mortgage Association—An association which was organized by the RFC on February 10, 1938, under provisions of the National Housing Act. At one time grouped with other agencies to form the Federal Loan Agency, it was later transferred to the Department of Commerce in 1942, and September 7, 1950, under Reorganization Plan 22, was made a part of the HHFA.

Over a period of years it was authorized to purchase or to commit for purchase FHA and VA loans totaling $3,650,000,000. Funds for mortgage purchases were obtained by FNMA by borrowing from the United States Treasury. On July 31, 1953, FNMA owned loans with balances of over $2,500,000,000 with additional commitments to purchase $500,000,000 more loans. The new FNMA chartered under the Housing Act of 1954 started its activity with funds provided by government subscription of $93,000,000 of preferred stock available from accumulated funds of the former FNMA. The rechartered FNMA, among its several duties, will manage and liquidate the former FNMA portfolio. Under the present setup, sellers of mortgages to this agency must purchase nonrefundable (but transferable) capital stock of the new FNMA in an amount of three percent of their sales to that corporation. The new FNMA is authorized to sell debentures up to ten times the amount of its capital and surplus. It may purchase FHA and VA mortgages at market prices only. Hence, it is prohibited from paying more for loans than the existing market price.

Fee—A reward or wages given to one for the execution of his office, or for professional services, as those of a counselor or physician, or mortgage broker or lender.

Fiduciary—One who holds a thing in trust for another such as a trustee.

First mortgage—A mortgage that is a first lien on the property pledged as security.

Foreclosure—The legal process by which a mortgagor of real or personal property or other owner of a property subject to a lien, is deprived of his interest therein. The usual modern method is sale of the property by court proceedings or outside of court.

Garnishment—An attachment of assets in the possession of a third person.

Grant—A generic term applicable to all transfers of real property.

Grantee—He to whom a grant is made.

Grantor—He by whom a grant is made. The seller of real property, i.e., the grantor in a deed, gives up title.

Hazard insurance—A contract whereby, for an agreed premium, one party undertakes to compensate the other for loss on a specific subject by specified hazards, such as acts of God or war.

Homestead estate—The rights of record of the head of a family or household in real estate, owned and occupied as a home, which are exempt from seizure by creditors.

Hypothecate—To pledge a thing without delivering the title or possession of it to the pledgee.

Income property—That property which produces a money income rather than yielding satisfaction to the owner.

Incumbrance—Any right to, or interest in, land which may subsist in third persons, to the diminution of value of the estate or tenant, but not preventing passing of the fee.

Institutional lender—A mortgage lender that invests its own funds in mortgages and carries a majority of such loans in its own portfolio, i.e., mutual savings banks, life insurance companies, commercial banks, savings and loan associations. Although individuals hold mortgage loans and service them, they are not generally classified as institutional lenders.

Intangible tax—In some states, a tax imposed, upon the transfer of real property.

Irrevocable—That which cannot be revoked or recalled.

Junior mortgage—A lien that is subsequent to the claims of the holder of a prior mortgage.

Late charge—Penalty permitted by both FHA and VA covering any monthly payment not made by the 15th of the month in which payment is due. Both permit four percent of the monthly payment. Some lenders exact a late charge for delinquencies on installments of conventional loans.

Lease—A species of contract for the possession and profits of lands and tenements either for life or for a certain period of time, or during the pleasure of the parties. (Tenements in such cases means estate or interest.)

Legal description—A description of a parcel of land sufficient to identify the property.

Lender's fee—A charge imposed by some financial institutions for delivering a loan.

Lessee—A tenant under a lease.

Lessor—One who leases.

Level-payment mortgage—One that provides for the payment of a like sum at periodic intervals during its term, part of the payment being credited to interest for the time involved and the balance of the payment being used to amortize the principal.

Levy—To raise, for example, to levy or raise a tax or an assessment; or to seize, for example, levy an execution, to raise money for the payment of a judgment.

Lien—A hold or claim which one person has upon the property of another as a security for some debt or charge.

Liquidity—A term referring to that condition of an individual or business, a huge percentage of the assets of which can be quickly converted into cash without involving any considerable loss by accepting sacrifice prices.

Loan—The letting out, or renting, of a certain sum of money by a lender to a borrower to be repaid with or without interest.

Loan-closing charges—A term applied to those charges which arise out of the final closing of a loan and the compliance with all the instructions of the mortgagor and mortgagee.

Loan trust funds—In connection with FHA and VA loans, the accumulation of funds to take care of taxes, fire insurance, and FHA premiums as they become due and payable.

Loan-value ratio—The relationship between the amount of the loan and the appraised value of the property usually expressed as a percentage.

Mechanic's lien—A claim created by statutory law in most states, existing in favor of mechanics or other persons who have performed work or furnished materials in and for the erection or repair of a building. A mechanic's lien attaches to the land as well as the building.

Merchantable title—One which a court of equity considers to be so clear that it will force its acceptance by a purchaser.

Moratorium—A period during which an obligor has a legal right to delay meeting an obligation, especially such a period granted in an emergency as to debt or generally by a moratory law.

Mortgage—A contract by which specific property is hypothecated for the performance of an act without the necessity of a change of possessions.

Mortgage insurance premium—The price paid by the borrower for insurance under FHA loans, furnished by the federal government in favor of the lender, insuring payment of the loan in event of default by the borrower after foreclosure.

Mortgage note—A negotiable promissory note secured by a mortgage on certain specific real estate.

Mortgage portfolio—The aggregate of mortgage loans held by the lender.

Mortgage risk—The hazard of loss of principal and/or interest in the loaning of funds secured by a mortgage.

Mortgagee—The lending party under the terms of a mortgage.

Mortgagor—The borrowing party who pledges property.

Mutual Mortgage Insurance Fund—A fund (established under the National Housing Act) into which all mortgage insurance premiums and other specified revenue of the FHA are paid and from which losses are met.

Mutual Mortgage Insurance System—A plan (established by the National Housing Act and administered by the FHA) for insuring lending institutions against hazards in connection with mortgage loans.

Net income—That part of the gross income which remains after the deduction of all charges or costs.

Net worth—The equity of the owners in the business, i.e., the net assets determined by subtracting all liabilities from the value of the assets.

Net yield—The yield of certain property, real or otherwise, clear of all charges and deductions; that part of the gross yield which remains after the deduction of all charges or costs.

Open-end mortgage—Mortgage, or deed of trust, written so as to secure and permit additional advances on the original loan.

Operative builder—A builder for his own account who erects houses for sale to others at an expected profit; a speculative builder.

Origination fee—A fee imposed on the borrower by a mortgage broker/banker or financial institution for making a loan.

Package mortgage—A mortgage or deed of trust including certain items which are technically chattels, such as stoves, refrigerators, washing machines, and garbage-disposal units.

Personal property—Estate or property which is not real property, consisting of things temporary or movable-chattels.

Plat—A map showing dimensions of a piece of real estate based upon the legal description.

Power of attorney—An instrument in writing, whereby one person, the principal, authorizes another, the attorney in fact, to act for him. The powers are determined by the express terms of the instrument itself; they are not implied, except insofar as may be necessary to carry out the powers expressly granted.

Prepayment penalty—Penalty for the payment of a debt before it actually becomes due.

Price—The consideration in money given for the purchase of a thing.

Property mortgage—A mortgage on the right and interest which one has in lands and chattels to the exclusion of other persons.

Purchase money mortgage—Mortgage given to the seller to secure in whole or in part the purchase price of real property.

Quitclaim deed—A deed of release. An instrument by which the grantor relinquishes all right, title, or interest he may have in the property.

Real property—Land and generally whatever is erected on, or growing upon, or affixed to, land.

Recording fees—A fee charged by a governmental agency to record mortgage documents.

Refunding—The process of refinancing a debt which cannot conveniently be paid when due.

Rental value—The estimated amount of rent which could be obtained for the use and occupancy of a property.

Reproduction cost—The sum of money which would be required to reproduce a building less an allowance for depreciation of that building.

Reserve—This term has a number of technical meanings. In banking, it most frequently refers to the legal reserve which banks must maintain on deposit with the Federal Reserve System. The Federal Reserve Systems Board of Governors has the power to raise and lower reserve rates, within statutory limits, to control the supply of credit.

Right of redemption—The right of the owner to reclaim title to his property, if he pays the debt to the mortgagee within a stipulated period of time after foreclosure.

Risk rating—A process by which the various risks are usually divided as to (1) neighborhood, (2) property, (3) the mortgagor, and (4) the mortgage pattern are evaluated. Usually the system employs the use of grids to develop precise and relative figures for the purpose of determining the overall soundness of the loan.

Roof inspection—A fee imposed upon borrower for independent inspection of roof.

Sales agreement—An agreement by which one of two contracting parties, called seller, gives a thing and passes the title to it, in exchange for a certain price in current money to the other party, who is called the buyer, or purchaser, who on his part agrees to pay such price.

Satisfaction—A written instrument that evidences the payment in full of a mortgage debt, and extinguishes the mortgage lien.

Secondary financing—A loan secured by a second mortgage or deed of trust of real property.

Security—Something given, deposited, or pledged to make secure the fulfillment of an obligation or the payment of a debt.

Servicing—The collection of payments of interest and principal, and trust fund items such as fire insurance, taxes, etc., on a note by the borrower in accordance with the terms of the note. Servicing by the lender also consists of operational procedures covering accounting, bookkeeping, insurance, tax records, loan-payment follow-up, delinquent-loan follow-up, and loan analysis.

Setback—The distance from a lot line which by law, regulation, or restriction in the deed must be left open; the linear distance between the lot line and the buildings or building line.

Shiftability—A quality that renders an investment exchangeable in the market with little, if any, variation in price.

Special assessment—A special charge against real estate such as a street assessment or sewer assessment for installation of public improvements from which the property benefits.

Subordination—The act of a creditor acknowledging, in writing, that the debt due him by a debtor shall be inferior to the debt due another creditor by the same debtor.

Subpoena—A writ commanding the person designated in it to attend court under a penalty for failure.

Surety—One legally liable on default of another.

Survey—To determine the boundaries, form, extent, area, position, contour, etc. of a tract of land or means of linear and angular measurements.

Tax service—Prorated taxes.

Teller—One who receives payments of any nature to apply on a mortgage loan, including pay-offs, which are tendered in person by the borrower at the office of the lender. Makes entry of payment in passbook, or issues other type of receipt used by lender. Balances receipts and disbursements at end of each day in accordance with accounting procedure of lender.

Term—The period of duration of a note, acceptance, time draft, bill of exchange or bond; synonymous with tenor and usance.

Term mortgage—One having a specific term, usually not over a 5-year maturity, during which interest is paid, but the principal is not reduced.

Termite inspection—An independent inspection to determine termit or other pest infestation of the structure.

Title—The means whereby the owner oflands has the just possession of his property.

Title theory and lien theory—Some states in the nation, known as "title-theory states," have the view that a mortgage gives the mortgagee some sort of legal title to the land. Other states, called "lien-theory states," have the view that the mortgagee has mearly a lien to secure the debt.

Title insurance—Protection against loss due to problems or defects in connection with the title not identified by title search and examination.

Torrens certificate—A certificate issued by a public authority, known as register of titles, establishing title in an indicated owner. Used when title to property is registered under the Torrens system.

Trust deed—An agreement in writing conveying property from the owner to a trustee for the accomplishment of the objectives set forth in the agreement. Trust deeds are generally used in many states rather than mortgages to secure loans on real property.

Trustee—A person, real or juristic, holding property in trust.

Unemcumbered property—Property that is free and clear of any assessments, liens, easements, or encumbrances of any kind.

Valuation—The act of establishing the value of real property.

Vendee—The person to whom a thing is sold.

Vendor—Seller.

Waiver—The relinquishment of a right or refusal to accept a right.

Warrant—A covenant whereby the grantor of an estate and his heirs are bound to warrant and defend the title. (*See also* Deed)

Zoning—A legislative process by which restrictions are places upon the use to which real property may be put.

Index

About the Author

Arthur Kramer, currently a real estate consultant in Florida, owned and operated a major regional financial lending institution, providing the public with FHA/VA insured mortgages and FNMA, FHLMC and private institution direct-mortgage financing. Throughout his 25 years in the real estate and financial services industries, Mr. Kramer has also served as executive officer, CEO and president of major national and regional organizations. His personal leadership and supervision has been responsible for securing hundreds of millions of dollars in consumer mortgage financing for clients to achieve home ownership.